SPIDERS
The Ultimate Predators

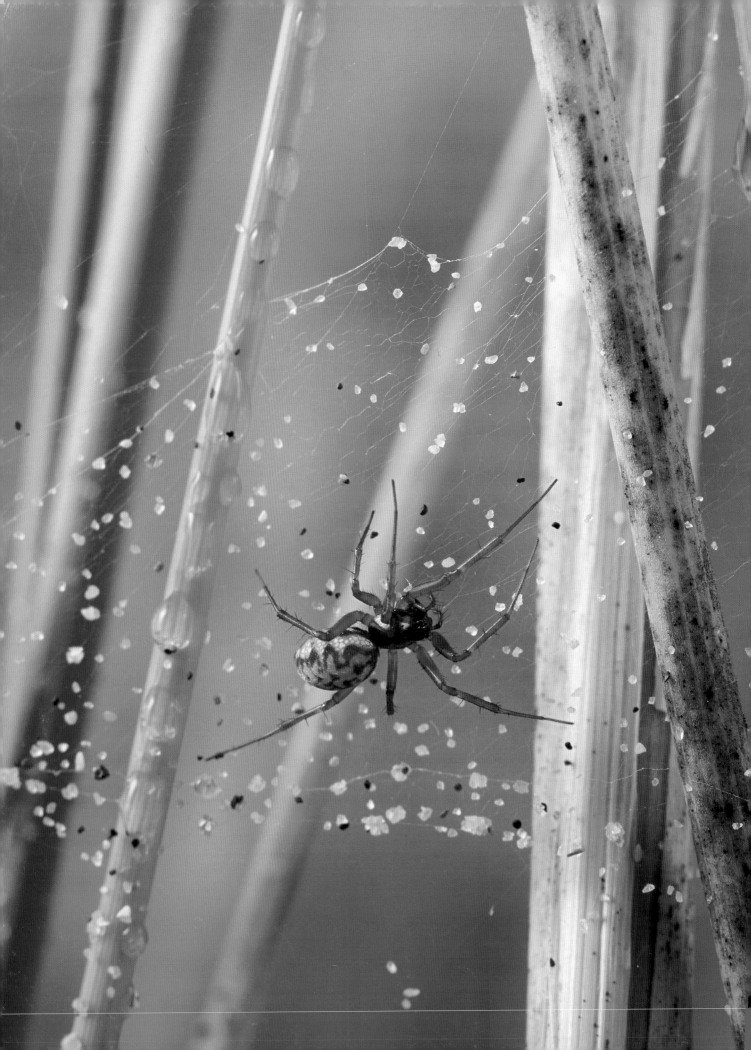

SPiDERS

The Ultimate Predators

Stephen Dalton

FIREFLY BOOKS

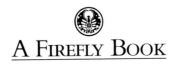

A FIREFLY BOOK

Published by Firefly Books Ltd. 2008

First printing

Publisher Cataloging-in-Publication Data (U.S.)
Dalton, Stephen.
Spiders : the ultimate predators / Stephen Dalton
[198] p. : ill., col. photos. ; cm.
Includes bibliographical references and index.
Summary: An illustrated exploration of the predatory techniques of spiders.
Includes descriptions and examples of many spider species, as well as an overview
of spider anatomy and directions for photographing spiders.
ISBN-13: 978-1-55407-346-7
ISBN-10: 1-55407-346-4
1. Spiders. I. Title.
595.44 dc22   QL458.4.D35   2008

Library and Archives Canada Cataloguing in Publication
Dalton, Stephen
Spiders : the ultimate predators / Stephen Dalton.
Includes bibliographical references and index.
ISBN-13: 978-1-55407-346-7 [bound]
ISBN-10: 1-55407-346-4 [bound]
1. Spiders. 2. Spiders—Pictorial works. I. Title.
QL458.4.D348 2008   595.4´4   C2008-900203-2

Published in the United States by
Firefly Books (U.S.) Inc.
P.O. Box 1338, Ellicott Station
Buffalo, New York 14205

Published in Canada by
Firefly Books Ltd.
66 Leek Crescent
Richmond Hill, Ontario L4B 1H1

Cover and interior design by Kathe Gray Design

Printed in China

The publisher gratefully acknowledges the financial support for
our publishing program by the Government of Canada through the
Book Publishing Industry Development Program.

Contents

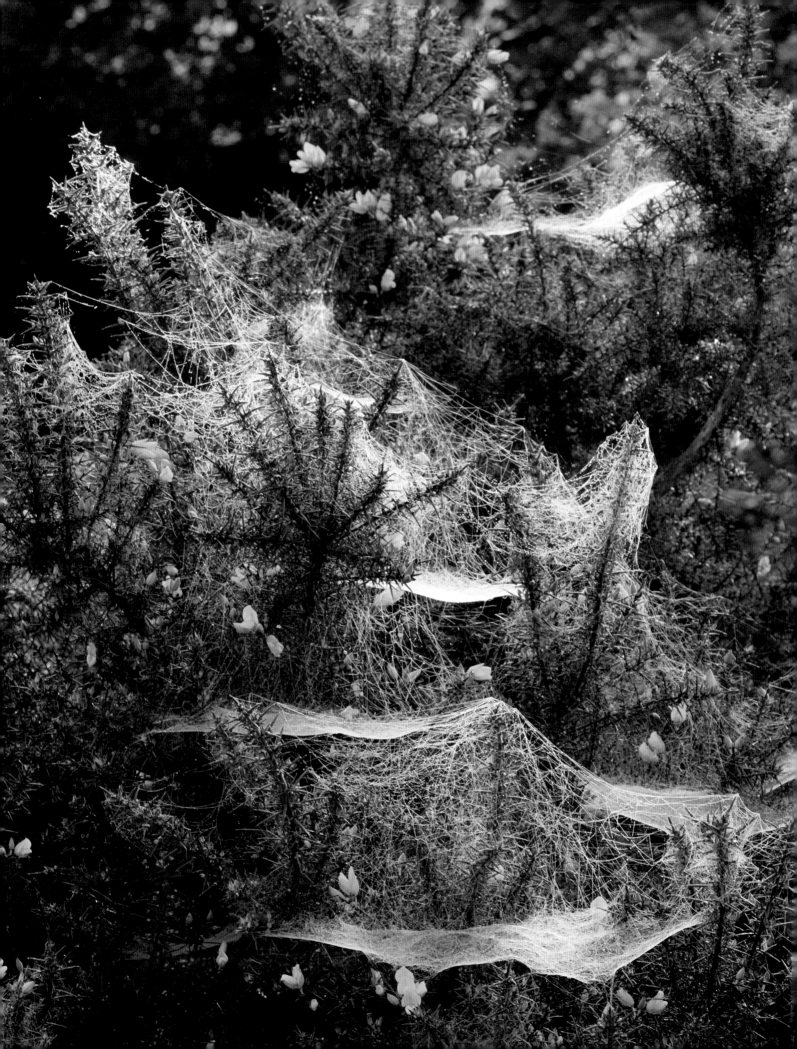

Introduction

Wherever we are, there is likely to be at least one spider within a few feet of us. It may be weaving a web, floating by on a gossamer thread, dancing to its mate, sucking the juices from an anesthetized fly or simply resting under our chair. Whatever it is doing, we are privileged to share the planet with about 40,000 known species of these remarkable animals.

Spiders are the most successful terrestrial predators on earth, occupying almost every niche possible. They are found from mountaintops to seashores and from ponds to deserts. They can even be found thousands of feet up, traveling vast distances as they balloon through the air on threads of gossamer. Spiders have been around for some 400 million years now and were pivotal in the evolution of insects, the most abundant class of animals on earth. Spiders consume more prey than all other carnivores. The late W.S. Bristowe, a British arachnologist, established that at certain times undisturbed meadows can support an astonishing population of more than two million spiders per acre, and that the weight of insects consumed per year by spiders easily exceeds the weight of the entire human population of England.

The success of spiders is almost wholly due to the formidable and astonishing array of techniques they have evolved for trapping insects and other small creatures. Their tactics are the result of a 300-million-year arms race fought against the insects. These range from a variety of ingenious traps in the form of webs to a host of other devious methods, including lassoing, jumping, stealing, chasing, ambushing, spitting, fishing, masquerading as other animals and even attracting prey by

◄ Webs on an autumn morning.

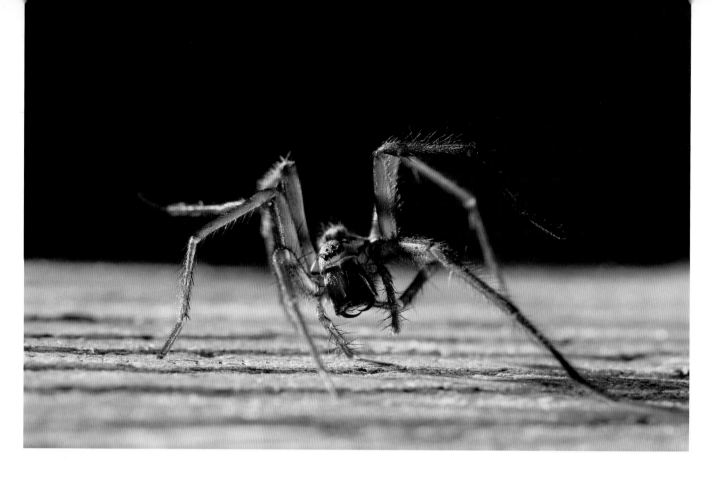

European house spider (*Tegenaria domestica*) using its chelicerae, or jaws, to clean its foot.

mimicking the prey's pheromones. My fascination with this stunning diversity of hunting techniques largely inspired the creation of this book.

It seems unfortunate that many naturalists and organizations concerned with conservation have tended to concentrate on the more obviously attractive groups of invertebrates, such as butterflies and dragonflies, as is clear from the many books on those subjects. The vast majority of spiders are not brightly patterned and colored; being tender and vulnerable creatures and surrounded by a profusion of enemies, they rely on merging with the subtle shades of their surroundings. Their coloring is usually composed of beautifully delicate patterns of browns, greens and grays, as reflected in the photographs in this book.

Another reason for their comparative neglect is that spiders are often tricky to positively identify. More than half are only 0.04 to 0.2 inch (1–5 mm) long, and the differences between many species can be discerned only under a microscope. Here, though, we are concerned mainly with the larger and more significant species. The difficulties of spider identification are hardly made easier by their numbers—more than 640 named species in England alone and about 3,700 in North America. In contrast, there are only about 65 British butterflies and around 700 in North America.

Spiders also have an image problem, so this book attempts to offset their creepy reputation. They possess rather a lot of legs to worry about; they are known to have a poisonous bite; they sneak about in dark places, scuttle across the floor at high speed and leave untidy webs all over the place. Paradoxically, though, many spiders are actually creatures of sunlight and are not at all creepy. The jumping spiders, by

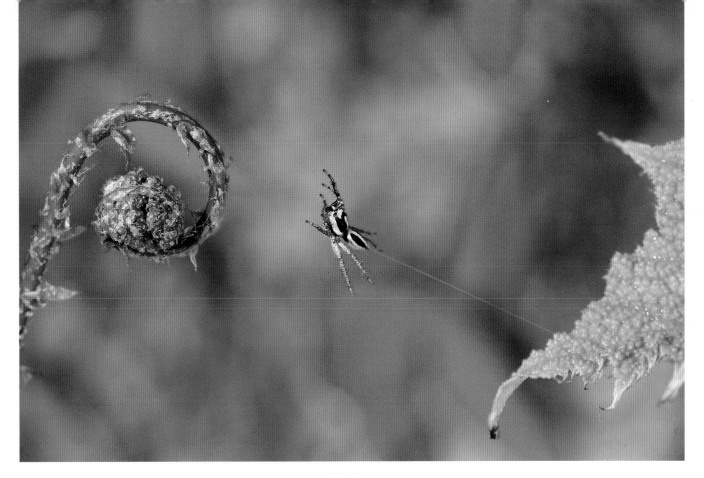

Pantropical jumping spider, from a family of sunshine lovers.

far the most numerous single group, have an enchanting and, some would say, almost cuddly appearance as they run jerkily over rocks and tree trunks, their large eyes following our every movement.

The aspect that most concerns many of us is actually the last thing we need to worry about—their bite (apart from some notorious exotic species). Even the few non-exotics that can nip do so only in self-defense, when severely provoked or squashed against our body. In reality most spiders are very nervous and retiring creatures because, unlike insects, which are protected by a tough exoskeleton, spiders have soft and vulnerable bodies. They do everything possible to keep out of harm's way, disappearing into their hiding places at the slightest disturbance or sign of danger. Many come out into the open only at night, spending the day hiding in some crevice or curled up in a leaf.

Spiders, like so many other animals, including humans, are predatory carnivores, but they are more humane than most others, albeit unconsciously so. This might seem like anthropomorphizing, but many of the predators we admire—such as owls, eagles and tigers—usually tear their relatively intelligent victims limb from limb while they are still alive, while the spider will first anesthetize its prey or, more likely, kill it with a lethal injection! We should also bear in mind that the nervous system of a spider's invertebrate prey is thousands of times less elaborate than that of any vertebrate, so their capacity to suffer is insignificant compared with the prey of larger carnivores.

There are a number of ways of organizing a book of this nature; for example, by family or habitat. Most spider books are based on classification, which is a sensible approach for identification and more serious study of the subject, but a slightly different course has been adopted here. In view of the range of ingenious hunting methods used by spiders, in this book they are grouped as follows: those that hunt down their prey by chasing, those that lie in wait and ambush, spiders that leap onto their victims, and of course the majority, which spin webs to trap insects, the latter being subdivided by different types of webs—orb webs, sections of orbs, sheet webs and funnel traps. Finally there are spiders that don't neatly fit into any of these categories—the nonconformists, those that tend to employ even more freakish techniques such as spitting, fishing and raiding other spiders.

It will soon become clear that these demarcations are not set in stone, as some species within one group often share the characteristics of another. For instance, many spiders that are capable of chasing down their prey may sit and wait for prey to come within reach before making a quick dash, so these could equally be described as ambushers. Similarly, some of the web builders do not actually trap prey in their webs but dash out of a hole or tunnel at high speed as soon they sense an insect touching a strand; and there is a good case for classifying fishing spiders with the chasers instead of bundling them with the nonconformists. Nevertheless, the broad divisions adopted here do help to demonstrate the range of hunting styles employed by these astonishing animals.

Unless it is unusually spectacular, I have avoided explaining much about courtship and mating behavior, particularly as several other books, including W.S. Bristowe's *The World of Spiders,* cover this topic in lavish detail. What has been included is a rough-and-ready translation of the scientific names. Whereas most of the names appear sensible and logical, others do not seem to have any obvious connection with the spider's appearance or way of life. Nevertheless I find them interesting—and at times amusing.

This book would not be complete without mentioning its omissions. For instance, we hardly touch upon the many minute spiders that require high magnification to see, let alone identify. These spiders mostly belong to a single vast family, the Linyphiidae; two of the larger species are portrayed here. Also excluded are many families specific to the tropics and Australasia and Africa. What is covered are the most important families common to both northern Europe and North America, together with a few representative "special" spiders that thrive on one continent but not the other. For example, the ladybird spider (*Eresus*) and the water spider (*Argyroneta*) are both European species that are not found in North America, while the black widow (*Latrodectus*), the golden orb spider (*Nephila*) and tarantulas do not enrich the lives of English country folk (perhaps global warming may change this!).

It may prove surprising to learn that there is considerable overlap between the actual species: over 30 percent of those described in this book are common to both continents, while a larger number of others are very similar. Many species have been introduced by shipments of plants, furniture and other imports from Europe, and a few species such as the European house spider (*Tegenaria*) and the daddy longlegs spider (*Pholcus*) have worldwide distribution. The species that are very similar have for the most part evolved over the eons from the same sources as temperate Eurasian fauna.

➤ A garden spider, the archetypal European spider that is also found in North America, in its freshly made symmetrical web.

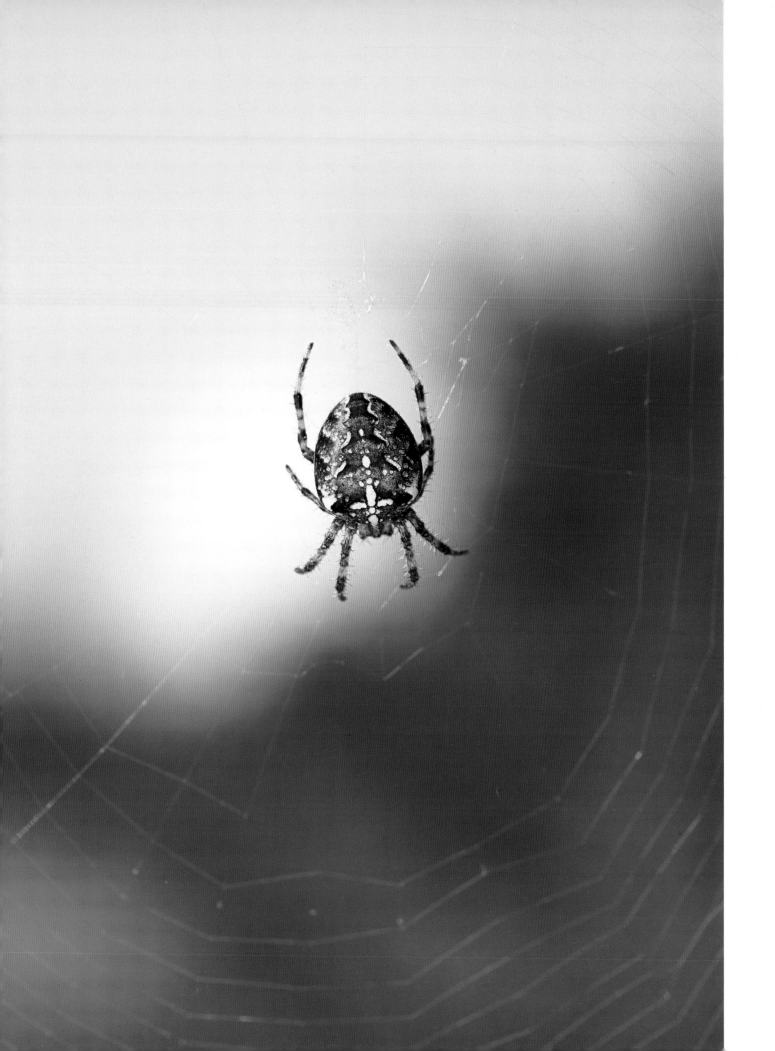

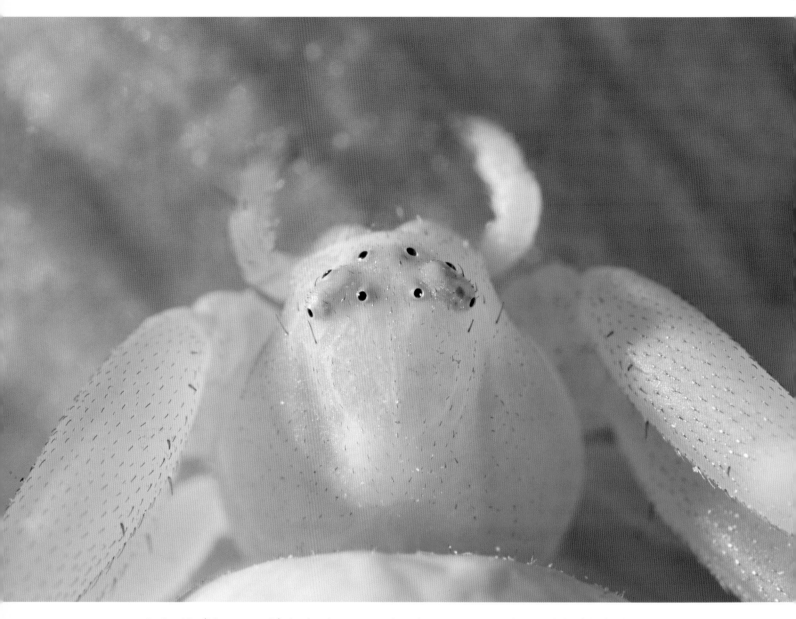

Crab spider (*Misumena vatia*) showing the crescent-shaped eye arrangement characteristic of the family.

I am often asked, "What is the point of spiders?" I am tempted to reply, "What is the point of humans, or anything for that matter?" Does there have to be a point or reason for the existence of a particular species? Life has evolved as a result of the universal process of natural selection, just as everything has since the big bang. What is certain is that all plants and animals rely on one another for their continued existence. In fact, the small and "lowly" creatures on which larger animals depend are more crucial in the scheme of things than lions and pandas. Over the eons, evolution ensured that living things remained generally in balance with their environment and with each other—until, that is, man began to overpopulate the planet and destroy this balance. Now, in a relative twinkling of an eye, nature as we used to know it is ending.

So what specific roles have spiders played? It is estimated that, worldwide, spiders are largely responsible for about 99 percent of the insect mortality rate—although spiders are incapable of discriminating between the so-called harmful and beneficial insects. Trials have proved that spiders can control large numbers of insect pests in agricultural areas, but since spiders have been so poorly studied their explicit function in nature has not been fully demonstrated. Spiders are food for a huge variety of animals such as birds, mammals and fish, while their silk is used in nest construction by many birds. Clearly, by virtue of their enormous population, the effect spiders have on maintaining the balance of nature is enormous.

Compared with studies of other, diverse terrestrial groups of animals, spider surveys are relatively simple to conduct, as few time-consuming dissections are required for their identification. This fact, together with their wide range of sizes—0.016 to 4.8 inches (0.4–120 mm)—and as much range in their biology as their size, now causes many ecologists to believe that spiders are the ideal subjects for assessing habitats and biodiversity, because they more easily provide information about the value of habitats than higher plants or vertebrates.

Economics and benefit to mankind seem to be the only language that many of us understand, so in addition to their importance as insect predators, we need also to take account of spiders' ability to produce silk and venom. Researchers are still struggling to work out how to take advantage of the combined strength and elasticity of spider silk so that it can be mass-produced. Venoms too are being studied for their potential for treating pain, epilepsy, strokes and Alzheimer's disease.

Perhaps we should also consider the spiritual and aesthetic value of these animals. Few of us, including arachnophobes, can fail to wonder at a dew-laden web on an autumn morning or to admire the spider's subtlety of form and color. Being moved and absorbed by the lives of spiders and all living things, however small and superficially insignificant they may appear, helps us to value all life as well as our own and realize that everything is intimately connected to everything else. Spider watching isn't only about spiders; it's about the whole natural world. In my view if such a holistic approach was embraced by everyone the world over, survival of Earth's natural beauty and life as we know it would be guaranteed.

According to E.O. Wilson, the farsighted American ecologist, we have a genetically inbuilt love for wild places and living things—he calls it biophilia—although for many of us this affinity is being increasingly suppressed by our material and anthropocentric approach to modern life. As Wilson says, humanity is exalted not because we are far above other living creatures, but because knowing them well elevates the very concept of life.

I quote a prophetic article from the *Illustrated London News* written more than a hundred years ago: "Man cannot wait for the cooling of the earth before consuming everything in it from teak trees and hummingbirds to snakes and spiders. In a hundred or two years hence he will be perplexed by a world in which there is nothing except what he has made." *Perplexed,* I think, is an understatement. We share the world with tigers, whales, hummingbirds and, yes, spiders too. The world would be a poorer place without any one of them.

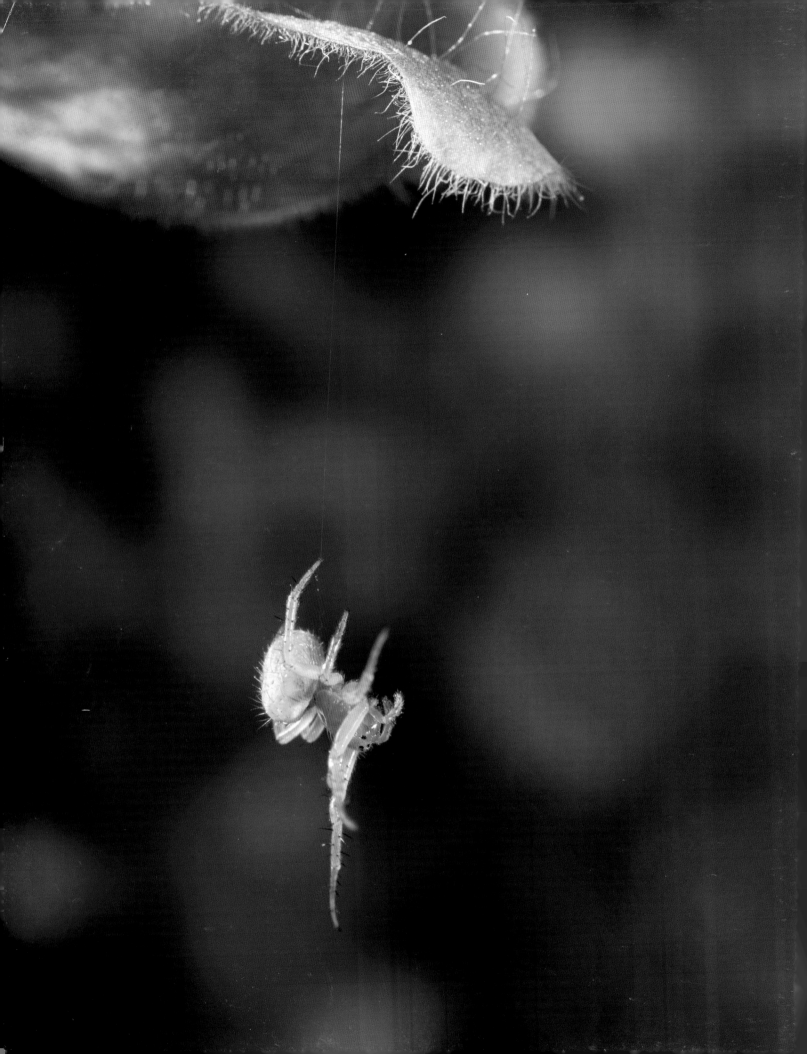

1

What is a Spider?

Before delving into the spiders themselves, it should prove helpful to give some general background information about these animals—how they differ from other invertebrates, how they are classified, how they build webs and mate.

Structure

The most obvious characteristic of a spider is its eight legs. Insects have only six. Unlike insects, whose adult bodies are divided into three parts, the spider's has only two parts. Also unlike insects, there is no larval or pupal stage—apart from color, pattern and reproductive organs, the young generally look like miniature versions of their parents immediately after hatching. The eggs are protected in silken egg sacs that come in a wide variety of sizes and designs. As the spiderlings become older, they shed their exoskeletons to accommodate their increasing size. The number of moults depends largely on the size of the spider; the smaller species undergo two or three while the larger ones moult up to about a dozen times. Lost or damaged limbs are often regenerated during or after the moult.

In contrast to their relatives, the mites, harvestmen and scorpions, which have their heads fused with the body, the two parts of a spider's body are connected by a very narrow stalk, although this is normally out of sight. Spiders also boast a unique feature—spinnerets. These are located at the tip of the abdomen for the all-important task of silk production.

◄ Cucumber or green orb weaver spider.

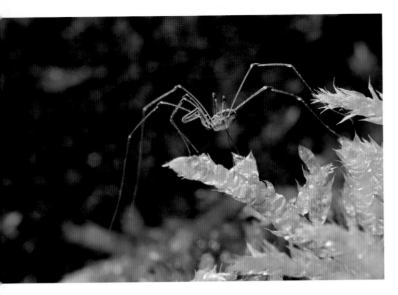

Harvestman (*Mitostoma chrysomelas*).

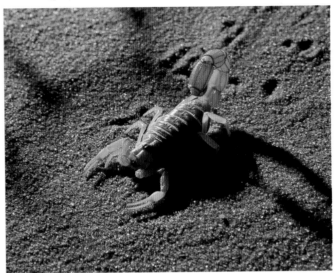

Scorpion from the Kalahari.

Cephalothorax

The front part of the body, the cephalothorax, consists of a fused head and thorax that is protected by a hard chitinous layer called the carapace. The front end accommodates the eyes—the vast majority of spiders have eight, although there are three families that possess only six (Oonopidae, Dysderidae and Scytodidae). The shape of the spider's face, the variety, number and arrangement of the eyes, and the shape of the jaws are key features in distinguishing one family from another. The eye color also can vary from a pearly luster to dark, but it can sometimes be difficult to see because of the presence of hairs.

Abdomen

The abdomen varies considerably in shape, markings and size. Even within a single species the size can vary enormously, depending on feeding or the stage of any eggs developing inside. The upper side frequently has a cardiac mark and four depressed brownish spots called sigella, which mark the internal muscle attachments. At the top of the underside are two pale patches (four in certain groups) that mark the position of the book lungs—air-filled cavities containing blood-filled leaves.

The tip of the abdomen holds the spinning organs, or spinnerets. Primitive spiders have eight spinnerets, but most present-day species appear to have lost the front two completely. In some the front two spinnerets have evolved

Spider eyes

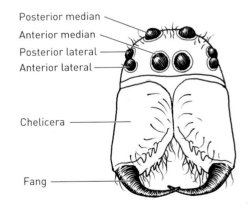

Posterior median
Anterior median
Posterior lateral
Anterior lateral

Chelicera

Fang

➤ Mouse spider showing ventral surface with book lung patches.

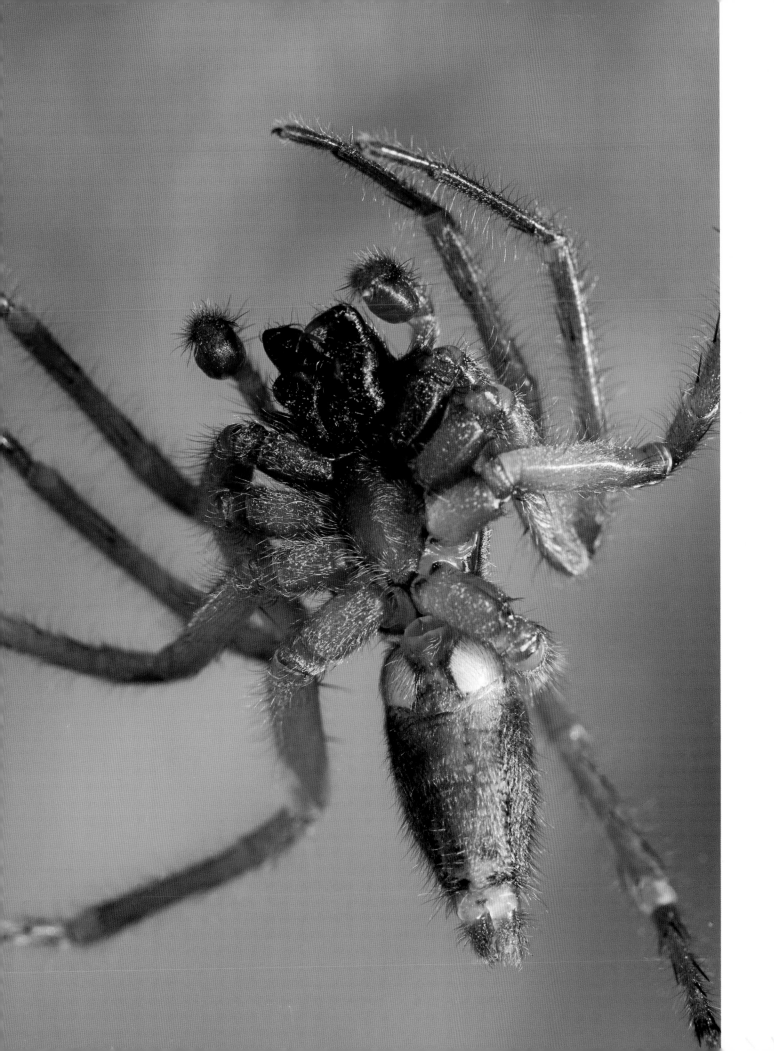

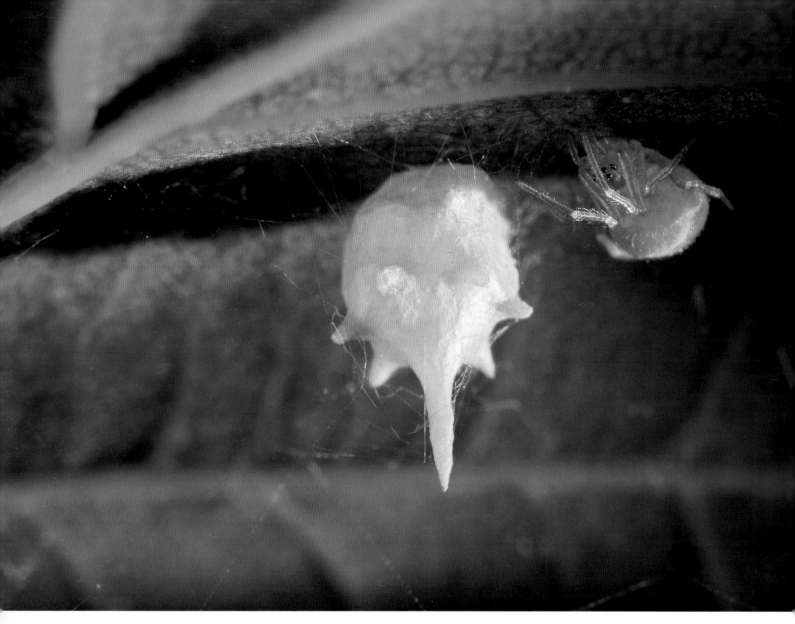

A scaffold-web spider (*Theridian pallens*) protecting its egg-sac.

into a single flat plate, the cribellum, which produces thick bands of bluish tangling silk. Just below the book lungs of most adult females may be seen the epigyne, the genital opening with a complexly shaped plate that is the lock to the male palpal key.

Jaws

The jaws, or chelicerae, are the spider's main weapon and are used for subduing prey. They are divided into a stout basal segment and an articulated thorn-like fang. The tip of the fang

has a fine opening through which venom can be injected from a duct supplied by a gland in the cephalothorax. When not in use, the fang

Structure of Mouthparts

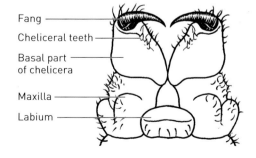

Fang

Cheliceral teeth

Basal part of chelicera

Maxilla

Labium

External structure of a female spider

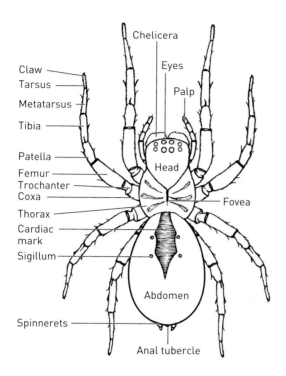

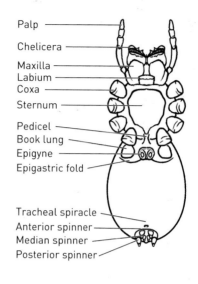

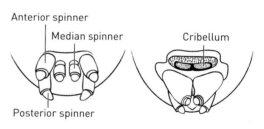

folds into a groove in the basal section, which is often bordered by teeth on the front and rear edges. The relative size of the chelicerae varies greatly between different species, which is also a useful feature in identification. Behind the chelicerae is the mouth, which is used for sucking up the liquid contents of prey.

Palps

Spiders have palpal organs at the front of the head that are really a fifth pair of small modified legs. These are important sensory organs and are used in prey manipulation. In the male the palps also perform an extraordinary role in reproduction. Male spiders are unique in the animal world because they pick up and carry sperm cells ready to be injected into the female. Moreover, the palps fit like complex keys into a lock-like plate on the belly of the female. The complexity and diversity of these organs can be fully appreciated only under the microscope. Because every species has its own special lock and key, the male palps and the female epigyne are vital characteristics for positive identification of most species.

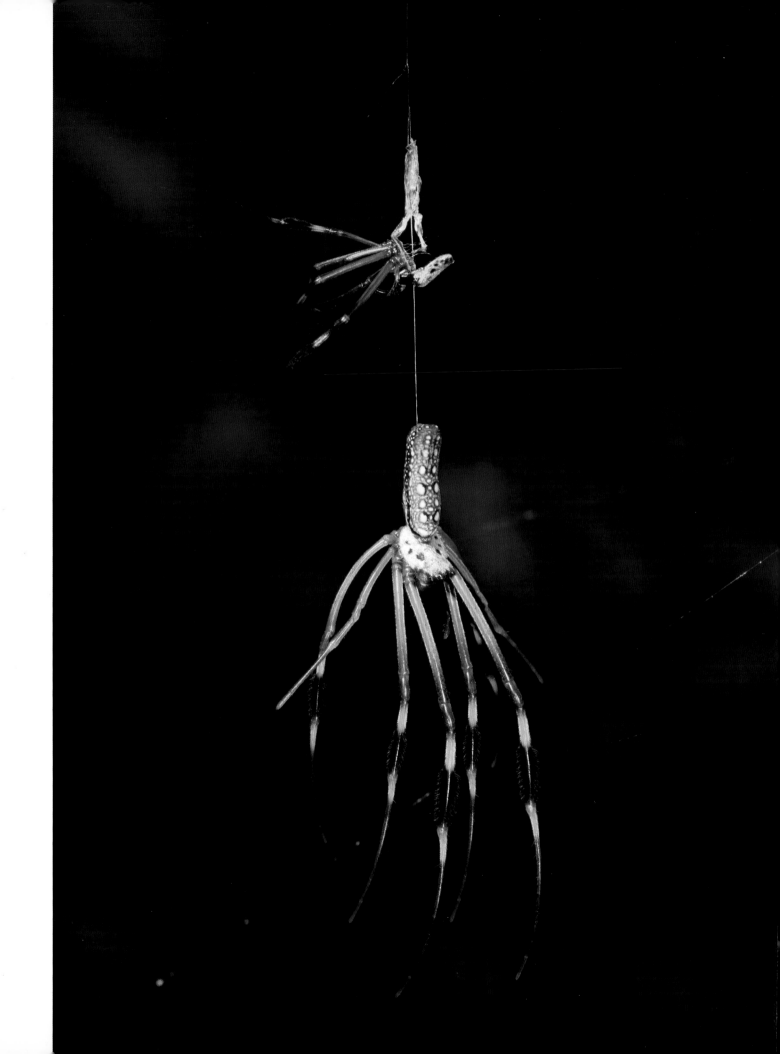

Legs

The four pairs of legs are divided into several joints; the tip of the terminal segment, the tarsus, has claws. Web spiders generally have three claws that are used for web control (see page 25), while some wandering and hunting spiders have lost one claw, often replacing it with a tuft of hairs (scopulae) that give a better grip. Some families have a series of curved bristles called the calamistrum running along the dorsal edge of the metatarsus of the fourth pair of legs. This is used to comb out a viscid substance from the cribellum that, when combined with ordinary silk, produces a thick, lace-like, fluffy bluish web.

The legs are clothed in a wide variety of types of hairs and spines, each of which has a special role. Most have a sensory function and possess their own nerve supply at the base. Some hairs are sensitive to touch; some at the end of legs are chemosensitive, allowing taste by touch; while other, fine vertical hairs, the trichobothria, are highly sensitive to air currents and vibration. More robust hairs are spine-like and assist in prey capture. Jumping and lynx spiders often have flat hairs rather like the scales on butterfly wings, which reflect light to produce iridescent colors.

Other sensory organs capable of detecting pressure, humidity and heat may also be present on the legs or body in the form of hairs or slits.

◄ Golden orb spider (*Nephila clavipes*) moulting.

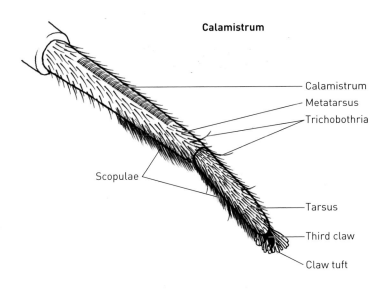

Calamistrum

Calamistrum
Metatarsus
Trichobothria
Scopulae
Tarsus
Third claw
Claw tuft

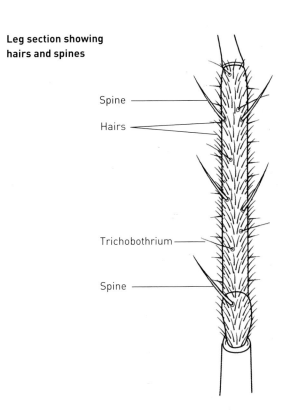

Leg section showing hairs and spines

Spine
Hairs
Trichobothrium
Spine

Spider names and classification

Together with other jointed-leg creatures such as crabs, scorpions, millipedes and insects, spiders are classified as arthropods. Unlike adult insects, which have six legs and usually wings, spiders and their kin, including mites and scorpions, possess eight legs and belong to the class Arachnida. Within Arachnida all spiders belong to the order Aranea (not to be confused with the Araneidae family of orb weavers; see page 30). On the basis of structure and behavior, spiders are further classified into two suborders and over a hundred families.

Earth supports some 40,000 named species of spiders but there may be three times as many yet to be discovered—if their habitats are not destroyed first. Even in a country as heavily populated with naturalists as Britain, species new to science are discovered regularly, adding to the 650-odd that have already been identified. In North America there are undoubtedly many species yet to be named.

Clearly some intelligent way of dividing spiders into groups with similar characteristics is vital if we hope to make any sense of such vast numbers. Very few species have been given English names—or, for that matter, names in other languages—and even if they had, the names would most likely be based on different characteristics anyway.

Internationally agreed-upon scientific names are vital if chaos is to be avoided. The name "house spider" could refer to any of several species—indeed, the American house spider belongs to an entirely different family from the European "house spider," while the name "jumping spider" could refer to any of 5,000 species! English-language family names can also give rise to much confusion. Take, for example, the Theriidae. This family has been

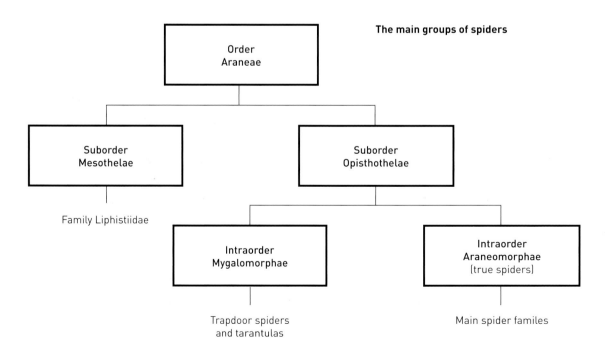

The main groups of spiders

Order
Araneae

Suborder
Mesothelae

Suborder
Opisthothelae

Family Liphistiidae

Intraorder
Mygalomorphae

Intraorder
Araneomorphae
(true spiders)

Trapdoor spiders
and tarantulas

Main spider familes

The classification and meaning of *Heliophanus favipes*

Kingdom	Animalia	as opposed to plant kingdom
Subkingdom	Metazoa	many-celled (as opposed to single-celled)
Phylum	Arthropoda	literally "jointed limbed"
Class	Arachnida	includes harvestmen, ticks, mites and spiders
Order	Aranea	spiders
Suborder	Araneomorphae	spiders with pinching jaws
Family	Salticidae	jumping spiders
Genus	*Heliophanus*	from Greek for "found in the sunshine"
Species	*flavipes*	red-legged

given at least four different names in the English language alone: scaffold-web spiders, space-web spiders, cobweb spiders and comb-footed spiders.

Scientific names are not devised willy-nilly but are closely linked with structural or other qualities that reflect the relationship between one group and another. Classification, or taxonomy, is simply a filing system for living organisms based on evolutionary relationships, taking the form of a branching hierarchy. At the top sits the kingdom, which is further divided down the tree into subkingdom, phylum, class, order, suborder, family, genus and finally species. Sometimes to complicate the matter (or to simplify things, depending on which way you look at it), extra subdivisions are added, such as subfamily or even subspecies.

By convention, family names end in *idae,* but they are often used adjectivally as well—for example, the family Araneidae may be referred to as araneids. In this book only the proper family name is capitalized.

The table above shows how a common little jumping spider, *Heliophanus flavipes,* is classified.

At this point it is worth saying something about the suborders into which spiders may be placed. It concerns the fundamental differences in structure between spiders from which the various families spring.

Suborder Mesothelae

The Mesothelae are a very ancient group of spiders from which all subsequent spiders have derived. There is only one family within the Mesothelae surviving today and it contains a small number of species; all are found in Southeast Asia, so they are not discussed in this book. The interesting feature about these spiders is that, like insects but unlike present-day spiders, they have a segmented abdomen. They also have eight spinnerets in the center of their abdomen. All live in caves or underground burrows covered by trapdoors.

Suborder Opisthothelae

All the spiders in this book are members of this suborder. They are further divided into two infraorders, the Mygalomorphae and the Araneomorphae.

Infraorder Mygalomorphae

Spiders in this group are familiar to most people as the huge, hairy bird-eating spiders, or tarantulas, but they bear no relationship to the true tarantulas from Spain, which belong to the wolf spider family, Lycosidae.

The mygalomorphs are a relatively primitive group consisting of 11 families and characterized by large, forward-projecting chelicerae that operate with a parallel upward and downward movement of the fangs. These spiders also have two pairs of book lungs as opposed to the single pair in "modern" spiders. Like the Mesothelae, the majority of mygalomorphs live in underground holes, often with a trapdoor entrance—hence their other name, trapdoor spiders. Whereas North America has several species, northern Europe has only one representative, the purse-web spider, *Atypus affinis,* although it is rare and localized in England (see page 174).

Infraorder Araneomorphae

The araneomorphs, sometimes called the true spiders, comprise the vast majority of spiders and are regarded as being more highly evolved. The difference between these spiders and those in the other two suborders is the way in which the chelicerae are attached to the head and their sideways action, which allows them a greater biting span. They are also capable of making many different kinds of silk and have evolved tracheae for breathing, having dispensed with one of the two pairs of book lungs of the mygalomorphs (insects have taken this further in having only tracheae).

The many families (more than 80) that form the Araneomorphae reflect the great diversity of body forms and lifestyles that has allowed this group to colonize all corners of the globe. Spiders from different families are usually clearly different in many ways.

Finally, within the many families of spiders there are one or more genera. The name of the genus, which always starts with a capital letter, forms the first part of the scientific name. Within each genus there may be one or more species, and the specific (species) name forms the second part of the scientific name; by convention this binomial name should always be printed in italics. Typically the species within a genus look fairly similar and tend to have a similar lifestyle, but they may be adapted to different habitats.

Because spiders have been rather neglected over the years compared with most other animal groups, and as new species are discovered, taxonomists frequently revise their ideas about the relationship between one spider and another. As a consequence scientific names are changed and species are sometimes transferred from one genus to another. So beware—the names used in one book frequently disagree with another! In the near future, though, DNA analysis may change our view of spider family relationships.

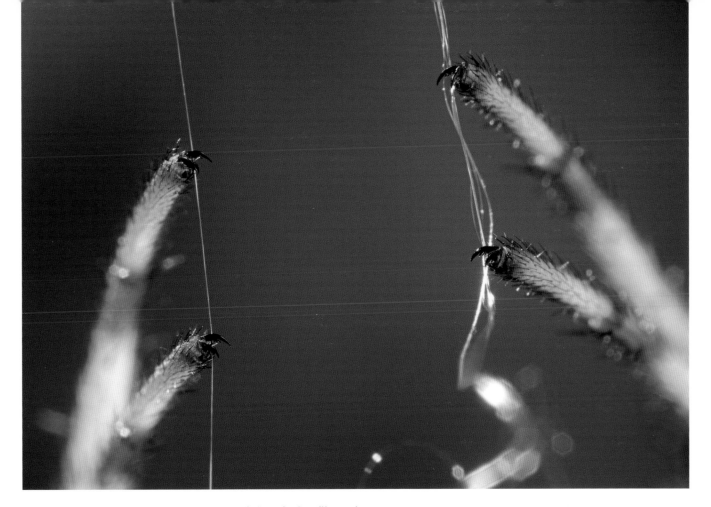

Showing orb web spider's use of claws for handling web.

Spider silk

Various invertebrates produce silk—certain insect larvae and mites, for example—but no animal approaches the spider in the versatility or variety of ingenious ways it is employed. The silvery strands of silk are woven into almost every aspect of a spider's life, and it is silk that is largely responsible for spiders' huge success over the past 300 million years, allowing them to compete with insects. Apart from making silken snares for catching prey, spiders can produce several different types of silk with a variety of characteristics from up to six different silk glands: sticky, viscid silk; silk for attaching threads; a sticky substance for depositing on thread; silk for wrapping prey; woolly cribellate silk; dragline silk; silk to protect egg-sacs; and "gossamer" silk suitable for ballooning tiny spiders thousands of feet up into the sky.

Silk is a fibrous protein made up of chains of amino acids produced by special glands in the abdomen. Although it appears as a single thread to the naked eye, in fact it is made up of several very fine strands of between one-millionth and four-millionths of an inch (0.00025–0.001 mm) in diameter. It starts as a liquid that is pushed through long ducts leading to microscopic spigots on the spider's spinnerets, but the extrusion process causes the liquid to solidify into strands. Most spiders have two or three pairs of spinnerets at the rear of the abdomen.

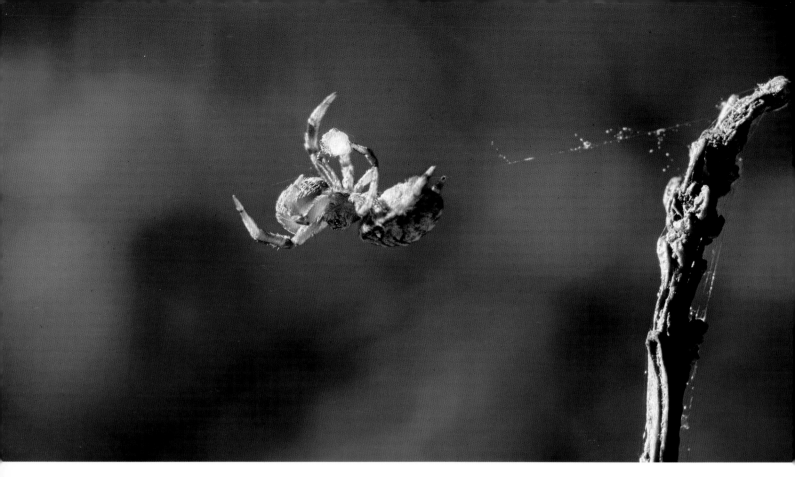

Triangle spider wrapping up old web prior to re-cycling it. The slight blurring of the legs is due to their rapid movement while rolling-up the silk (also see pages 135-137).

Valves on the spigots control the thickness and speed of the extrusion. As the spigots release the liquid out of the ducts into the air, its molecules are stretched out to form long strands that are finally wound into a strong silk fiber by the spinnerets. Watching spiders do this with the aid of a magnifier or through the camera lens is quite mind-blowing, for as well as manipulating the spinnerets or cribellum they can sometimes be seen to operate all eight legs simultaneously, each tarsal claw either working with the separate threads or holding the spider onto its web.

The whole operation is of course instinctive but it always reminds me of an organist playing a Bach fugue with ten fingers and two feet.

Each of the spider's several silk glands is optimized to produce a different quality of silk. Thus, by winding a range of varieties of silk together in varying proportions, the spider can form an assortment of webs. Furthermore, silk can be made into multiple layers, followed by a coating of a variety of substances suited for different purposes—sticky or waterproofing materials, for example.

The strength and elasticity of spider web is legendary, some types being five times stronger than steel of the same thickness, and it is capable of being stretched to about 10 times its original length. The secrets of its composition are still not totally understood to this day.

Silk is expensive in terms of body resources, so when the web is taken down after it becomes damaged or the spider wants to move to a fresh location, it is recycled. The spider does this by rolling up the silk into a ball and eating it as it climbs up or moves along the web.

Construction of a typical orb web

The most difficult part in the construction of an orb web is the first thread. This needs to be a sturdy horizontal line from which the rest of the web will hang. So how does the spider place this thread between the two connecting points? The answer is simple. It makes use of the wind and some luck: the wind carries away a thin silken thread from its spinnerets, and if the spider is lucky the thread sticks to a convenient spot. It then strengthens this primary thread with extra strands. When it is sufficiently robust to take the load of the whole orb, the spider hangs a second line in the form of a Y below the primary thread, making up the first three radials of the orb. Once all the radials are in place, it makes a temporary spiral before constructing the final, more finely pitched spiral, eating the temporary spiral on the way.

Web visibility

The human eye is incapable of detecting objects with a diameter smaller than 25 microns at a distance of 4 inches (10 cm), but the average diameter of a thread of orb web is around 0.15 microns, the thinnest threads being only 0.02 microns thick. The only time we can see the thread is when it is covered with dust or dew or when sunlight or another bright light source catches it. This is why much of the orb web's construction is invisible to us; only portions of the web catch the light at any one time. For this reason diagrams show the construction better than photographs.

▼ Construction of a typical orb weaver web.

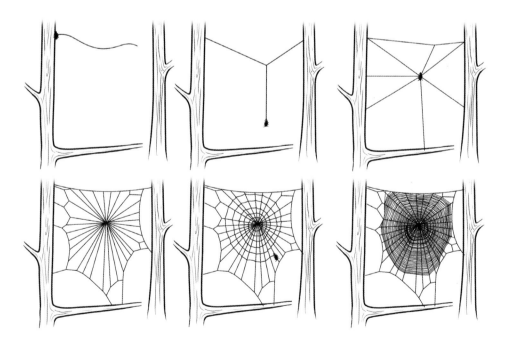

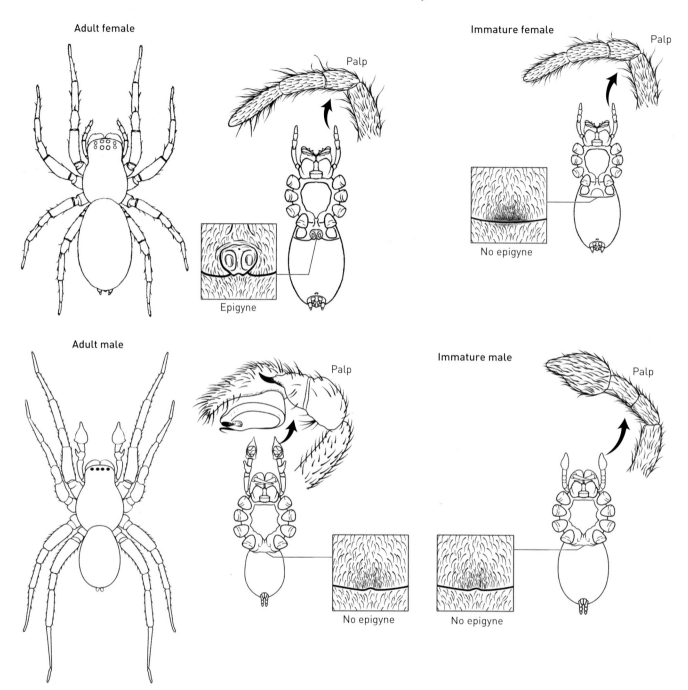

Differentiation of sex and maturity

Adult female

Palp

Epigyne

Immature female

Palp

No epigyne

Adult male

Palp

No epigyne

Immature male

Palp

No epigyne

Sexing a spider

Spider identification is not a priority here, as several books accomplish this extremely well (see bibliography), but it is still very useful to be able to determine the sex of a spider, especially as this is the first step in their identification. Many species of spiders, especially the smaller ones, can be identified with certainty only by careful examination of the palps or epigyne under the microscope. Immature specimens are best tossed away!

Courtship and mating

The courtship and mating practices of spiders are among the strangest acts in the animal kingdom. The genital organs, their physiology, the elaborate courtship and the bizarre copulation behavior that follow would seem to stem from science fiction rather than planet Earth. Male and female spiders are often strikingly different in color, size or shape; commonly adult males are often smaller than females and can be readily recognized by their conspicuously large palps.

The genital openings of both sexes are located on the underside of the abdomen between the book lungs. In addition, the male has extraordinarily complicated ancillary sex organs on the terminal joint (tarsus) of each palp. The anatomy of these structures is completely different for each species, and there is no connection whatsoever between these and the testes in the abdomen. The genital organ of the female, the epigyne, is positioned just above the genital opening (epigastric furrow) between the book lungs. Its complexity does not compare with the male's equipment, but the important point is that the two are designed to interlink perfectly during copulation, rather like a lock and key.

The initial stages of the long drawn-out mating process work as follows. The male builds a sperm web, a small rectangle or triangle of silk onto which he deposits a small drop of seminal fluid containing the spermatozoa. Now the palps come into play as they dip into and suck up the liquid rather like a fountain pen filling with ink—whether this operates by suction or capillary action is uncertain. The sperm is stored there until the male finds a mate.

The male's next task is to look for a mate. This may take anything from a few minutes to several days, depending on the type of spider and the density of the local population, but once the male senses the presence of a female, the game is on. In some spiders the courtship may be very brief or nonexistent—they simply fling their legs over each other and mate—but in the majority of species it has evolved into an elaborate ritual often surpassing the most inventive and flamboyant displays of birds.

There are sound reasons for this ritualistic behavior. Mating is often a particularly dangerous time for male spiders, as not only are the female's instincts strongly predatory but she is also usually considerably larger than her mate. Unless the male approaches her in the right way and adopts the prescribed prenuptial ritual, he

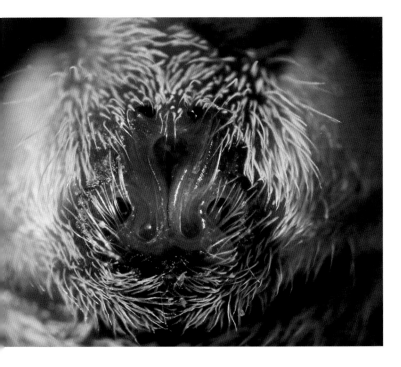

Epigyne of female spider (*Pisaura*).

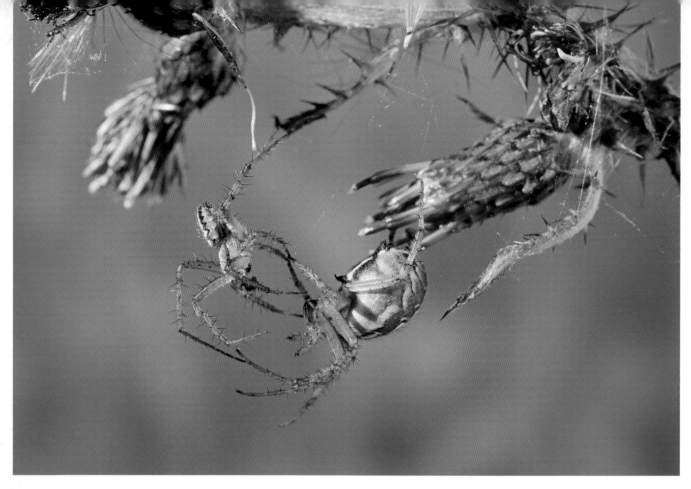

A male orb weaver (*Neoscona*) tentatively approaches the female.

stands a grave chance of being mistaken for prey and ending up as a meal instead of a mate.

The nature of courtship depends on the lifestyle of the spider and the importance attached to its various senses. In the case of web builders, the web acts as the communication line during courtship. The male begins by delivering a series of gentle tweaks to the web in such a manner that the female recognizes the coded signals. If she is happy, the male is allowed into her home and mating can take place. In the unlikely event that the incorrect code is transmitted or she is not ready, the male will have to watch his step. One genus of tropical salticid spiders, *Portia,* has learned to take advantage of this by mimicking the coded signals of male web-spinning spiders and so gaining access to the female, which is promptly attacked and eaten. *Portia* even seems to have a genetically programmed built-in database of signals from which it can make a selection according to species. It is also capable of flexible trial-and-error adjustment of signals in response to feedback from the prey. Whereas the preprogrammed repertoire of signals is consistent with animals governed by instinct, trial and error is an example of problem-solving behavior that is less expected in an invertebrate.

Hunting spiders depend on sharp eyesight for finding prey, so they have evolved a visually based courtship. Once the male has found a suitable mate, perhaps by tracking her down by pheromones in a similar way to some insects, he signals his intentions by a complicated display of leg and palp movements. The spiders that win all the prizes for chivalry are the enchanting and perky little jumping spiders. As

➤ The male inserts his palps into the female's epigyne. Note the inflated palps.

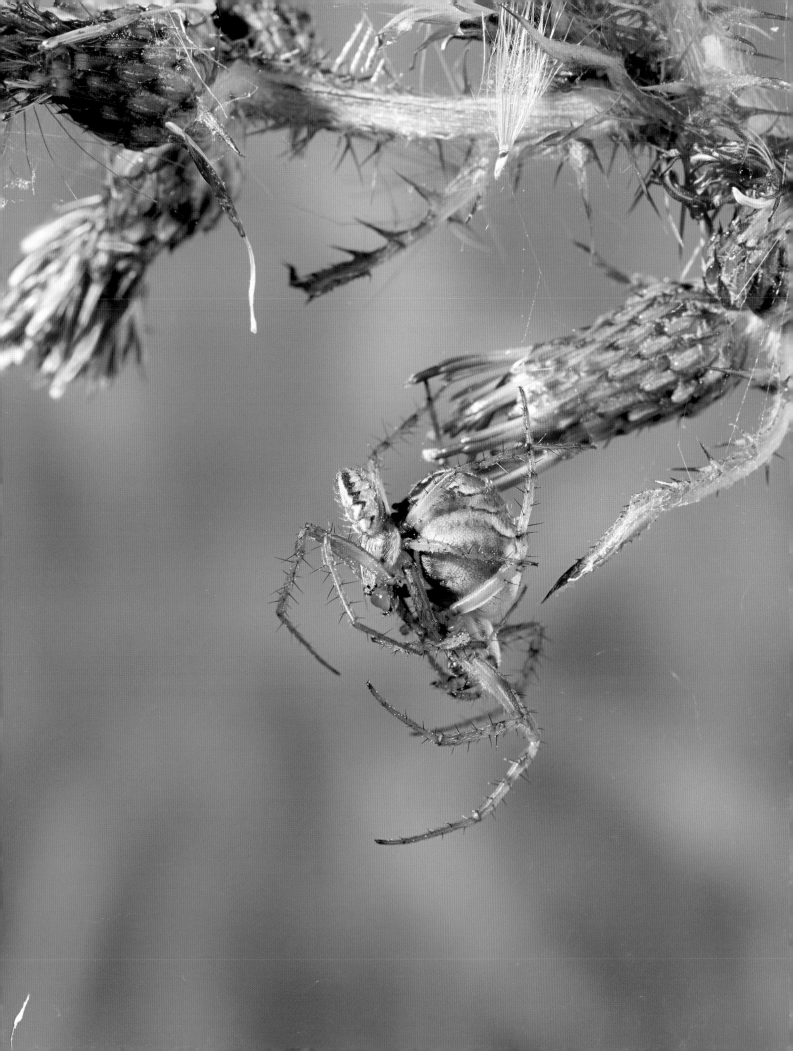

they possess the most acute eyesight of all, they perform the most elaborate dances, involving much waving of legs and vibration of palps, the nature of the display being specific to each species. Such spectacular performances may be enhanced by adornments of bright metallic colors and ornamental tufts of hair on head and legs.

Other families adopt simpler courtship strategies. For example, among the relatively primitive mygalomorphs, where the female lacks an epigyne and the male has simple palps, courtship is generally done by touch alone. Then there are spiders that may emerge only at night and live underground under stones or bark or in caves, which gain information about their surroundings almost entirely by touch or taste, using special sense organs on their legs. It is unlikely that such encounters are left to chance, as this would lead to an evolutionary blind alley, especially when populations are at a low point for some reason. Such spiders, like the hunting spiders, probably rely on pheromones.

Some male spiders, such as the nursery-web spiders *Pisaura*, practice a form of bribery by presenting their mate with gifts of wrapped prey, so distracting their partner's predatory instincts elsewhere. One of the most freakish techniques is adopted by *Xysticus* crab spiders, which employ what can only be described as bondage. Here the male circles around and over the female, stroking her gently with his legs until she is in a submissive state. As he does so he covers her with a thin veil of silk, effectively immobilizing her so that he can mate without risk to himself. After the male has left she escapes from her bonds to lay her eggs.

As with courtship, the physical act of copulation varies widely among different families. The main object of the exercise is for the pair to adopt such a position that the previously charged male palp is coupled with the female's epigyne, so allowing the seminal fluid to be transferred. The details of the procedure depend largely on the complexity of the palps and the epigyne, but it is beyond the scope of this book to describe the physiology of these here. The spermatozoa are stored in the female's abdomen until needed to fertilize the eggs.

Some male spiders ensure their paternity by fabricating a biological chastity belt by sealing their mate's epigyne. In other species the same object is achieved by the couple simply remaining together in harmony, leaving the male to repel other would-be suitors. The males of many spiders leave their mates to wander about looking for other females to couple with, but as they become weaker they may fall prey to another female of the same species. As humans we may find this horrific, but from the spiders' perspective such a fate is far better for the survival of the species than being snapped up by a bird or simply dying of exhaustion or old age.

Spider bites

Unlike those of the majority of insects, the bodies of spiders are soft and easily injured. Also, spiders are not equipped with claws, large mandibles or stings and most are weak and timid. The capacity to stop enemies and prey is critically important to them—hence the web and a venomous bite are crucial to spiders' survival. Paradoxically the most venomous species are typically quite small; they depend on their powerful venom to instantly immobilize dangerous prey.

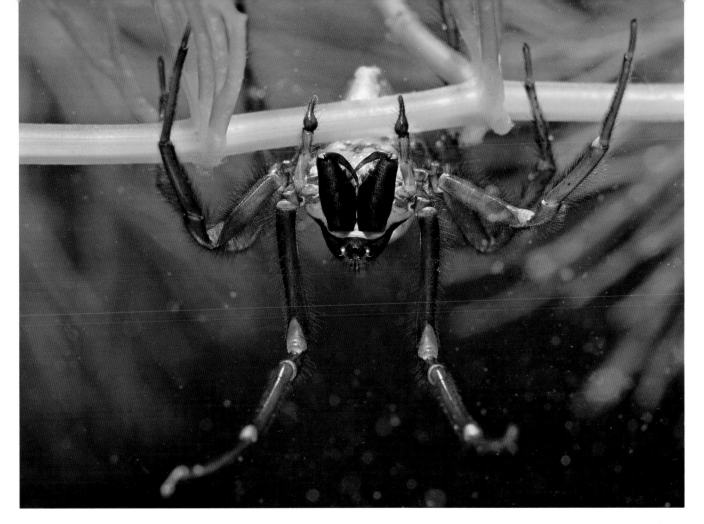

Male water spider (*Argyroneta*) showing its large jaws.

Spiders rarely bite, even if provoked. To a spider human skin is merely another surface to walk over and so there is no point in biting it, besides which the vast majority of northern European spiders are far too small to be capable of breaking its surface. Their biting instincts are geared to respond to small moving or vibrating objects such as a fly rather than a finger. Most bites are the result of a spider becoming accidentally trapped against the skin.

Only a handful of European species have the potential of biting a human, and the effects are unlikely to be much worse than a small pinprick and perhaps minor irritation. In spite of the abundance of spiders, bites are extremely rare. We all know that in hotter parts of the world there are a few nasties around—the black widow (*Latrodectus*) and brown recluse (*Loxosceles*)

are notorious examples from North America, and another is the Sydney tunnel-web spider (*Atrax*) from Australia, which is reputed to be the most dangerous spider in the world. But there have been few confirmed fatalities as a result of spider bites, while bees and wasps kill thousands of people a year. Fortunately none of the potentially dangerous spiders are found in northern Europe.

The fallacies surrounding tarantulas start with their name, which arose during the Middle Ages from the village of Taranto in Italy, where a bite from a certain spider was blamed for a range of symptoms from severe pain and vomiting to spasms and exhibitionism. The supposed cure was to perform a frenzied dance—the tarantella—until the victim dropped from exhaustion. Curiously, the species of large wolf

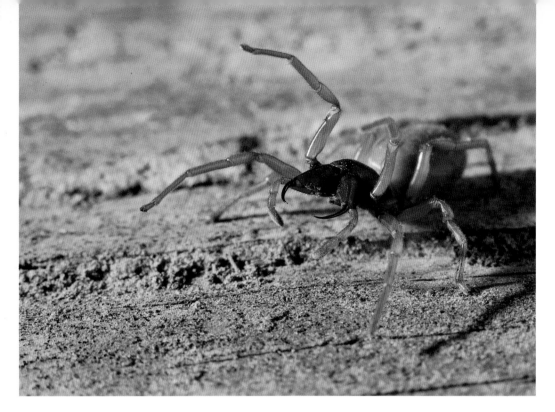

Woodlouse spider (*Dysdera*) in threat pose.

spider allegedly responsible spends most of its life in an underground burrow; it's unlikely to bite anybody and its venom is relatively harmless to humans. The culprit, if there was one at all, may have been a theriidid, *Latrodectus tredecimguttatus,* an attractive red-spotted spider closely related to the black widow.

Even the large, hairy bird-eating spiders or tarantulas are misrepresented. Although their impressive fangs can easily break the skin, the venom from most species has little effect on humans. Perhaps one of the most famous tarantulas of all time was Thomas, a spider I owned in the 1960s, which was found in a bunch of bananas. In his starring role in the first James Bond film, *Doctor No,* Thomas was persuaded—albeit reluctantly, I should add—to walk over the naked chest of Sean Connery ... but that's another story!

That being said, there are a few exceptions in both northern Europe and North America. Some of the larger species such as the house spider (*Tegenaria*) and the garden spider (*Araneus*) are capable of giving a little nip if carelessly handled or imprisoned by a hand. The water spider (*Argyroneta*) and woodlouse spider (*Dysdera*), both large-jawed species, have a reputation for biting without much provocation, and there are a number of reports of mouse spider bites, but the reason is quite understandable in the latter case. The mouse spider is not only common but has a predilection for creeping around the walls of houses at night in search of prey. Come twilight it often takes refuge in garments scattered on the floor, especially in corners or against the floor edges. When the spider's slumbers are disturbed by being thrown against an armpit or some other sensitive part of the human anatomy, it naturally tries to defend itself by using the only weapon it possesses. I have been bitten by the uncommon *Araneus marmoreus* (page 102) in exactly these circumstances; the spider must have crept into my shirt while it was hanging out to dry on the clothesline near some bushes. It was only a pinprick, but if you are worried, shake out your clothes before dressing.

Another European spider capable of biting is *Segestria,* a huge creature with flashing green

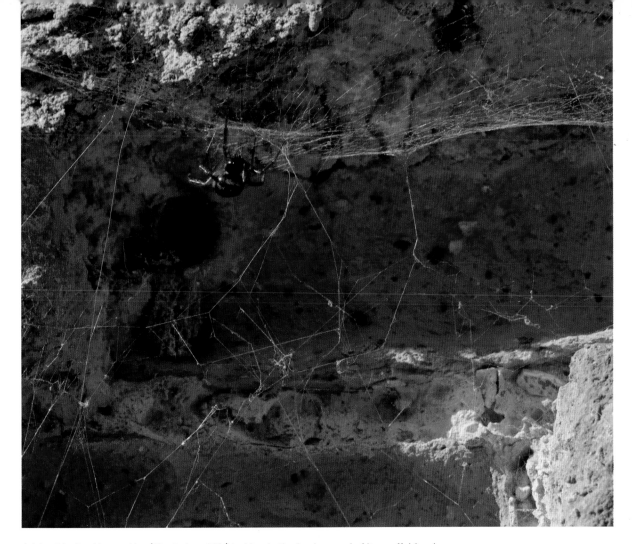

A false black widow spider (*Steotoda nobilis*) lurking in the background of its scaffold web.

jaws that bites fiercely at anything hovering near the entrance of its characteristic tunnel in a wall—a finger, for instance (page 168). A friend of mine was brave enough to try this, whereupon the spider shot out like a moray eel, grabbed his finger and held on for more than 10 seconds before finally letting go. His finger remained numb for two days!

More recently there have been reports of an alien spider establishing itself in the United Kingdom, imported from Madeira and the Canary Islands; like the black widow spider it lives around houses and outbuildings. Its bite causes intense local pain and swelling. It is a theridiid spider a little smaller than the garden spider, but with a round, shiny dark brown body. Its name is the false black widow (*Steotoda nobilis*) (see above and page 148). Apparently its neurotoxic venom initiates production of a neurotransmitter, and it appears to mimic the venom produced by the black widow (*Lactrodectus*), to which this spider is closely related. It has been found in sheds and porches hanging upside down in tangles of web. The spider is clearly spreading—I found one on a bridge over a country stream some way from human habitation. Perhaps best avoided!

There can be little doubt that, apart from the bites of a very few particularly poisonous spiders, the physical effects of stings from wasps and bees are more painful and potentially more serious. For most people the psychological effects of a spider bite are more traumatic than the actual bite.

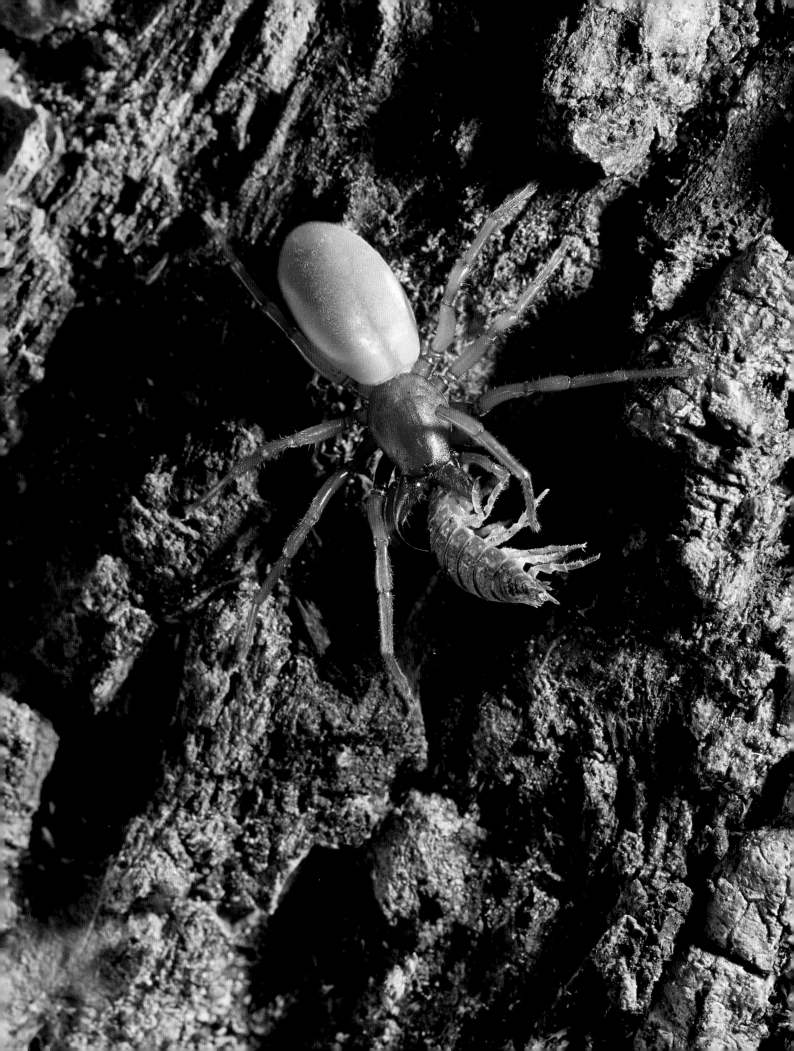

2

Nocturnal Hunters

The prey-catching techniques of nocturnal spiders, which hunt at night, do not depend on web traps or keen eyesight but rely instead on scent, touch or vibration to locate prey. Many spiders are particularly active at night, including many orb weavers, spitting spiders and house spiders, but the spiders described here are those that actively hunt at night. They are generally much duller in color than the daylight species, most being brown, black or gray, and are often furnished with fine hairs. Their habits too are less spectacular, as they prefer to creep about rather than making the high-speed dashes of daylight hunters. Their eyes are correspondingly much smaller than those of their more active diurnal counterparts. During the day these nocturnal hunters hide away in silken retreats under stones, in holes in logs and trees or curled up in leaves.

A common European nocturnal hunter—a species that is also spreading in North America—is the mouse spider, *Scotophaeus blackwalli*. It wanders about in houses at night looking for prey, then makes a short sprint and pounces on its victim. Another, less common species is the more brightly colored woodlouse spider, *Dysdera crocata*.

Nocturnal hunting families

The **Gnaphosidae** family, commonly known as ground or stealthy spiders, are mostly gray or black, lacking in pattern, and are furnished with short silken hairs, but some species are subtly iridescent. They have protruding and widely spaced cylindrical spinnerets.

Gnaphosids are primarily ground dwellers, only rarely occupying arboreal habitats. They spin tubular silken retreats in rolled leaves or under stones, hiding during the day and emerging only at night. These spiders rely on scent, touch and stealth to find prey.

Gnaphosids are often the most abundant spiders to be found in open and drier areas. About 250 species occur in North America and 15 in northern Europe.

◄ Woodlouse spider.

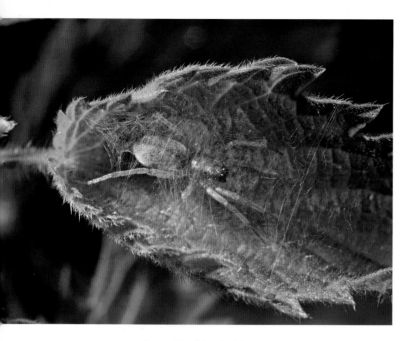

Sac spider (*Clubionia*) in cell.

Another family of nocturnal hunters are the **Dysderidae**, the woodlouse or long-fanged six-eyed spiders. Dysderidae are relatively primitive nocturnal short-sighted spiders, all of which have a rather long, smooth abdomen with no clear pattern or markings. In common with other ground spiders, they do not construct webs for catching prey but make silken retreats under logs and stones.

Their jutting jaws give them a menacing appearance. They possess six eyes only, which are arranged in a circular pattern. The female has no epigyne, while the male's palps are of simple design. This spider is a specialist in catching creatures that most other spiders reject or are unable to tackle—woodlice. Hence the impressive fangs, which are adapted to pierce the tough body armor of these animals and similar arthropods.

Four species occur in northern Europe, while only one is recorded from North America.

The **Clubionidae** family, sac or foliage spiders, are a largish family of mostly nocturnal spiders that bear a superficial resemblance to Gnaphosidae, the night prowlers. The easiest way to tell the two apart is to examine the

spinnerets, which in Gnaphosidae are cylindrical and more widely separated; those of the clubionids are more pointed and generally appear smaller. In addition, sac spiders are typically foliage hunters. The majority of these spiders are brownish or gray, with little in the way of markings except for the subtle shadings of their velvety coat, although there are a few exceptions. Most species can be reliably identified only by microscopic examination.

Sac spiders are so named for their habit of resting during the day in a silken cell hidden in a rolled leaf among vegetation or under stones or bark. Some occur in dry situations at ground level, similar to the gnaphosids, while others prefer damper situations higher up in bushes and trees. North America has 58 species and 35 may be found in northern Europe.

Prowling or long-legged sac spiders, the **Miturgidae** family, are similar to the sac spiders and were once bundled together in the same family, but the former have longer legs and more robust bodies. Like sac spiders they are nocturnal wandering hunters that hide during the day in silken sacs. Most species are ground dwelling, living in forest, scrub and rocky deserts. This is a small family with only about 40 species worldwide. Twelve are found in North America.

The nocturnal spiders of the **Anyphaenidae** family, known as buzzing or phantom spiders, occur mostly in the foliage of trees and in leaf litter, hiding during the day in tubular silk retreats. Under a lens the family can be identified by the displaced tracheal spiracles, which are midway between the spinnerets and the epigastric furrow. Rather than trapping prey in webs, buzzing spiders hunt down insects in a similar manner to the running crab spiders, Philodromidae. There are 37 species in North America and one from northern Europe.

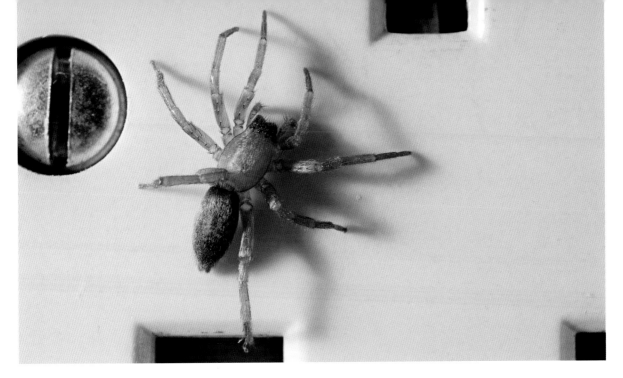

Mouse spider on electrical socket.

Mouse spider (*Scotophaeus blackwalli*)

Scotophaeus from Greek *scotos* (darkness); *blackwalli* after John Blackwall, a 19th-century spider expert

One of the most frequently seen spiders in houses is the mouse spider, a member of the Gnaphosidae family. Rather than spending its time hiding away on its web in dark corners like the house spider, the mouse spider stalks stealthily around the walls and ceiling at night in search of prey. It can often be seen in the form of a gently moving dark blob that pauses every now and again for a rest.

Although it does not build a web for trapping prey, like so many spiders the mouse spider trails a thread of silk as it stalks about, pouncing with speed and ferocity on any prey it encounters, such as mosquitoes, moths and flies. When not creeping around the house, the mouse spider spends the day in a silken cell hidden away in a crevice behind a picture or in the folds of curtains or clothing. Able to survive for months without water, it is well suited to a domestic environment.

A fully mature female mouse spider is about 0.5 inch (12 mm) long, and this size, coupled with her dark, velvety-sleek mousy appearance, gives her a slightly creepy aura. Although not aggressive, this spider has occasionally been known to nip more delicate areas of the skin. But such bites are insignificant when compared with the assaults of most other small creatures such as wasps and horseflies!

The mouse spider can be seen at any time during the year in the warmer parts of Europe, under bark or in holes in walls, but in England it lives only in and around houses. The species is now well established in North America, where it was imported from Europe.

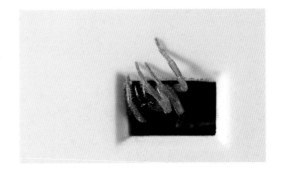

Mouse spider peeping out from retreat in electrical socket.

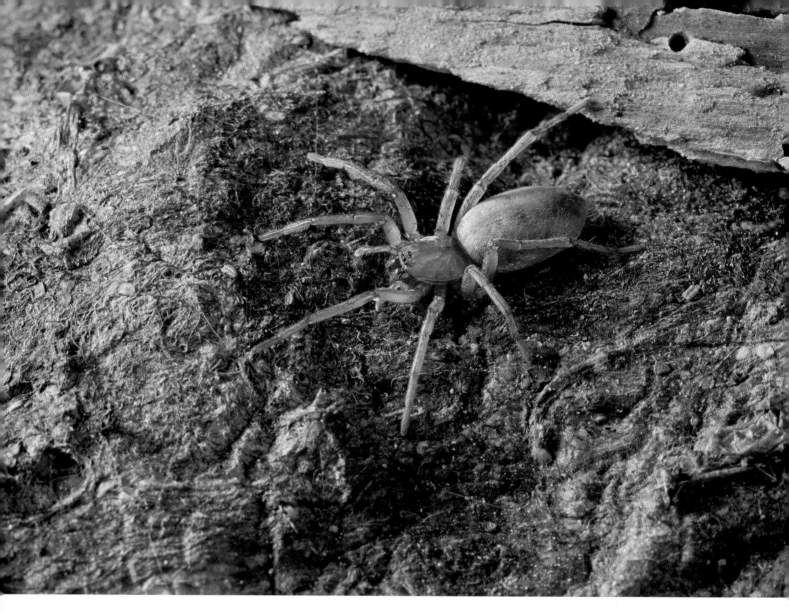

A ground-living nocturnal hunter (*Drassodes*) showing typically somber colors associated with its lifestyle.

Ground spider (*Drassodes lapidosus*)

Drassodes from Greek "active on the road"; *lapidosus* from Latin "stony"

Another common but larger ground spider is *Drassodes lapidosus*. It is the largest and fiercest of the northern European gnaphosids, reaching about 0.7 inch (18 mm) in length. It is a sleek and mousy-looking spider with a pinkish gray abdomen and is lithe in movement, capable of moving rapidly when disturbed from its daytime retreat under a stone or log or at the base of a grass tussock. At night *Drassodes* emerges from its silken cell to prowl around like a panther in search of food.

There are several species of *Drassodes* in the genus, *D. lapidosus* being found all over Europe. Identification of some of them is possible only by careful examination with a powerful lens or microscope. There are six species of *Drassodes* in North America; one of the common ones is *D. neglectus,* a yellowish or light gray spider that has an indistinct pattern of chevrons toward the rear of the abdomen.

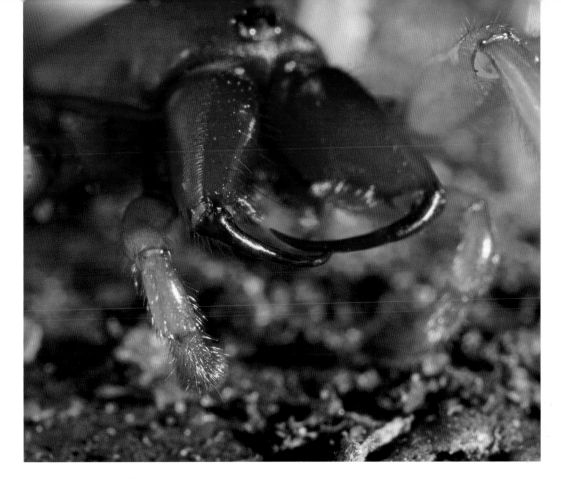

Fangs of woodlouse spider.

Woodlouse spider (*Dysdera crocata*)

Dysdera from Greek "without a fleece"; *crocata* from Latin "saffron yellow" (referring to its hairless yellow abdomen)

The bright orange legs and a carapace with contrasting cream abdomen, together with the massive protruding chelicerae with their wickedly sharp fangs, imbue the woodlouse spider, *Dysdera crocata*, with a sinister appearance. This member of the Dysderidae family (known as the sow bug killer in North America) favors slightly warm and damp habitats, often around buildings, spending the daylight hours in a silken cell under logs or stones. Come nightfall it wakes up to wander about in pursuit of suitable prey.

There are two similar European members of the genus, *D. crocata* and *D. erythrina,* and they are difficult to tell apart. The former species is also found sporadically in North America, where it was probably imported from the Mediterranean.

Most nocturnal spiders spend the day in a silken cell.

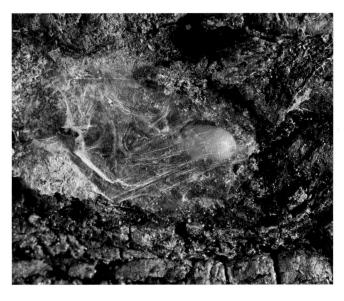

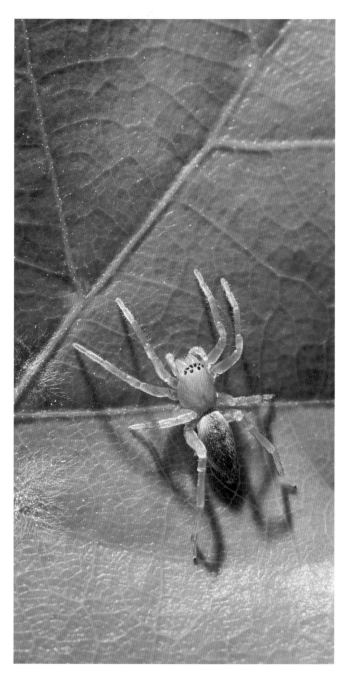

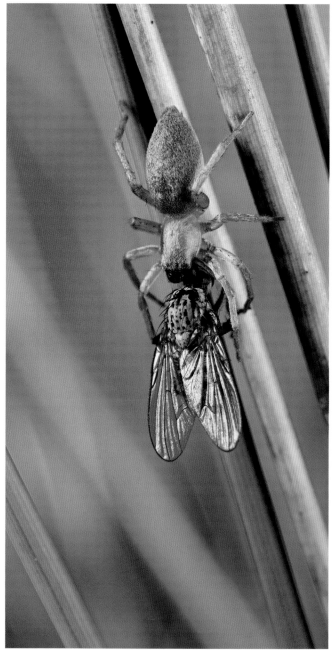

Sac spider on a nocturnal prowl.

Sac spider with prey.

Clubiona phragmitis

Clubiona from Greek "cage" (referring to the silken sac); *phragmitis* from Greek "reed"

The habits of spiders in the Clubionidae family are broadly similar to one another, although they occupy a range of slightly variable habitats, depending on species. Two European species are illustrated here: *Clubiona lutescens*, a common species that lives among low vegetation, shrubs and bushes, often in damp places, and *C. phragmitis*, which prefers drier habitats—this one was photographed in marram grass growing on a coastal sand dune. Neither of these two species occurs in North America, but there are many with similar appearance and habits.

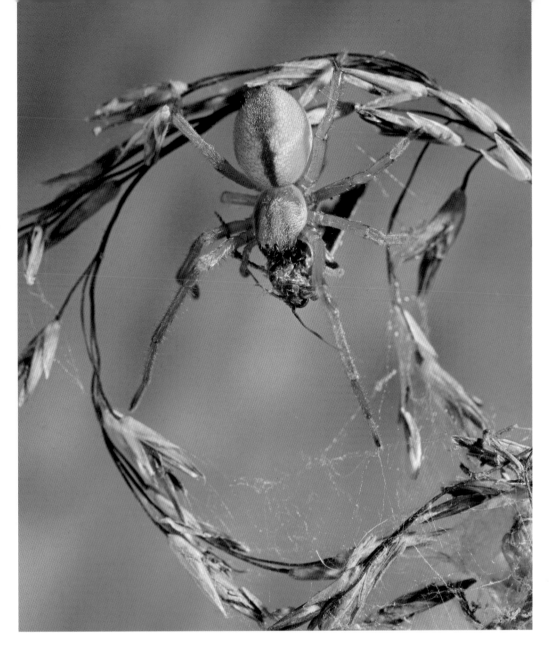

Grasshead prowling spider with prey.

Grasshead prowling spider

(*Cheiracanthium erraticum*)

Cheirocanthium from Greek "thorned hand"; *erraticum* from Latin "wandering"

The spider illustrated, *Cheiracanthium erraticum*, is the commonest and prettiest member of this genus. Unlike other spiders of the Miturgidae family, which prefer a more arboreal lifestyle, it lives among low plants such as heathers and grasses. It also differs from the clubionids in having a longer, slimmer first pair of legs and narrowing, forward-slanting chelicerae.

One way to find *C. erraticum* is to look out for its silken cells interwoven with dead grass heads, which protect both the spider and her eggs; when backlit the spider can often be seen sandwiched within.

C. erraticum is widespread in Europe, while a similar species, *C. mildei*, occurs in both southern Europe and North America, where it was introduced. A few of the larger species have a reputation for biting people and causing necrotic blisters.

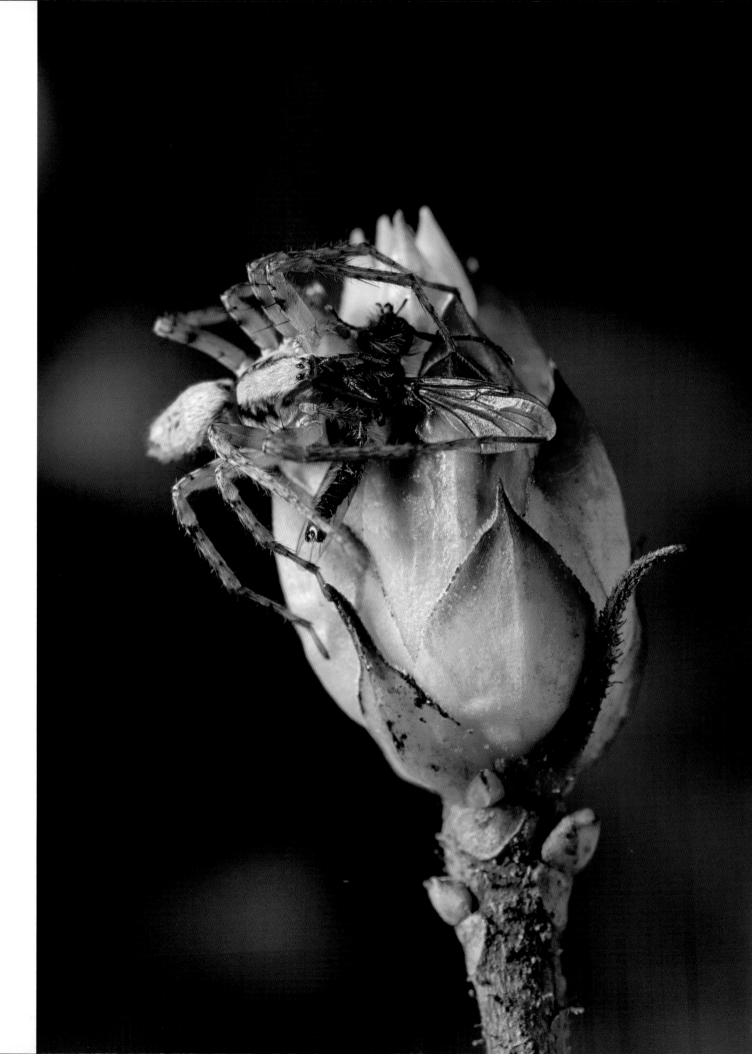

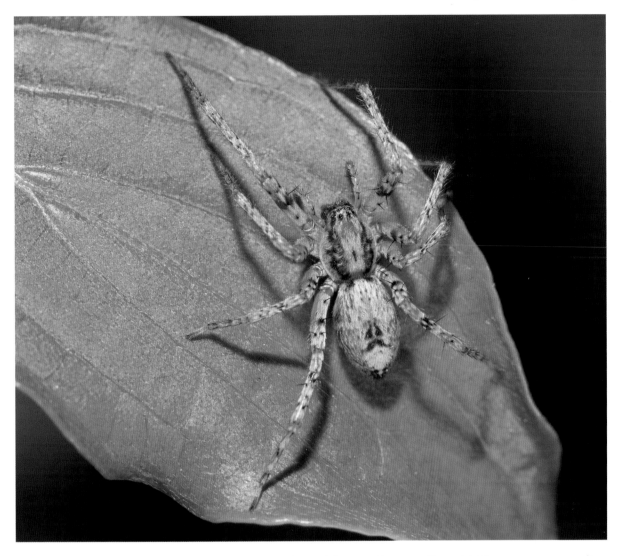

Buzzing spider showing characteristic double chevron marks on abdomen; with prey on flower (right).

European buzzing spider
(*Anyphaena accentuata*)

Anyphaena from Greek "without web";
accentuata from Latin "sings to others"

Few spiders make audible sounds, but the buzzing spider is an exception. As part of an elaborate courtship display, the male raises his front legs and violently taps his abdomen against the leaf beneath him, producing a high-pitched buzzing like a tuning fork on paper.

Anyphaena accentuata has the distinction of being the only member of the Anyphaenidae family found in northern Europe, but in North America, where the family has its headquarters, its relatives are quite common. *A. accentuata* can generally be recognized by distinct pairs of dark marks on the abdomen, although the female turns gray and loses her markings once she lays eggs.

Buzzing spiders are particularly adept at leaping rapidly from leaf to leaf, pouncing on insects such as small flies and leafhoppers that take their fancy. To help them cling to the leaves and twigs of shrubs and trees, they are equipped with special tufts of hair on their claws known as scopulae. The best way of finding a buzzing spider is to beat the lower branches of trees and shrubs, particularly oak trees, in early summer, although few males survive into June.

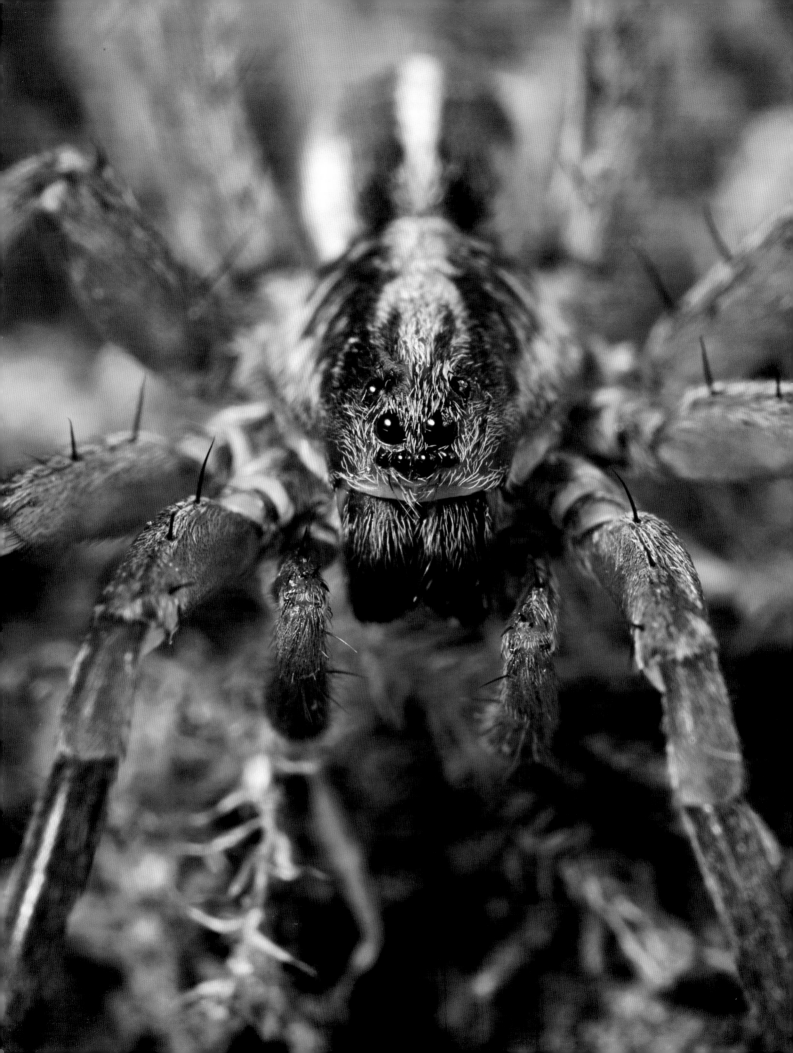

3 Daylight Visual Hunters

When compared with most other groups of spiders, the prey-catching methods used by the daylight hunters are relatively conventional. Rather than relying on cunning techniques such as web traps or spitting, they locate prey visually and run them down or ambush them. Many wolf spiders, for instance, execute this at high speed, rather like cheetahs chasing antelope, with the odd little jump thrown in from time to time. These spiders, which include mainly the jumping, wolf, nursery-web and lynx spiders, rely heavily on their eyesight for prey capture and so can generally be recognized by their large eyes.

The wolf spiders are the most familiar—anyone who has wandered around the countryside in spring or early summer will not have failed to notice restless movements on the dry, leafy woodland floor or open fields as these ground-loving hunters sprint off to safety. Indeed, any spider seen dashing around on terra firma is most likely to be a wolf spider. As most wolf spiders spend their lives on the ground, they tend to be brown or gray in color, although some species are blessed with brighter markings that become evident only when examined closely. Almost all wolf spiders hunt in daylight, so they need keen eyesight, this being provided by the two large, forward-pointing median eyes. Although frequently found in large numbers, they do not hunt in packs, as their name suggests!

Other spiders with a similar predatory lifestyle include the hunting spiders, Pisauridae—the best known of which is the handsome nursery-web spider, *Pisaura mirabilis*—and the lynx spiders, Oxyopidae. The latter hunt actively on vegetation, often leaping from leaf to leaf like jumping spiders. Three species of lynx spiders are found in Europe but only one member of the family lives in England, where it is rare and restricted to a few Surrey heathlands; more colorful and larger species are found in North America. Another family included here are the ghost spiders, Zoridae. These resemble sac spiders in some respects but unlike them are basically daylight hunters.

◄ Lycosid wolf spider showing eye layout (*Trochosa*).

Daylight visual hunting families

The dark, furry appearance of **Lycosidae**, or wolf spiders, together with their ability to chase down prey at high speed, has earned them their family name. They need excellent eyesight for their active hunting technique and so have especially large anterior eyes set in an arrangement that is characteristic of the family. It is one of the largest groups of spiders, with about 3,000 species worldwide, superseded in numbers only by jumping spiders (Salticidae), money spiders (Linyphiidae) and comb-footed spiders (Theridiidae).

Wolf spiders are largely free-living and can be seen scurrying over the ground as they run for safety at our approach, especially on warm days. The females can often be spotted carrying their egg-sac attached to the spinnerets. Some dig burrows and pounce on or give chase to insects that wander close to the entrance. Some wolf spiders—*Trochosa* species, for instance—are nocturnal and can be detected at night with a flashlight, as their eyes reflect the light back in the same way as those of nocturnal mammals.

Like wolf spiders, the **Pisauridae**, or nursery-web spiders, are free-living, so they do not build webs to trap prey but rely on their excellent eyesight instead. They are usually larger than most wolf spiders, varying from 0.32 to 1.2 inch (8–30 mm) long. Females build large, conspicuous tent-like webs for protecting their offspring. Rather than carrying her egg-sac on her spinnerets like the wolf spiders, the female uses her jaws. This family includes the raft or fishing spiders described in chapter 9.

Like the wolf and nursery-web spiders, lynx spiders, or **Oxyopidae**, are agile daytime hunters, but even more so, relying on their large and efficient eyes to find prey. Once the target is located, lynx spiders slowly creep forward, cat-like, until within pouncing distance—which can be quite long. Indeed, their jumping abilities can sometimes almost match those of the true jumping spiders. They may also be found running and leaping through foliage and flowers in active pursuit of prey, sometimes stopping to crouch low before continuing their quest. They are largely a tropical family.

Lynx spiders are sun lovers and are often beautifully camouflaged. Most can be identified by their heavily spined legs, rather slim, pointed abdomen, high-domed head and eye arrangement, with one smaller pair positioned below a hexagonal pattern of six larger ones. North America can boast of 18 species, but Europe has only three.

To quote *Spiders of North America* by Ubick, Paquin, Cushing and Roth, "zorids have wandered about (in taxonomic terms) since the mid-1800s and have yet to find a comfortable placement." In the past **Zoridae**, the ghost or spiny-legged spiders, have been classed at various times with the Gnathosidae, Clubonidae, Lycosidae and Ctedinae. For the time being they have been given a family of their own, but maybe DNA analysis will reveal their true family origins.

Zorids are sprightly ground- and shrub-dwelling spiders that are active mainly during the day, having a similar hunting strategy to the clubionids. Ghost spiders do not build webs but hunt actively, chasing down their prey among low vegetation or at ground level in leaf litter, moss and the detritus of hedges and woods in a variety of dampish habitats. Seven species occur in northern Europe but only one in North America.

➤ Nursery-web spider (*Pisaura mirabilis*) guarding nest of spiderlings.

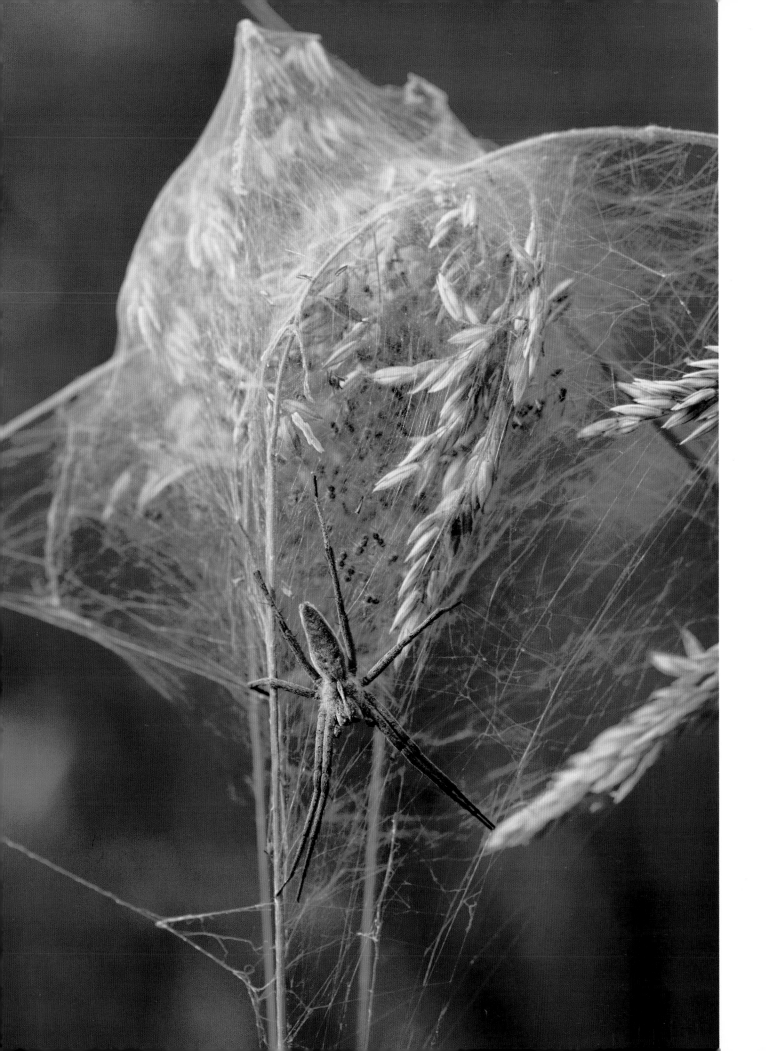

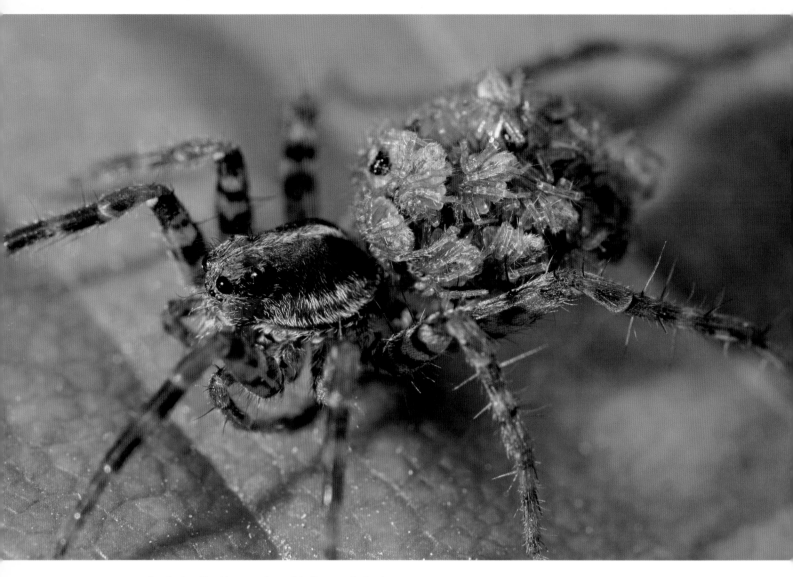

Spotted wolf spider carrying spiderlings on its back.

Spotted wolf spider (*Pardosa amentata*)

Pardosa from Greek "spotted like a leopard"; *amentata* from Latin "furnished with a strap"

The majority of Lycosidae wolf spiders carry their egg-sac attached to the spinnerets, which makes the females very conspicuous as they run about on the ground. This exposes the eggs to the warmth of the sun, accelerating their development. On hatching, the spiderlings climb onto their mother's back and are carried around by her for about a week. When viewed with the naked eye the female's abdomen looks fuzzy and irregularly shaped; a close inspection will soon reveal the individual spiderlings. The males are a little smaller than their mates; like many wolf spiders during courtship, they employ a system of semaphore, signaling with the palps and front legs.

Pardosa amentata is a ubiquitous species, being found in a wide variety of habitats—this one was living among a patch of wildflowers in my garden. It is one of the commonest species in Britain and can be seen any time from spring to autumn in northern Europe.

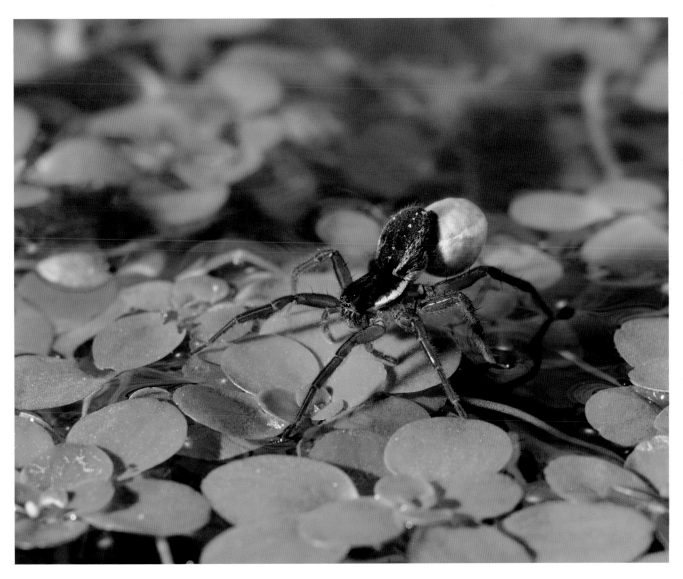

Common pirate wolf spider on pond surface with egg-sac.

Wolf spider (*Pirata piraticus*)

Pirata from Greek "sea-robber"; *piraticus* from Latin "piratical"

This velvety rust-brown wolf spider, with its white spots and smart white lateral stripes running down the full length of the body, is a lover of watery habitats. In hot weather this member of the Lycosidae family can often be seen running over the surface of ponds and bogs, where it hunts for insects on or just below the surface.

The female here is basking in the midday sun with her egg-sac attached to her spinnerets. When alarmed she will vanish beneath the surface, not to reappear for several minutes.

In North America this spider is known as the common pirate. Unfortunately this causes confusion with pirate spiders from an entirely different family, Mimetidae—spiders that really do lead a piratical lifestyle. Several very similar *Pirata* species are found in both Europe and North America.

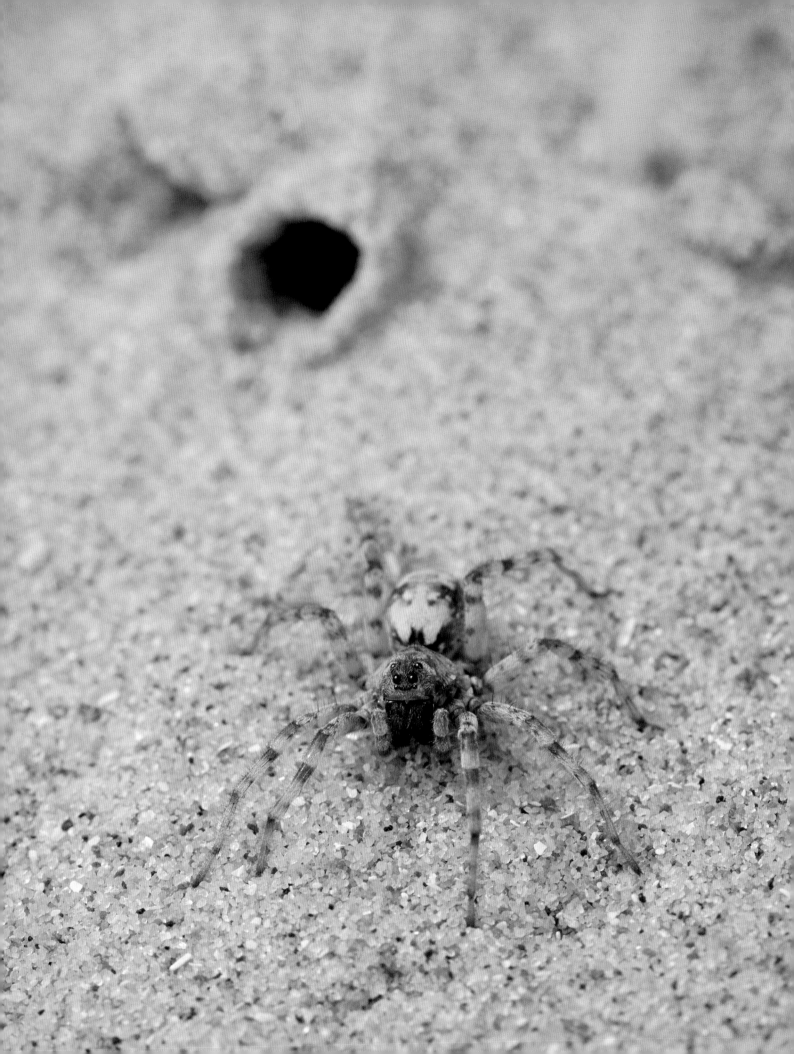

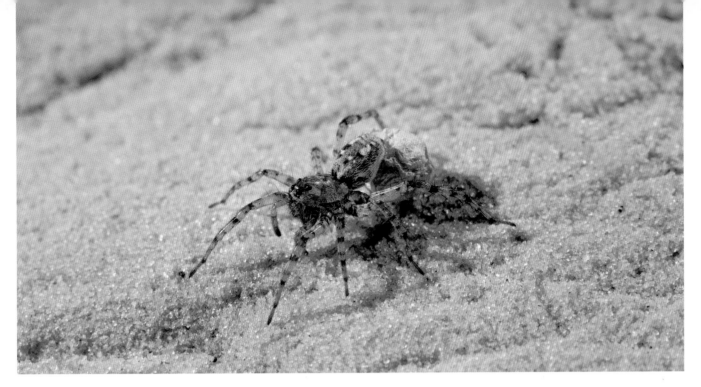

Sand-dune wolf spider with egg-sac.

Sand-dune wolf spider (*Arctosa perita*)

Arctosa from Greek arktos, "bear"; *perita* from Latin "skillful" or "experienced" (at camouflage?)

Living on sand requires special adaptations and camouflage, and this lycosid species clearly exhibits both. Attractively decorated with subtle pink and black markings and annulated legs, *A. perita* blends perfectly into its natural habitat of coastal dunes and light sandy soil. In North America the very similar *A. littoralis* is sometimes known as the sand-runner.

Perita spends most of its time inside a silk-lined burrow that it excavates in the sand. When the weather is sufficiently warm it peeps out of the entrance, waiting to pounce on some unsuspecting insect that may wander by. Members of this genus have a rather flattened carapace with the posterior eyes mounted on top so they look upward. Like all wolf spiders, *perita* has acute eyesight that can spot the slightest movement. At any sign of danger, for

◄ Sand-dune wolf spider leaving its burrow.

instance, a human walking past several yards away, it will bolt down its hole, not to appear again until the potential threat has vanished. If the danger seems especially grave, this spider will seal the burrow entrance with a curtain made from sand and silk. Recording its activity on film entailed lying flat in the sand with a long-focus macro lens and keeping stock-still for an hour or two. Just a twitch of a finger sent the spider bolting back down the hole.

Unfortunately for *perita*, it has a deadly enemy, one that is capable of detecting it even when buried out of sight beneath the sand in its closed burrow. This is a small hunting wasp, *Pompillus plumeus,* that depends on the spider to lay her egg on, thus providing fresh meat for the larva that hatches. When the wasp senses a spider underground, presumably by scent, it digs frantically down into the tunnel to find the spider—"like an excited terrier," according to W.S. Bristowe. *Perita* has a trick up its sleeve, though, which more often than not enables it to make an escape. The tunnel is Y-shaped, allowing the spider to execute a high-speed sprint through the alternative fork into the open—followed no doubt a second or so later by a frustrated wasp.

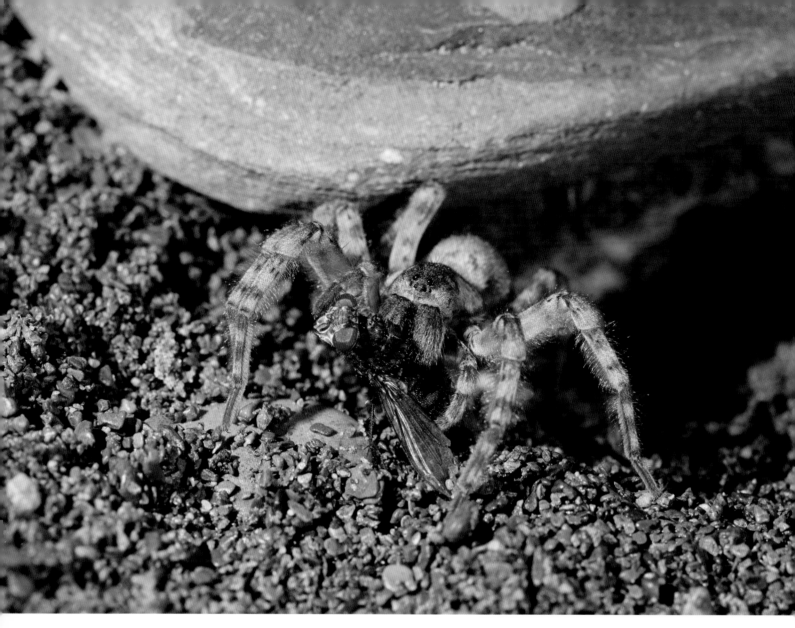

Wolf spider (*Arctosa cinerea*) with prey at entrance of its riverbank burrow.

Wolf spider (*Arctosa cinerea*)

Arctosa from Greek *arktos*, "bear"; *cinerea* from Latin "ash-colored"

This splendid lycosid is Britain's largest wolf spider, although both sexes lack the brighter colors of some of their smaller relatives. The female is shown here. It spends most of its life in a silk-lined burrow of its own making in the sand and pebbles of rivers and lakesides, where it waits in ambush for any invertebrate that comes within its field of vision. From time to time the spider will also venture out of its hiding place to hunt more actively.

Most *Arctosa* species are mottled with gray or brown markings and have annulated legs so that they blend into their preferred habitat among sand and stones. *Arctosa cinerea* does not occur in North America, although there are a number of similar species. One way of spotting these spiders is at night. If you hold a flashlight level with your eyes, the spider's eyes will reflect the light with a characteristic blue-green glow.

➤ Wolf spider basking on riverbank shingle.

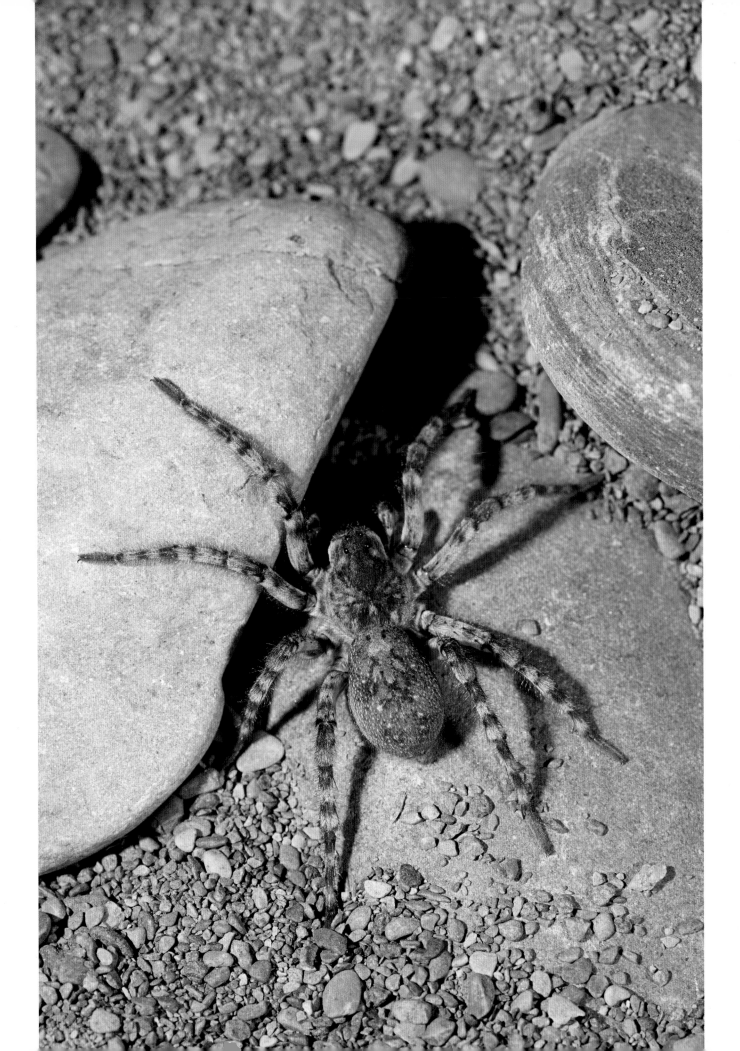

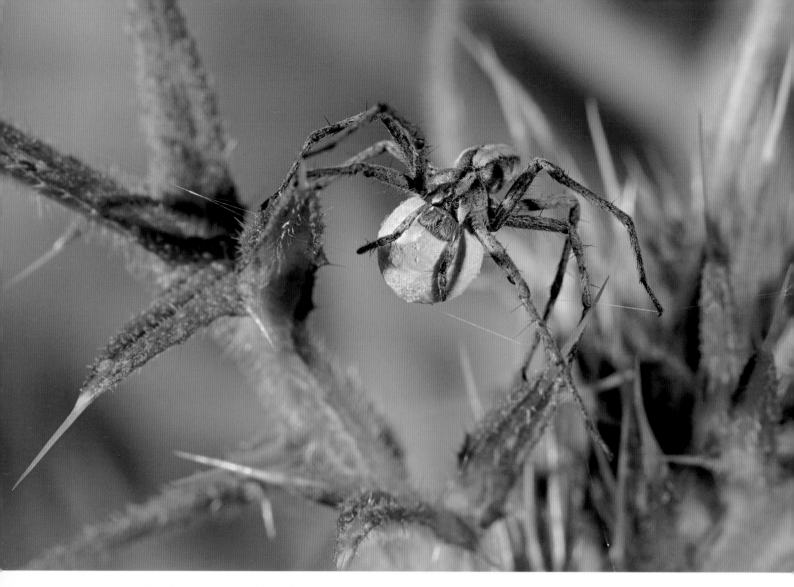

Female nursery-web spider with egg-sac.

Nursery-web spider (*Pisaura mirabilis*)

Pisaura from Latin *Pisaurum* (Pesaro) in Umbria, Italy; *mirabilis* from Latin "wonderful" or "extraordinary"

This large, handsome spider is a familiar sight to country dwellers all over England and northern Europe, where it can be found around heathland, grassland and woodland clearings. A very similar species, *Pisaurina mira*, is found in North America.

The most obvious evidence of *Pisaura*'s activities appears during late summer, when conspicuous nursery tents can be seen strewn among the low vegetation of their favorite haunts.

These serve to protect the egg-sac, which the female hangs up inside while she stands guard outside, ready to attack any intruder that dares to get too close.

This spider's color ranges from rich chocolate brown or light tan to light gray, with a pale narrow band running down the middle of the carapace and an abdomen bordered by wavy lines. There are three northern European species of hunting spiders in the Pisauridae family, all of which have long, robust legs and acute eyesight. All are active hunters either in low vegetation, like *Pisaura* and *Pisaurina*, or on the surface of water, as in the case of *Dolomedes* (described in chapter 9).

Like other hunters, the female does not spin webs to catch prey but runs around among low plants or on the ground in pursuit of her quarry. When at rest or sensing prey, she frequently can be seen with her two front pairs of legs held together and extended stiffly forward at an angle, like a pointer sniffing the air. Unless you approach very cautiously she will dart off to hide under a leaf or jump down into lower vegetation. During courtship the male presents his mate with a wedding present of a wrapped juicy grasshopper or some other insect, which acts as a diversion during mating. However, he has been known to cheat by wrapping up an empty carcass or even running off with the gift at the end of the mating ceremony!

Come July, the female may be found trundling about with a large spherical egg-sac beneath her sternum. When the eggs are ready to hatch she attaches the sac to some low vegetation, such as long grass or heather, and weaves the large protective tent all around it. On hatching, the spiderlings cluster together for a few days before molting and gradually wandering off on their own.

Female nursery-web spider.

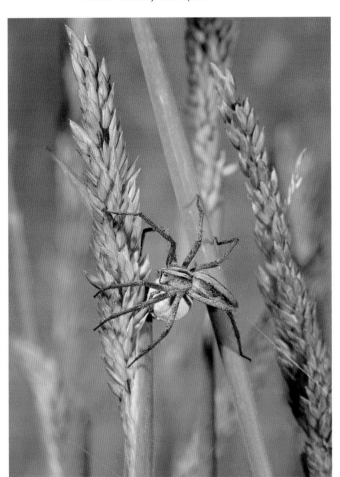

Male nursery-web spider.

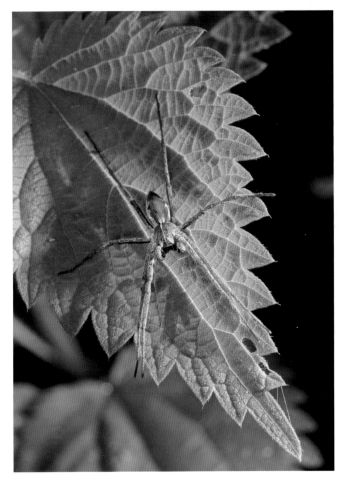

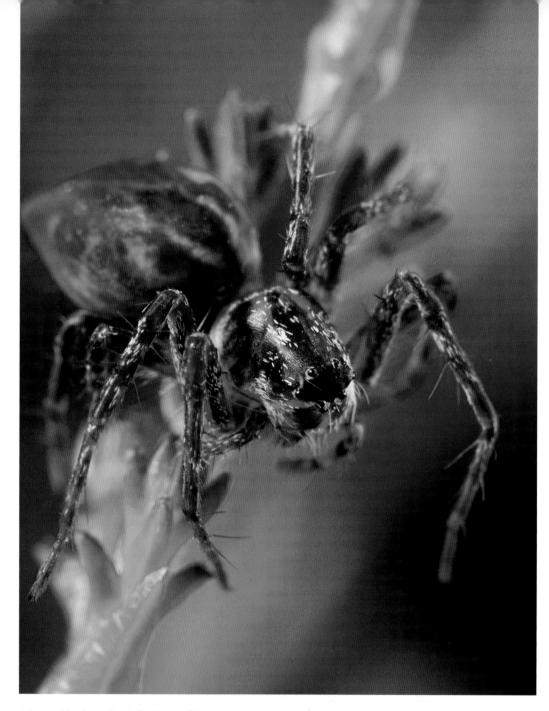

A lynx spider from Northern Europe (*Oxyopes heterophthalmus*).

Lynx spider (*Oxyopes heterophthalmus*)

Oxyopes from Greek "sharp"; *heterophthalmus* from Greek *heteros ophthalmos*, "different (other) eye"

Most of the 500-odd species of lynx spiders, the Oxyopidae, live in the tropics, although a few are found in Europe and North America. Britain has only a single representative, *Oxyopes heterophthalmus,* which is unfortunately rare, being restricted to a few heathland areas in Surrey, although it is widespread over much of Europe. One particularly attractive species from the southern United States, the green lynx spider, *Peucetia viridians,* will spit venom at any intruder that threatens her or her progeny from up to 8 inches (20 cm) away.

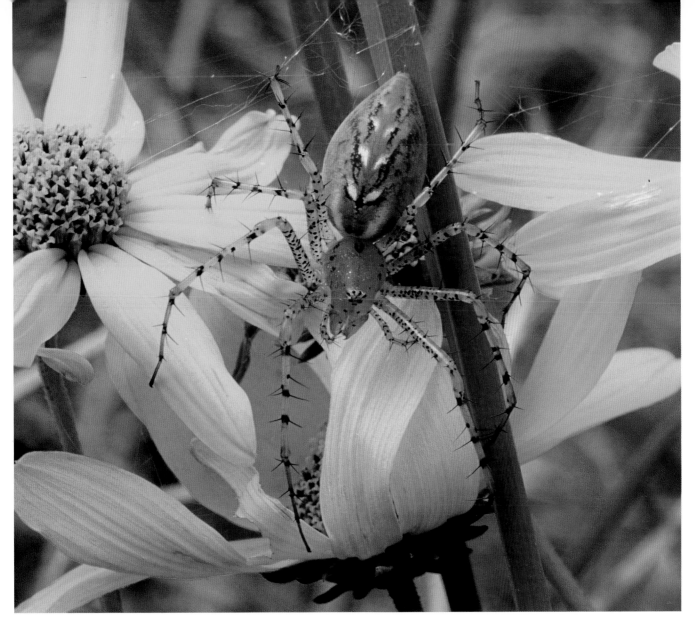

The green lynx spider from North America.

Green lynx spider (*Peucetia viridians*)

Peucetia—alternate name for Pasithea, one of the three graces of Greek mythology; *viridians* from Latin *viridis*, "green"

This handsome, vivid green spider is common in the southern United States and Mexico. Larger than its European counterpart, it is only a medium-sized spider measuring about 0.5 inches (15 mm). Although those from the southeastern states are bright green, specimens from the western side tend to be yellow or brown.

Like the European species *Oxyopes heterophthalmus,* this spider hunts prey by day, running with agility and leaping from one stem to another. It can also adopt a more passive approach by waiting for insects on flowers and stems, sometimes standing on its hind legs with front legs raised in a posture reminiscent of a praying mantis.

The female spins a large egg sac and extends lines of silk to nearby vegetation, forming a sort of nursery web. Here she stands guard, ready to spit venom into the face of any intruder.

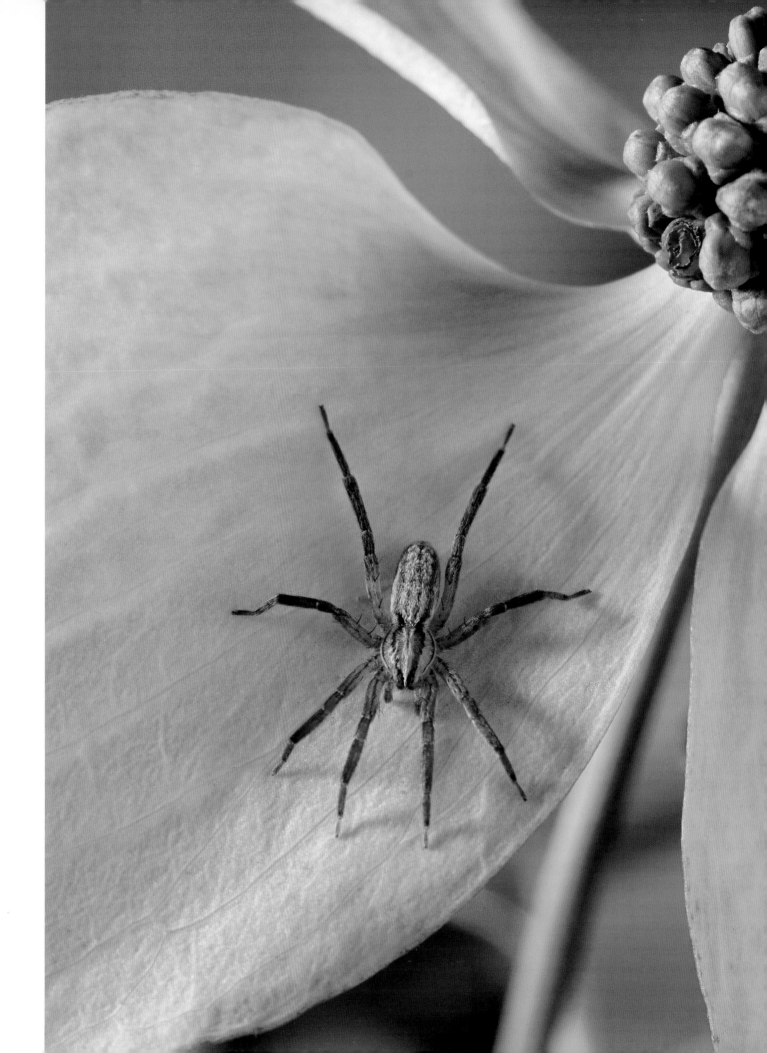

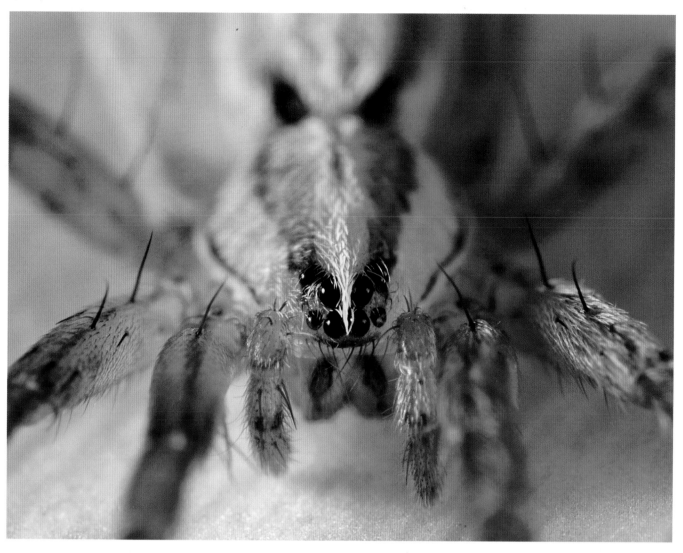

Close-up showing characteristic eye arrangement of ghost spiders.

Ghost spider (*Zora genus*)

Zora from Greek "violence"

Ghost spiders have a certain stylish charm of their own, although their full beauty can be appreciated only when examined under a magnifier; this reveals a background of pale yellow embellished with subtle darker brown striations.

The pointed carapace perhaps best identifies the Zoridae, together with their large, dark eyes set in two curved rows, the posterior row being so rounded that they almost appear to be in three rows. Most species are virtually impossible to tell apart without a microscope. Another characteristic of ghost spiders is their capacity to sprint at high speed and to jump when the need arises—abilities shared by many spiders, but perhaps with less elegance.

Ghost spiders normally live amid leaf litter and debris on ground level, although the one illustrated was found on a garden shrub.

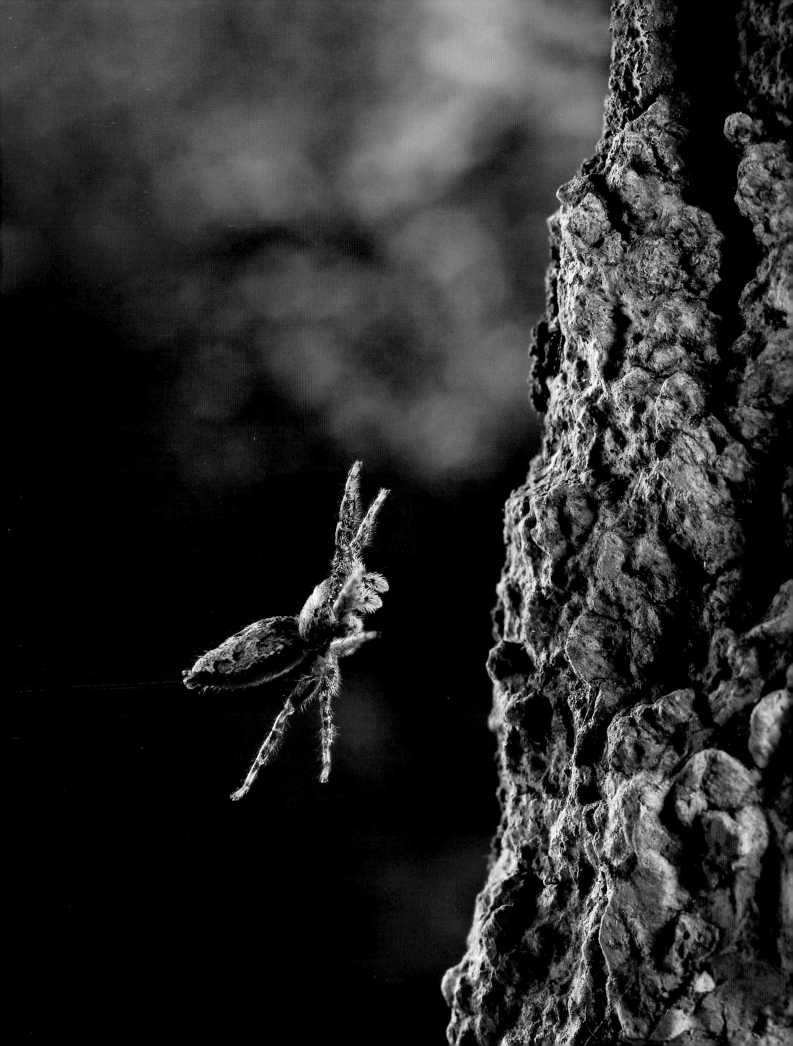

4

Jumping Spiders

Strictly speaking, jumping spiders should be bundled with the "Daylight Visual Hunters," but as their attributes are so exceptional, together with the fact that the family is by far the largest, I have accorded these spiders a special section of their own in this book.

Jumping spiders, or Salticidae, are the most fascinating and advanced family of spiders, capable of charming even hardened arachnophobes. Indeed, these spiders have evolved such exceptional physiological and behavioral abilities that the family has become the largest in the spider world, with more than 5,000 species named so far. Apart from their athletic prowess, some of the tropical species are the most colorful and bizarre-looking spiders to be found anywhere. A glimpse of a metallic red and blue *Chrysilla* bouncing through a patch of sunlight like a sizzling spark in an Old World jungle is an unforgettable experience.

These alluring spiders are also associated with bright sunshine, in which they may be seen walking or skipping on a warm summer's day. Jumping spiders are unmistakable in appearance, having two large, owl-like forward-facing eyes protruding from a square-faced head, as well as six other, smaller eyes. Sharp eyesight dominates their sensory universe, as it does ours. There is something beguiling about the way they watch us, swiveling their heads from side to side or up and down, sometimes following our every move. Vision also dominates their courtship behavior, which involves much waving of their often brightly colored legs and palps.

Jumping spiders are hunters that walk around in a series of jerks while spotting for prey from a considerable distance. Once the intended quarry is detected, the spider stealthily approaches until it is sufficiently close to leap onto its victim's back. Spiders from some other families are capable of jumping short distances, but only salticids make accurate vision-guided leaps onto prey or other objects. Over a narrow angle their spatial acuity is said to exceed that of large dragonflies by tenfold.

◄ Fence spider (*Marpissa muscosa*) about to land. Note the safety line.

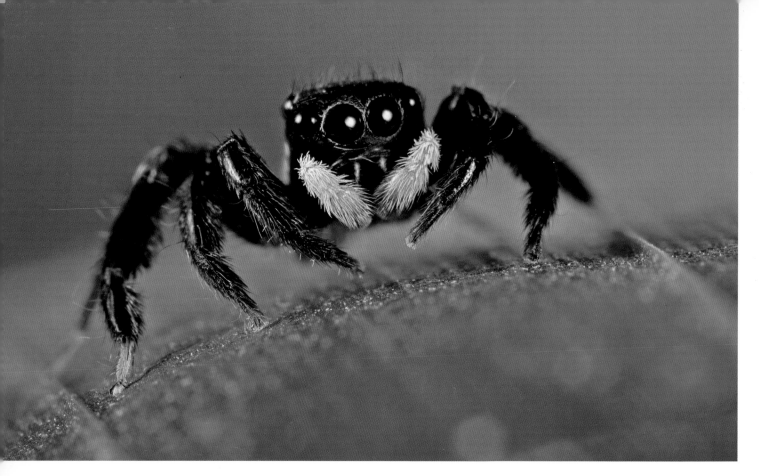

Unidentified jumping spider showing the impressive anterior eyes of salticids, and the bright palps, which are used for visual signaling.

It is this acute eyesight rather than their jumping prowess that makes these engaging little creatures so special. The optical and neurological equipment by which this is controlled is contained in the characteristic large, dome-shaped cephalothorax.

The eyes of salticids are physiologically unique among arthropods. As well as possessing high-resolution, full stereoscopic color vision, they are able to adjust the angle of view and focus by moving components inside the eye, including the retina itself! If you gaze into the eyes of a salticid you may be lucky enough to see a mysterious flicker or color change as the retina is moved. The eyes are constructed rather like binoculars, with a long- and a short-focus lens at each end of a long tube and a layered retina at the rear of the cephalothorax. This sophisticated mechanism allows the spider to locate, track, stalk and leap onto active prey. Using just visual cues, salticids can discriminate between prey and predators, mates and rivals. Recent research even suggests that their brains could be far more advanced than those of other spiders. Among other "intelligent" skills they have an almost uncanny ability to figure out complex paths to gain the best vantage points before pouncing on prey, much like lions.

Some salticids can jump more than 20 times their own length, and these Olympian leaps are powered not directly by muscles but by hydraulic action. All the internal organs and legs are immersed in a blood-like fluid, so when a large muscle in the cephalothorax suddenly expands, the legs are rapidly extended through hydraulic pressure. One would hardly imagine that this could result in an accurate jump, but it usually does, as proven by high-speed photography.

Around 315 species of jumping spiders have been recorded in North America and 75 in Europe.

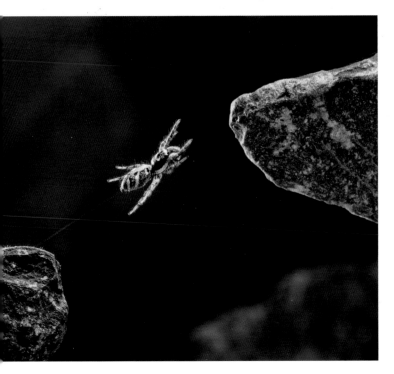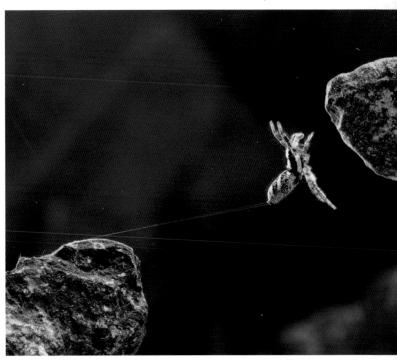

Sequence showing zebra spider during the latter stages of jumping. Note the safety lines, including one on the left from the previous jump.

Zebra spider (*Salticus scenicus*)

Salticus from Latin *saltus* (leap); *scenicus* from Latin "actor"

This charming little black-and-white-striped spider is the best known of the large Salticidae family of jumping spiders. It is found not only over much of North America but also in Britain and northern Europe. The zebra spider can be found almost anywhere that is sufficiently warm and sunny, especially around houses and gardens on walls, fences, plant containers and windowsills. Less frequently it is found away from human habitation, on sun-exposed rocks and sunny tree trunks, moving over the surface in its typically jerky manner.

When the warmth of the sun disappears, the spider vanishes too and hides away in some suitable crevice. Evidence of its activities can often be seen on the surfaces it frequents, in the form of crisscross strands of web—like so many spiders, it leaves a trail of draglines wherever it goes.

As in all salticids, the eyes of the zebra spider are spectacularly acute. Although the smaller eyes may not have high resolving power, they do provide a 360-degree field of view to spot any movement. Once some visual disturbance is detected, the spider will raise its head and orient itself so that the main anterior median eyes (the headlight ones) scan the potential prey in detail. Its gaze will even latch onto minute prey such as a greenfly offered on a pair of fine forceps from several inches away.

The series of photographs of a female shows the action of the hydraulically powered leap in detail, including the dragline and its anchor point. The relaxation of the flexor muscles of the two pairs of hind legs that provide standing-start takeoff power can be seen in the picture on page 69. Adult males have huge, unwieldy chelicerae that are used for elaborate courtship displays as well as bloodless sparring contests between rival males.

There are four similar species of salticids in the family, of which two are rare in Britain.

Fence spider (*Marpissa muscosa*)

Marpissa from Greek *marpto*, "to seize"; *muscosa* from Latin "mossy"

Although not a common species, the fence spider is the largest salticid to be found in Britain, adult females reaching 0.4 inch (10 mm) in length. Its natural habitat is around stone walls and the trunks of trees, especially those that are exposed to warm sun and have peeling bark, under which these delightful spiders hide away in their whiter-than-white silken cells. Man-made wooden structures such as fences are just as popular, particularly those with peeling bark or clefts in which to take refuge and protect their cocoons.

Marpissa is so well camouflaged that it is almost impossible to spot when resting on bark. Perhaps the best way of finding this spider is to examine the south-facing surface of a gate or fence, where it is much easier to spot while basking in the heat of the sun. Remember, though, to approach very slowly, as the super-sensitive eyes will readily detect your presence and the spider will dash off to hide on the other side or in some crevice. Although the fence spider does not occur in North America, other, similar species in the genus are found there.

The series of photographs clearly shows the action of the jump. Note the trail of thread that acts as a safety line in case of misjudgment.

➤ From top to bottom, the jumping sequence of the fence spider.

▼ The eyes from the side. Note the flat head for this species' crevice-dwelling life.

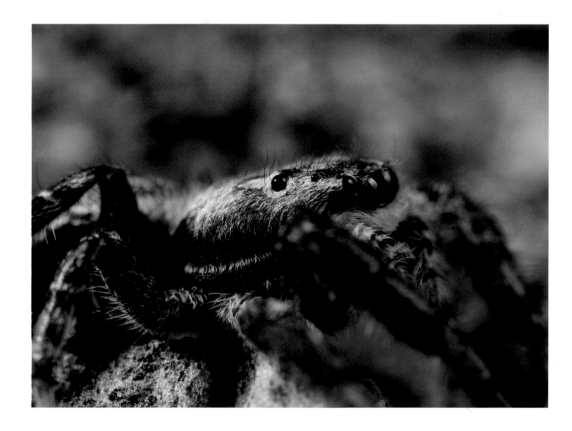

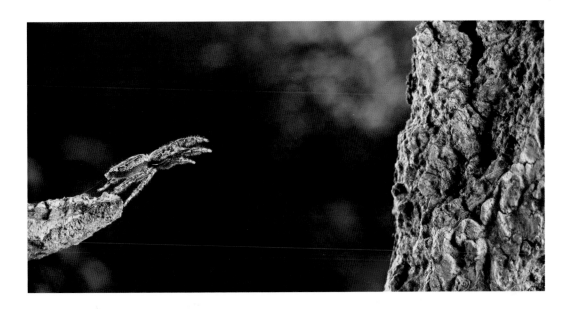

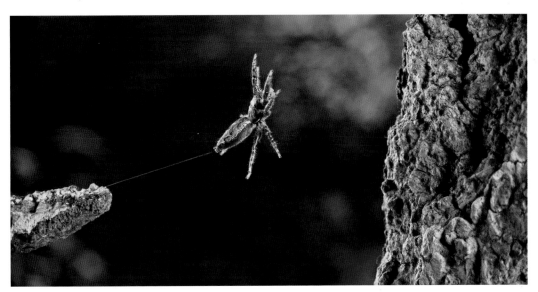

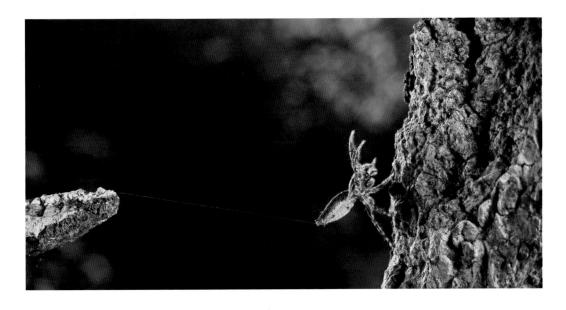

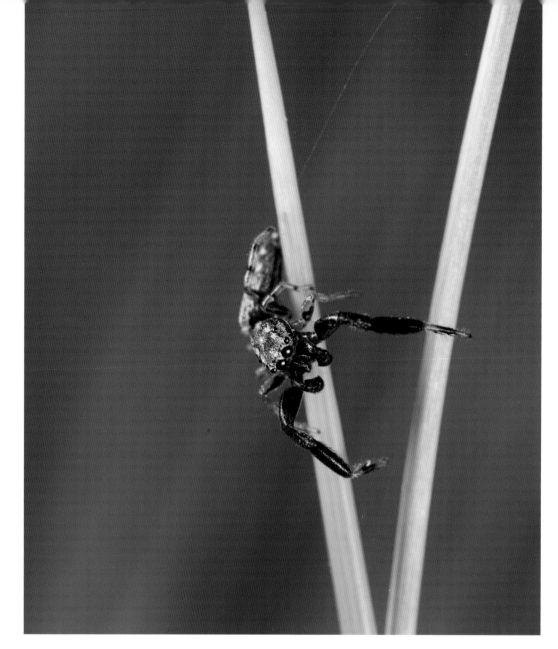

This elongated Marpissa species lives amid grass stems.

Marpissa nivoyi

Marpissa from Greek *marpto,* "to sieze";
nivoyi from de Nivoy, a 19th-century spider researcher

Another *Marpissa* jumping spider is *M. nivoyi*. It is more elongate than the fence spider, with a rather antlike appearance, and is adapted to a life among grass stems. Like the fence spider, its front legs are thickened.

This spider is rare in England; it is most likely to be found among marram grass on coastal dunes and, less often, farther inland in marshy areas. When not stretched out along a blade of marram, it lies concealed in a silken cell within the hollow stem. The spider has the rather non-spider-like trait of sometimes running backward like a pseudoscorpion, another arachnid that is often found in the same habitat.

A similar species, *Marpissa pikii*, is found in North America and favors similar surroundings.

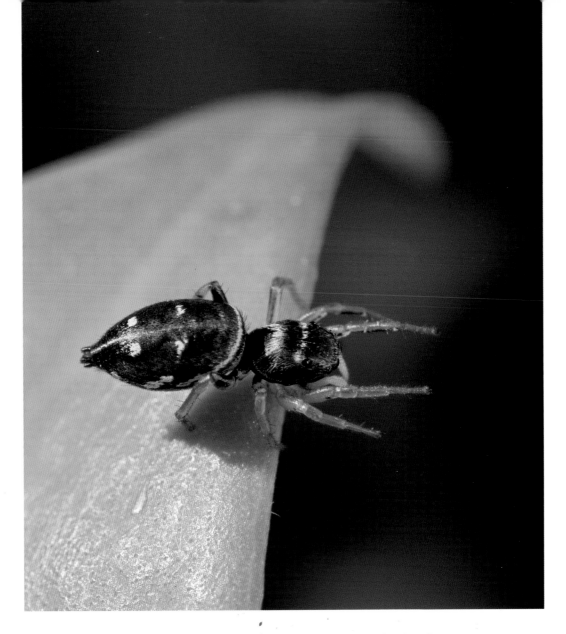

A sun-loving jumping spider (*Heliophanus cupreus*), caught a split second before jumping.

Heliophanus cupreus

Heliophanus from Greek *helio*, "sun"; *cupreus* from Latin *cuprum*, "copper"

Most of the *Heliophanus* genus of salticids can be readily identified in the field, as the females of most species have a striking color combination: a black body with pale yellowish-green legs. The males, though, are less impressive, tending to have darker legs and a subtly iridescent body—the species name *cupreus* refers to this spider's coppery appearance in bright sunlight. Both sexes have a thin white band around the front edge of the abdomen and white spots on each side of the dorsal surface.

As its generic name suggests, *Heliophanus cupreus* is a sun lover, like the majority of the family. It can be found on low vegetation and is most active near the top of plants in hot sunshine. This spider can be differentiated from other *Heliophanus* species by the black streaks down both sides of the femur and tibia on all four pairs of legs. Although absent from North America, the species is common and well distributed throughout Europe.

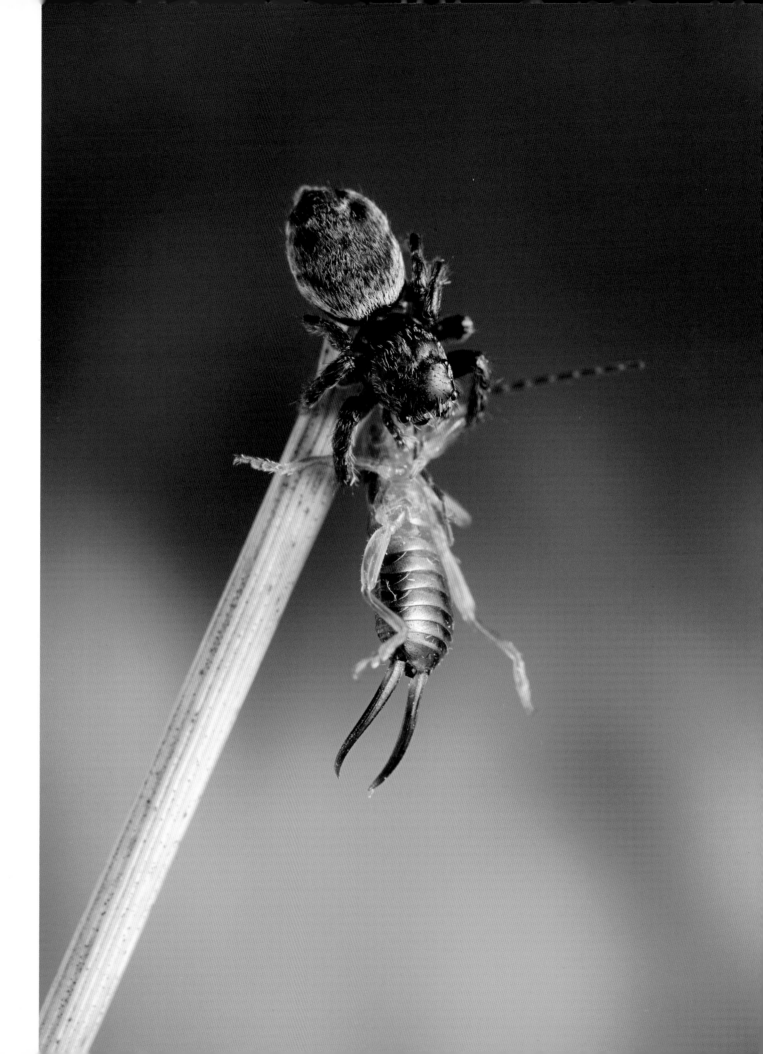

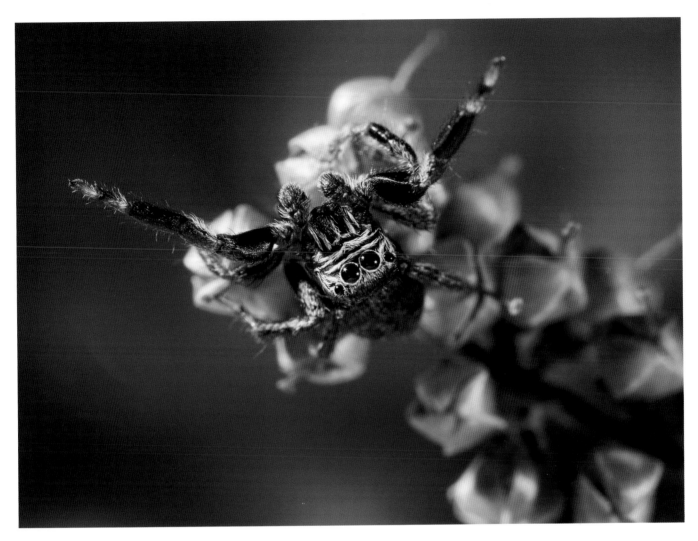

Male *Evarcha arcuata*.

Evarcha arcuata

Evarcha from Greek; *arcuata* from Latin "curved" (referring to the shape of the spider's epigyne)

This charming little jumping spider, along with the rest of its genus, shows wide variation between the sexes, as is clear from the photographs. Whereas the male E. *arcuata* is dark brown or black, the female is a tawny color marked with chevrons and thickly covered with white hairs.

◄ Female with earwig.

The courtship of spiders is often an elaborate performance, and that of jumping spiders is especially so. *Evarcha* species are quite energetic, with much waving of palps and front legs. After mating, the female lays her eggs within rolled-up leaves or, as is usually the case with *arcuata,* in sprigs of heather tied together with silk, and there she stands guard until the eggs hatch. Maturity is reached in midsummer, when the best place to find them is heathland in southern England, where these salticids are sometimes quite common.

This spider is widespread throughout Europe but absent from North America, where there are several other *Evarcha* species.

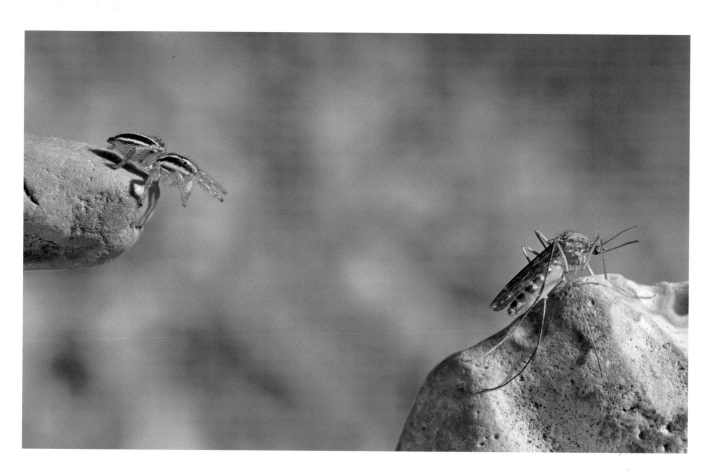

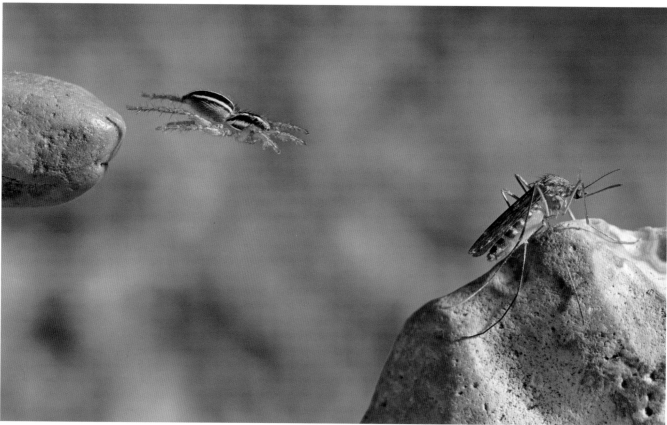

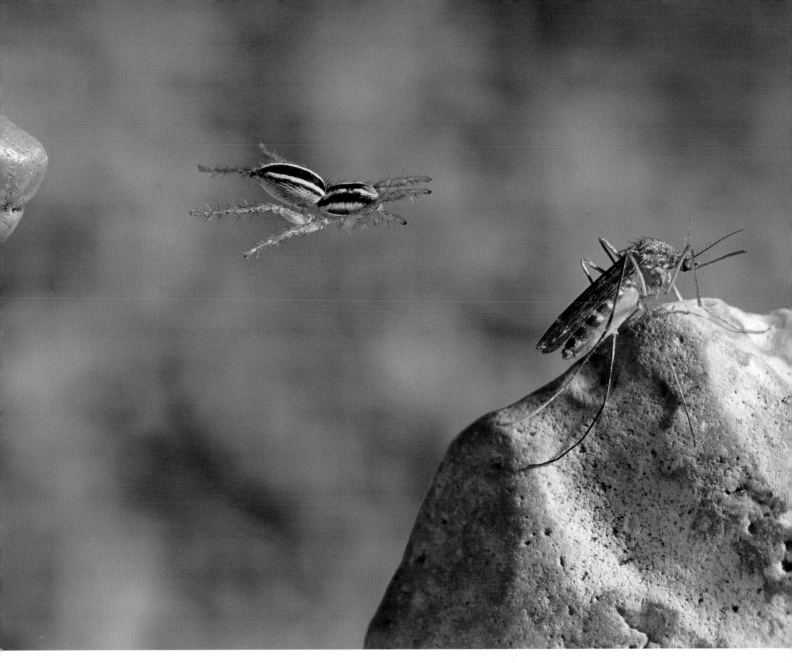

◄ ▲ Jumping sequence of *Phlegra* attempting to catch a mosquito.

Phlegra fasciata

Phlegra from a city in ancient Macedonia;
fasciata from Latin *fascia*, "band"

An inhabitant of coastal shingle and low vegetation around anthills, this dapper little dark-and-light-brown-striped jumping spider is difficult to spot unless seen moving. The male has a glossy abdomen and much more subdued markings than the female. The series of photographs shows a juvenile female leaping toward a mosquito (which actually managed to get away). It is clear that the spider shows no hesitation about tackling prey larger than herself—not that a mosquito poses much threat to her.

Phlegra is both rare and localized in Europe and North America. In England this salticid has been recorded only on a very few stretches of coastline in the south.

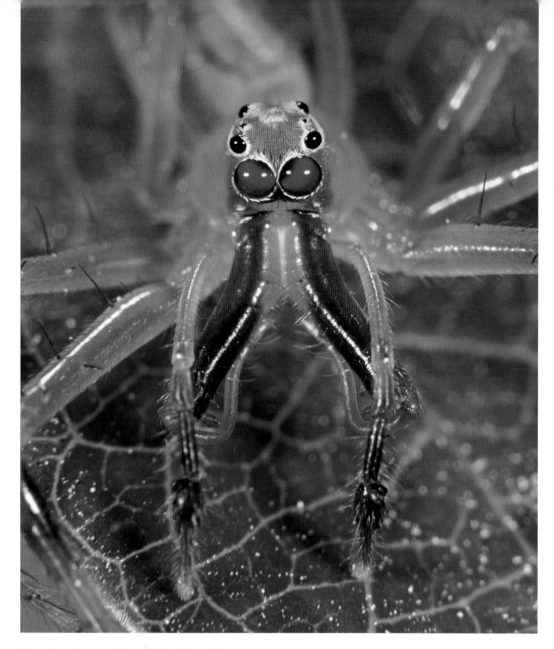

Face of male magnolia green jumping spider.

Magnolia green jumping spider
(*Lyssomanes viridis*)

Lyssomanes from Greek "raving mad" (referring to the spider's manic activity); *viridis* from Latin, "green"

This bizarre-looking, vivid, translucent green jumping spider from the southern United States hardly resembles a salticid at all and could be mistaken for a lynx spider at a casual glance. Both sexes have long legs and palps and are extremely active—even for jumping spiders. The awesome face of the male is dominated by his spectacular anterior median eyes. These appear to rotate in their sockets, but it is only the retinas, controlled by six pairs of muscles, that move behind the perfectly clear front lens. Adding to the inscrutable stare is their chameleon-like ability to move each eye independently.

Lyssomanes can be found living in all types of woodlands, particularly broad-leaved evergreens such as live oak and magnolia.

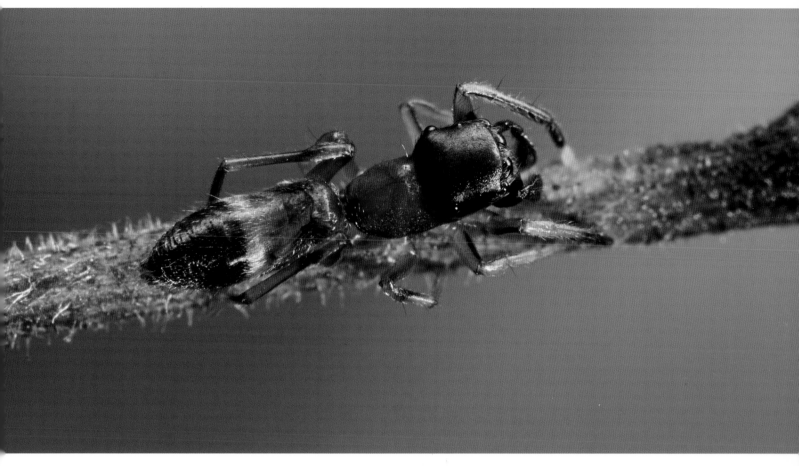

Many salticids mimic ants, including *Myrmarachne* seen here.

Ant-mimic spider

(*Myrmarachne formicaria*)

Myrmarachne from Greek "antlike spider"; *formicaria* from Latin *formica*, "ant"

What is so extraordinary about ant-mimic spiders, particularly those from the *Myrmarachne* genus of the Salticidae family, is that they not only look so much like ants but also move like them. As well as having long, slender legs and what appears to be the three-part (head–thorax–abdomen) body of an insect, the front legs are often raised and waved in the air like a pair of antennae to add further to the deception. The antlike head of this species, *M. formicaria,* also has a black metallic luster, and the jaws, especially in males, are enormously enlarged, projecting forward to make the spider look like

a soldier ant of the tropics. The imitation is so perfect that it is difficult to imagine that the animal is not an ant.

Some scientists believe that these spiders deceive their models by looking like them so that they can prey on the ants themselves. A more plausible explanation is that by copying the ants' physical appearance and manic movements, the ant-mimicking jumping spiders gain protection. Birds, spider-hunting wasps and other spider predators generally avoid ants, which may bite, sting or secrete formic acid when attacked.

As the genus is essentially tropical, only a single species of *Myrmarachne* is found in Europe. In England it is rather rare and locally distributed in the south and east. It lives in sunny sites among low vegetation and stones.

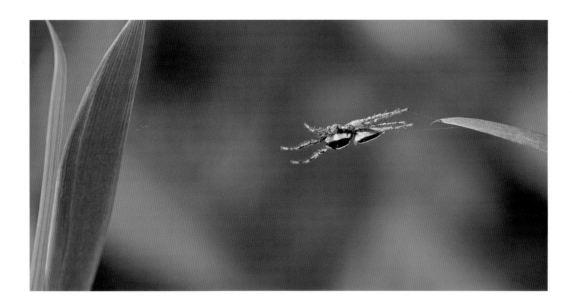

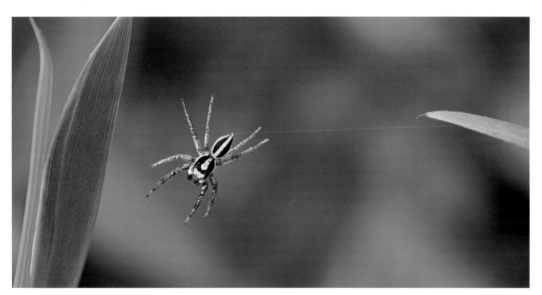

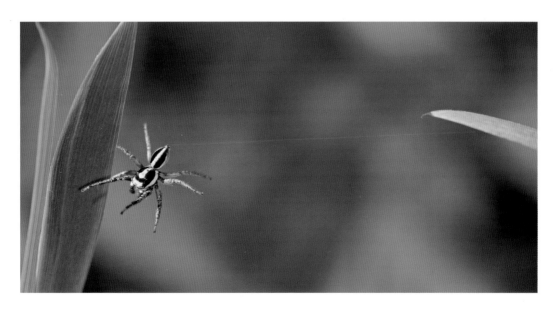

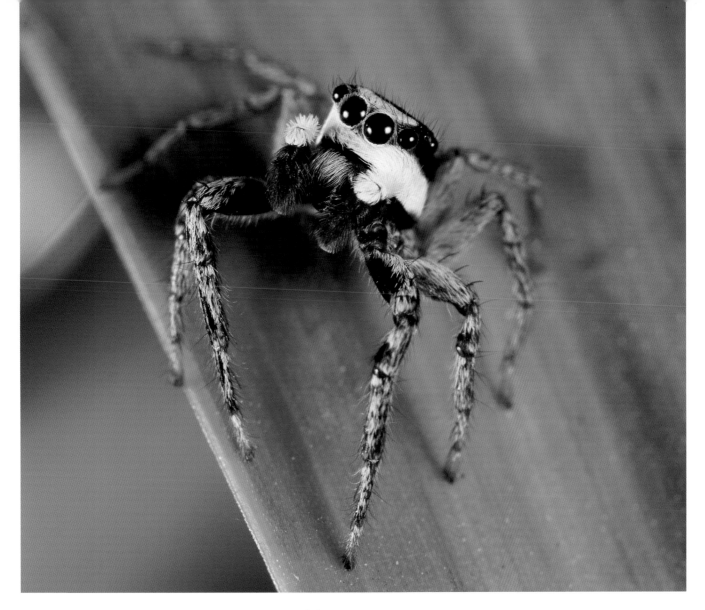

A pantropical jumper's eyes are alert to the slighest movement.

Pantropical jumper (*Plexippus paykuli*)

Plexippus from Greek "driving horses"

Many people who live in warmer regions of the world must be familiar with this natty and very active jumping spider. Not only has the pantropical jumper spread to most warm regions of the world, but it prefers to live around houses and other man-made structures, where

◄ A pantropical jumping spider leaping inverted. Jumping spiders are perfectly capable of jumping from any position — this one has rotated 180 degrees prior to landing.

it is readily noticed. Adding to its conspicuousness are its size—females are 0.4 to 0.5 inch (10–12 mm) long, large for a salticid—and the distinctive whitish bands that run down the entire length of the body.

The pantropical jumper was introduced to North America, where it is restricted to the warmer southern states. Unfortunately it is absent from northern Europe, although it survives well in the Mediterranean region. The species is very competitive, sometimes monopolizing structures such as old walls and even gas stations, where it tends to exclude all other species of jumping spiders.

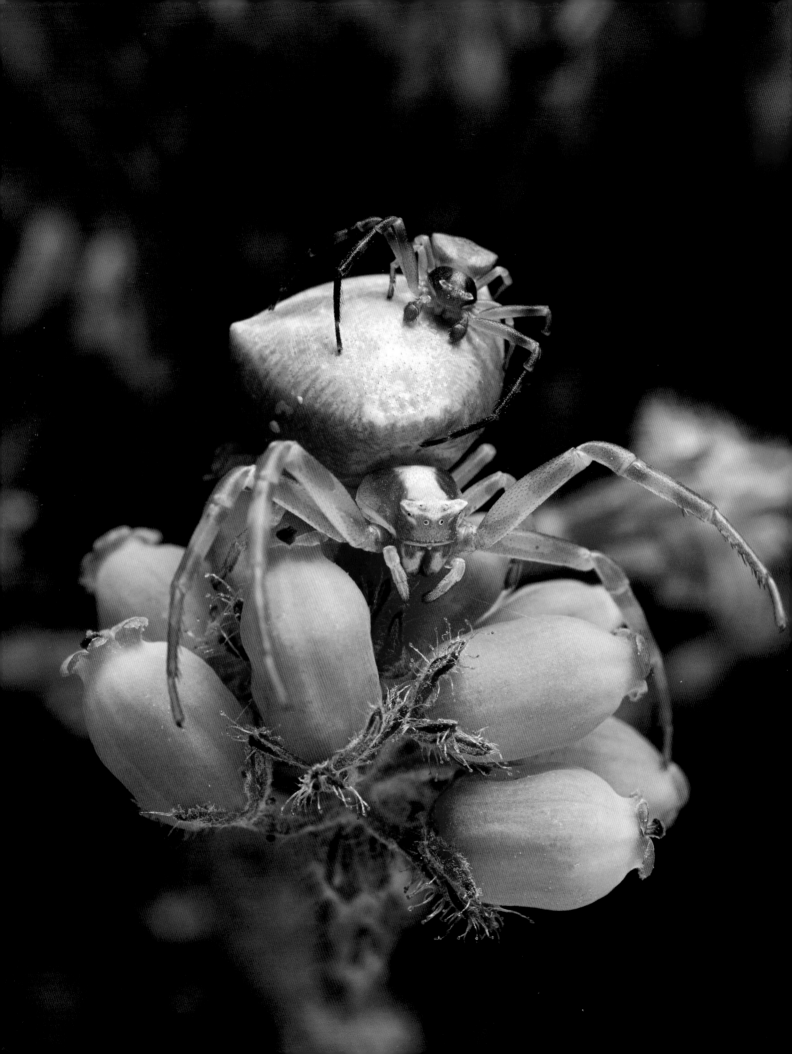

5 Ambushers and Lurkers

Whenconsidering the hunters and the ambushers, the overlap between the categories into which the spiders in this book have been divided is not always clear-cut. We have already seen that many of the so-called hunters frequently wait in ambush for prey, pouncing or giving chase at the last moment. By the same token, some spiders that are basically sit-and-wait predators can be divided into two groups. The first are those that sit in or close to their webs, lurking in nearby foliage or in tunnels that form part of the web; the web is instrumental in trapping or detecting the prey in the first instance. The second group does not rely on webs at all. Instead the spiders remain motionless, merging into the background until some unsuspecting creature falls into their arms, so to speak.

Crab or ambush spiders, the Thomisidae family, are masters at the second method. Instead of relying on webs, they use deception and camouflage, being adept at blending beautifully among the petals and stamens of flowers, where they wait motionless for their quarry. Some crab spiders are capable of changing color over several days to merge into the background yellow, pink, white or green of their chosen flower or foliage. Other species, especially those from the tropics, are able to mimic tree bark or even bird droppings.

Another group of spiders included here are the so-called running crab or small huntsman spiders, the Philodromidae, which are closely allied to the crab spiders (some experts bundle them into the same family with the Thomisidae). These too are capable of remarkable camouflage, remaining motionless and behaving much like the typical crab spider as they grab prey that ventures too close. However, as their name suggests, running crab spiders are usually much more active, being capable of running very rapidly in pursuit of prey or to escape predators. A common species of this type is the little running crab spider *Philodromus dispar* (page 89), which either chases prey or waits in ambush, employing both techniques with equal mastery.

◄ Male and female crab spiders (*Thomisius onustus*) prior to mating.

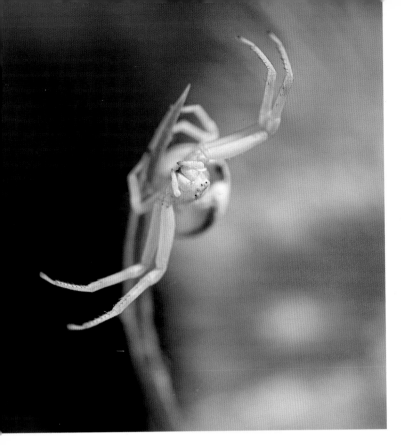

Female crab spider (*Misumena*).

In warmer parts of the world, including parts of North America, there are the larger and more scary huntsman or giant crab spiders from the Sparassidae family. In Europe this family has only one representative, a smaller and rather rare species, the green spider, *Micrommata virescens*.

Ambusher and lurker families

True crab spiders, the **Thomisidae**, have short, squat bodies with two pairs of atrophied-looking hind legs. By comparison the front two pairs are longer and more robust, designed to seize insects that wander too close. The males, in contrast to the sturdy-looking females, are slim, dwarf-like creatures. Crab spiders are lethargic by nature but, unlike spiders from other families, are capable of moving in any direction, like crabs. When alarmed they may be seen scuttling backward or sideways out of sight behind a flower or leaf.

Crab spiders come in a wide range of forms and colors, but most are crab-like, with an almost circular cephalothorax and a dumpy, squat abdomen; their two pairs of front legs turn inward and are considerably longer than the hind pair. They never build webs for trapping prey, preferring to lie motionless on a flower or leaf waiting for prey to visit, then grabbing it with the front pair of legs, which are held wide apart. Although thomisids have small chelicerae, the venom they produce seems to be highly toxic, as they have no trouble subduing large insects such as butterflies and bumblebees very rapidly.

There are 130 species in North America, but only 62 in northern Europe.

Whereas the Thomisidae are distinctly crab-like, the running crab or small huntsman spiders, **Philodromidae**, generally possess a longer, more oval abdomen; they have longer, thinner legs, with the hind pair nearly as long as the front pair, and are far more agile in their movements. In addition, to help these lively spiders clamber around actively in plants and execute lightning changes in position, they have scopulae on the soles of their feet. North America has about 96 species, while northern Europe has 62.

The **Sparassidae** family, or huntsman spiders (sometimes called banana spiders), are medium-sized to very large wandering spiders that are mostly tropical and rely on ambush to catch prey. Many species are crab-like and flattened, allowing them to creep into narrow crevices; they frequently get imported in banana consignments. Some species live in houses, where they are often encouraged, as they prey on household pests such as cockroaches. North America has 10 species, while northern Europe has only one.

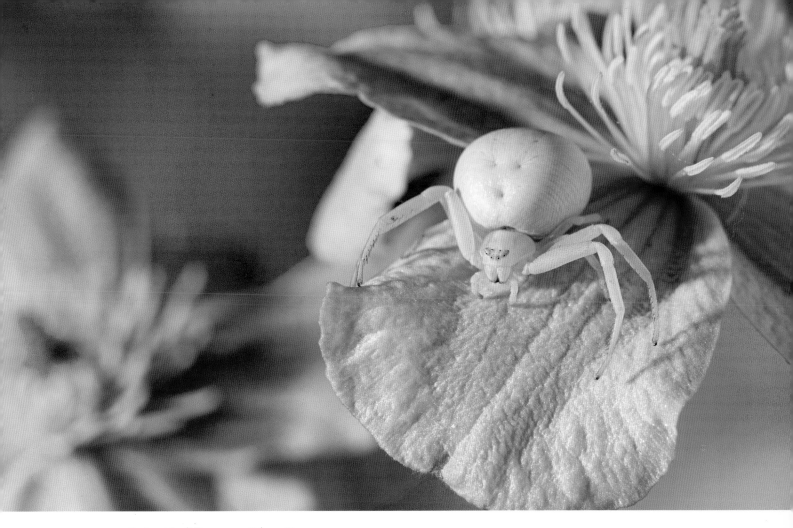

Crab spider (*Misumena vatia*) awaiting prey.

Crab spider *(Misumena vatia)*

Misumena from Greek *miseo*, "hate or wrath"; *vatia* from Latin "bowlegged"

One of the most familiar crab members of the Thomisidae family—found in both North America and Europe—is *Misumena vatia,* known in North America as the goldenrod crab spider. Its color can vary from white to yellow, green or occasionally bluish, depending on what flower it chooses to adopt, and sometimes it exhibits light red spots or stripes. If *Misumena* moves from one sort of flower to another of a different color, it is capable of changing color to match the new surroundings; this spider is most frequently found on white or yellow blooms, ox-eye daisies being a favorite. There it lies in wait for a visiting insect seeking nectar or pollen.

As an insect approaches, *Misumena* opens its two pairs of front legs and subtly aligns itself with the oncoming prey. Once sufficiently close the legs snap shut to embrace the victim, whereupon a bite is delivered without delay. Occasionally, if for some reason the toxic effects of the bite are slow to kick in, the spider will take flight on the back of a victim such as a large butterfly or bumblebee. However, such trips are short-lived—both spider and prey will tumble to the ground as the venom takes hold.

One way of finding flower-loving crab spiders is to keep a look out for immobile butterflies or bees on flower heads. The chances are that the unlucky insect is being held there by a crab spider.

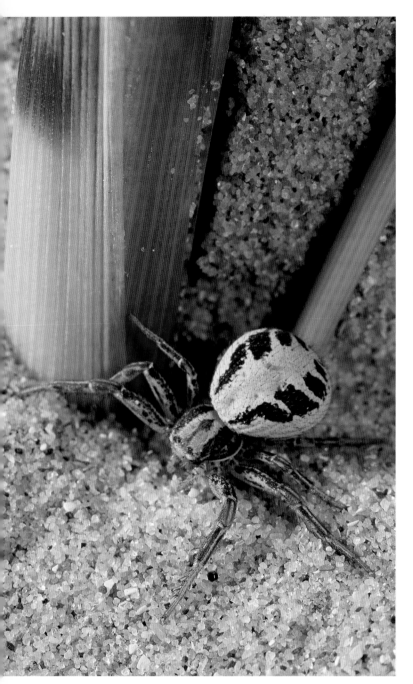
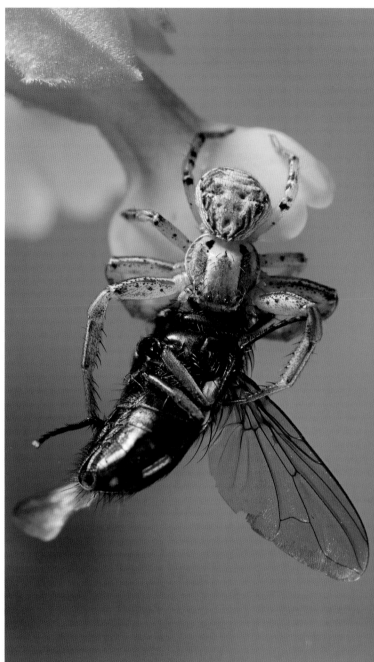

These two pictures of the same crab spider species (*Xysticus cristatus*) reflect their choice of habitats.

Crab spider *(Xysticus cristatus)*

Xysticus from Greek "scraper"; *cristatus* from Latin "tufted" or "crested"

Many thomisid crab spiders are prone to variation, *Xysticus cristatus* being particularly so, as these two photographs show. This species lives among low vegetation or at ground level in a wide variety of situations from heathland to hedgerows. The exceptionally boldly marked specimen shown here was living on a Sussex sand dune, while the duller one with the fly was found among low-growing plants in an open forested area. This is the commonest and most widespread species in the genus and occurs throughout Britain and northern Europe.

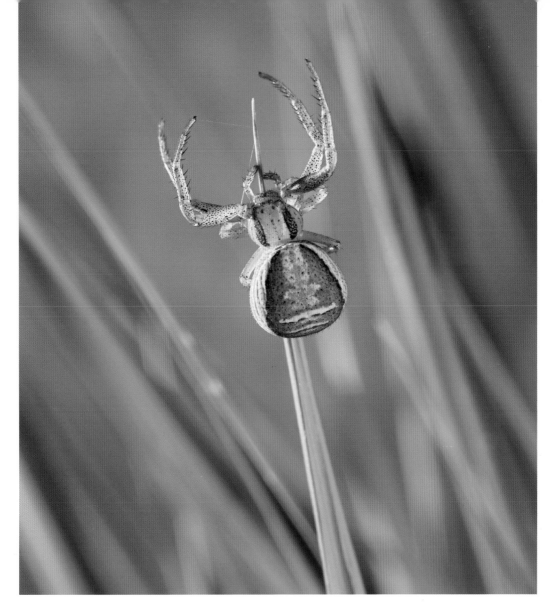

Marsh crab spider, with front legs extended, climbing a plant.

Marsh crab spider *(Xysticus ulmi)*

Xysticus from Greek "scraper"; *ulmi* from Latin *ulmus*, "elm"

Similar to *Xysticus cristatus* is another crab spider, X. *ulmi*, but this one is less catholic in choice of habitat, preferring damp, marshy places among low vegetation. It too is distributed throughout Britain and northern Europe, and is replaced by similar species in the United States.

The most astonishing thing about *Xysticus* spiders is their courtship and mating behavior. Indeed, their technique is so bizarre that many experts doubted the validity of the behavior when it was first observed in the middle of the

20th century. The smaller and more long-legged male begins wooing his mate by putting her into a submissive frame of mind. He accomplishes this in typical spider fashion by gently stroking her with his legs. Once this stage is completed, he ties down her head and legs with bonds of silk to whatever she is resting on. He is now free to lift her abdomen, crawl underneath and mate—a process that may last up to 90 minutes. Once these matrimonial activities have been completed, the female breaks away from her bonds, which by now have served their purpose of preventing her from grabbing her suitor during the dangerous time shortly after mating.

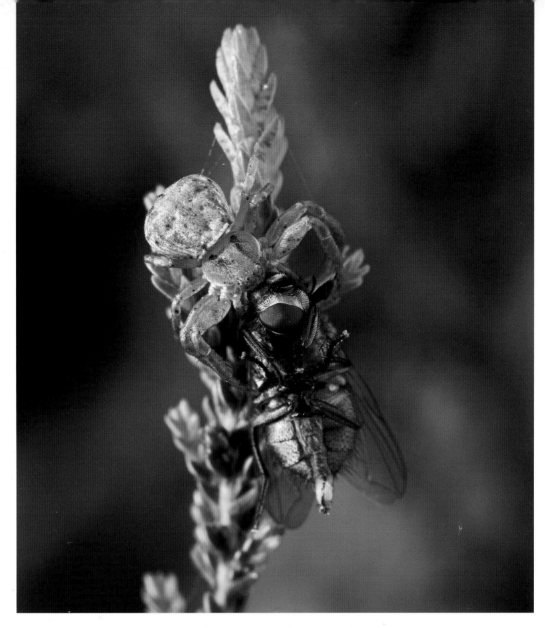

Toad-like crab spider. Crab spiders often take prey larger than themselves.

Toad-like crab spider (*Oxyptila* species)

Oxyptila from Greek "sharp feather down" (possibly referring to the spider's clavate hairs)

Other common crab spiders in the Thomisidae family are those from the *Oxyptila* genus. These are similar to *Xysticus* but tend to have a more rounded and marbled abdominal pattern; like *Xysticus,* many show wide variation in colors and markings within the species. *Oxyptila* crab spiders are particularly squat and toad-like. Several species occur in both Europe and the United States.

During the day *Oxyptila* species are found at ground level, sometimes deep amid the base or roots of vegetation. They can easily be overlooked because of their effective brown camouflage and very slow movements. Also, like many spiders they are prone to feigning death by drawing up their legs and remaining motionless for several minutes. At night they may crawl up the vegetation, where they can be spotted with the aid of a flashlight. They are reported to feed during both day and night.

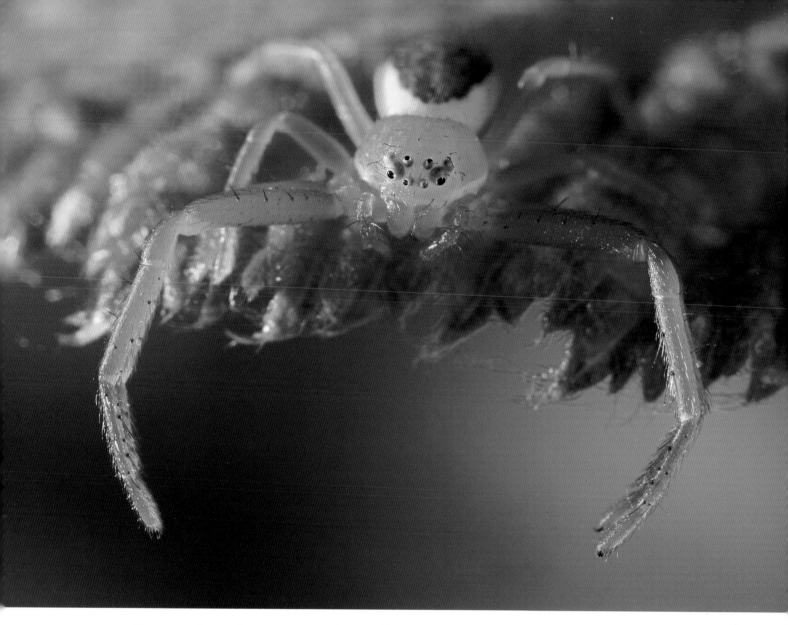

The green crab spider lives among leaves of trees and bushes.

Green crab spider (*Diaea dorsata*)

Diaea from Greek "during spring"; *dorsata*
from Latin *dorsum*, "back"

The vivid green legs and cephalothorax and
the yellow-margined, leaf-marked brown abdomen make this attractive medium-sized
thomisid spider unmistakable. Like so many
crab spiders, *Diaea dorsata* is beautifully camouflaged, making it extremely difficult to spot as
it waits in ambush among the leaves of shrubs
and bushes, especially young oaks. Individuals
within a single species can vary widely in color
and pattern, according to the color of the background they adopt. Some species are said to be
able to change color gradually to match their
selected leaf or flower. The spines on the front
legs aid in trapping insects and are typical of
crab spiders.

This spider is widespread in Europe but
commoner in southern parts. In England it is
rather locally distributed, mainly in the south.

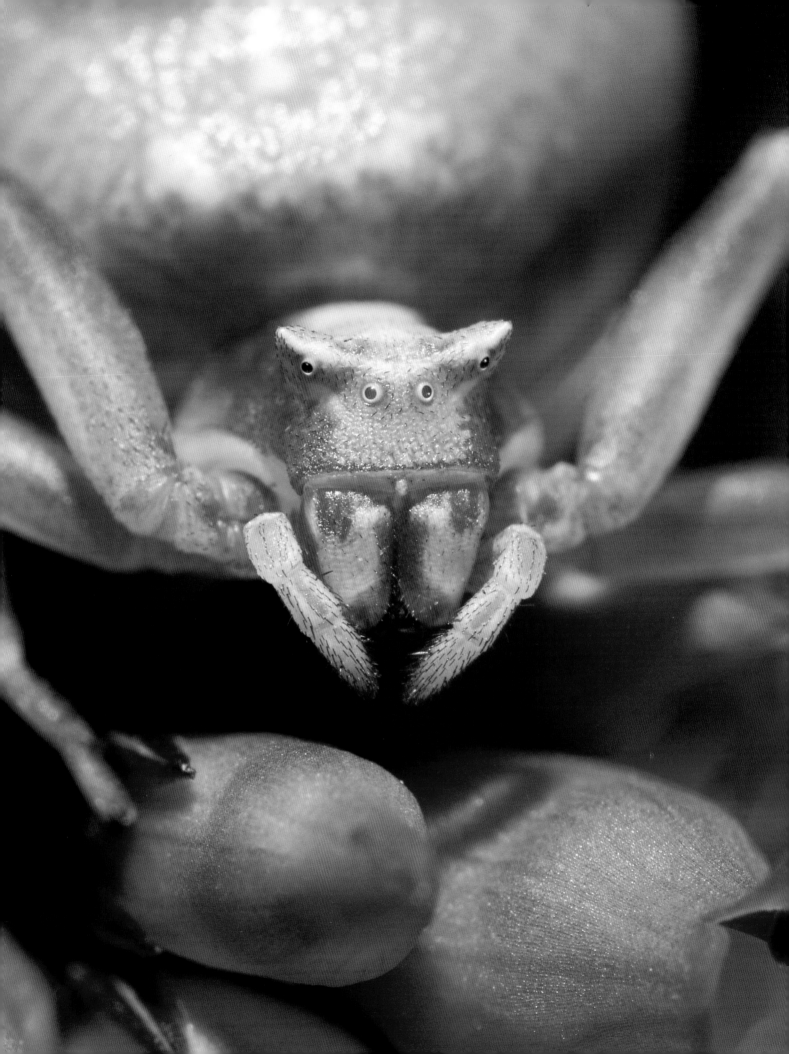

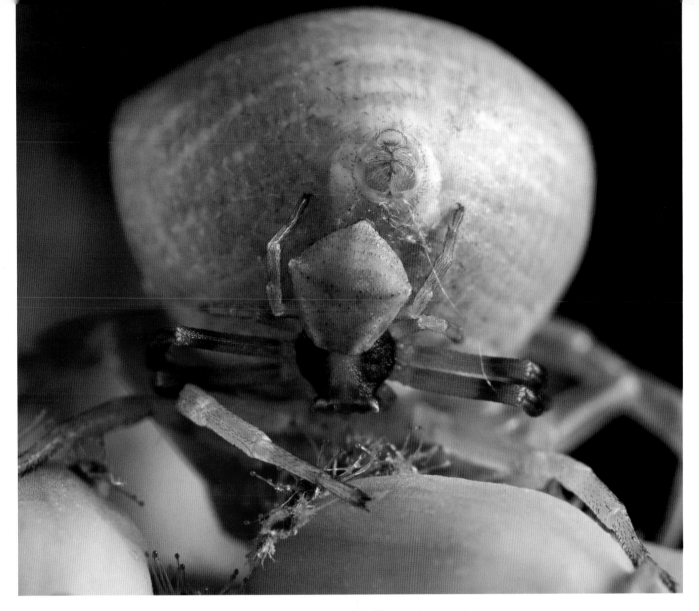

Rear view of mating crab spiders. Note the enormous size difference between the sexes.

Crab spider (*Thomisus onustus*)

Thomisus from Greek *thomis*, "sting"; *onustus* from Latin "loaded" or "filled"

The most splendid of northern European crab spiders is *Thomisus onustus*. Adding to its allure is its comparative rarity—although it is widespread in Europe, the spider is found only in small numbers in England, being confined to certain heathlands in central southern parts of the country.

With her angular pink abdomen sporting two conical humps and her devil-like horned head, it is impossible to confuse the female of the species with anything else. The male is much darker and, in common with many other thomisids, much smaller, as is manifest in the mating sequence. Like *Misumena vatia,* this crab spider is able to adjust its color to match that of the flower upon which it rests.

T. *onustus* lives among mature heather, where it lies in wait. At the approach of an insect it will make smooth and barely perceptible adjustments to its position. As the potential prey lowers its head in search of nectar, it is seized in a flash. This spider often grabs insects considerably bulkier than itself, such as bees or even bumblebees.

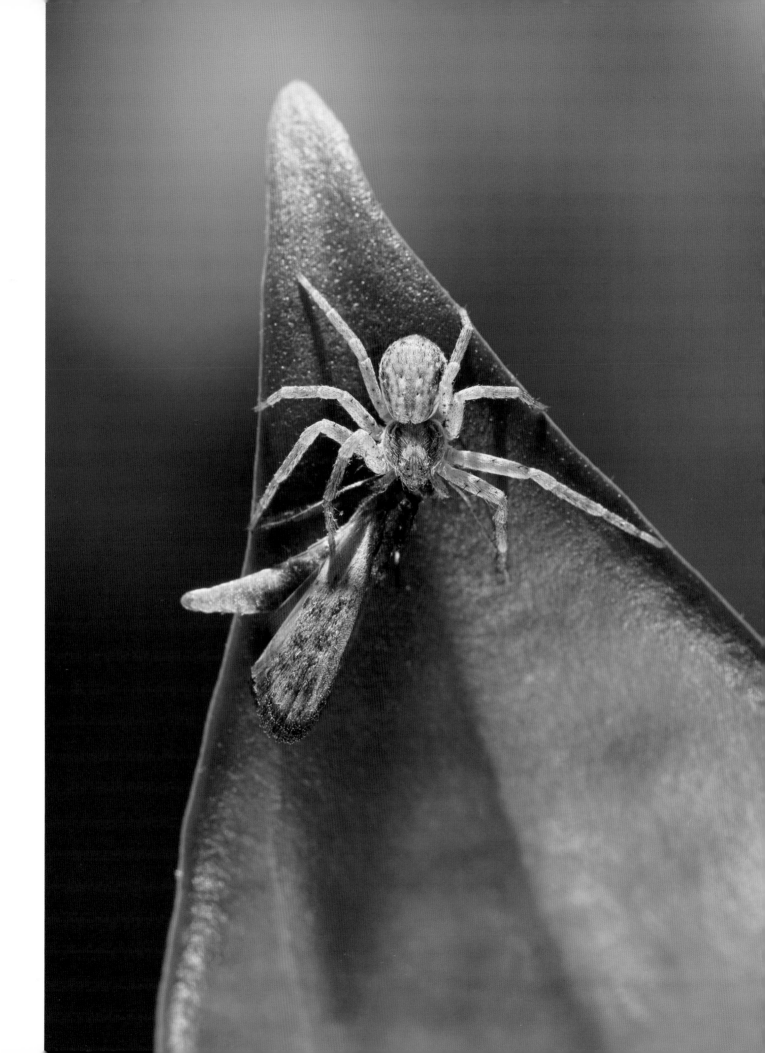

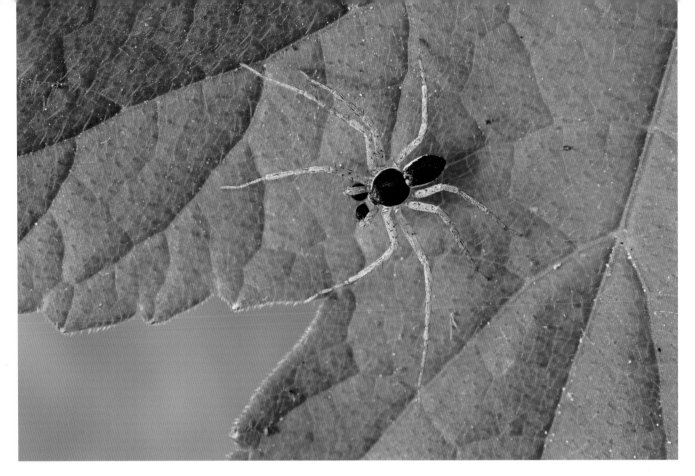

Male running crab spider (*Philodromus dispar*).

Running crab spider (*Philodromus dispar*)

Philodromus from Greek "loving to race";
dispar from Latin "different"

The male *Philodromus dispar* is a particularly dapper-looking fellow with his chocolate-brown, sometimes almost black, body contrasting with the bold cream lateral line all around and pale gray legs. The female, on the other hand, is like another species altogether, with a larger body and an overall brownish appearance, but she becomes more attractive when viewed through a magnifier. This sexual dimorphism is reflected in the spider's species name *dispar*.

This philodromid species is widespread throughout England and Europe and is also found in North America. It frequents bushes and low-growing vegetation, where it will either lie in wait or chase after its prey at lightning speed. When seriously threatened, this spider, like many species, will sham death by lying on its back with its legs curled over the body (below). *P. dispar* frequently finds its way into houses, where it seems to survive quite happily.

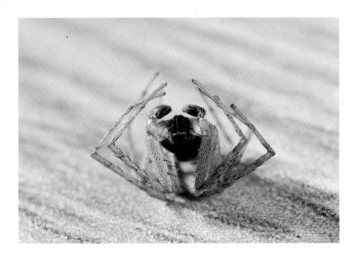

◄ Female running crab spider.
➤ Running crab spider shamming death.

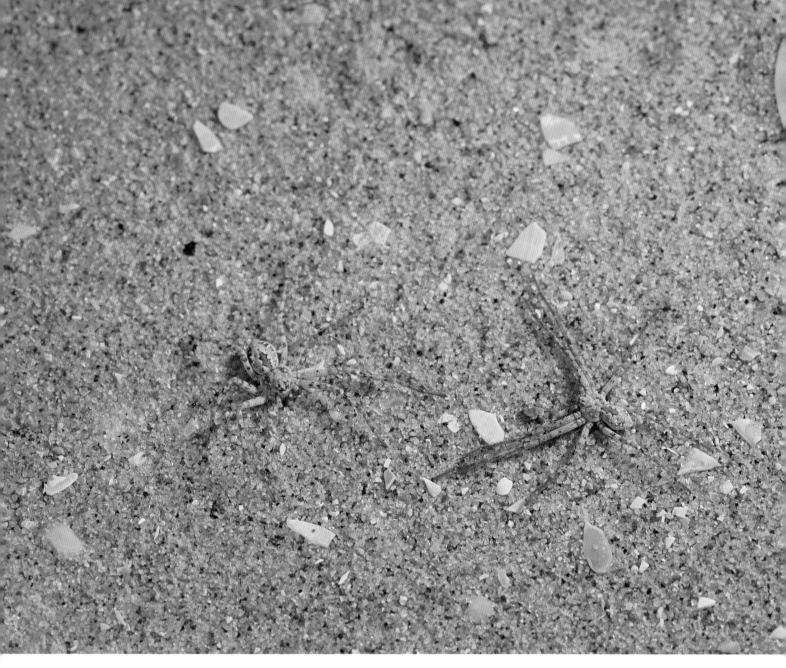

Male and female sand-dune running crab spiders.

Sand-dune running crab spider

(*Philodromus fallax*)

Philodromus from Greek "loving to race"; *fallax* from Latin "deceptive"

Most running crab spiders of the Philodromidae family actively climb around in shrubs and trees, but this splendid species, *Philodromus fallax*, is an exception. It spends its life running about on sand dunes and lurking within clumps of marram grass, its yellow-gray mottling effectively blending in with the surroundings. The depth of color of this spider varies to match the color and tones of its sandy habitat.

P. fallax is locally distributed around the coasts and sometimes on sandy riverbanks of England and northern Europe, but is absent from the United States. The spider is widespread in Europe but commoner in southern parts. In England it is rather locally distributed, mainly in the south.

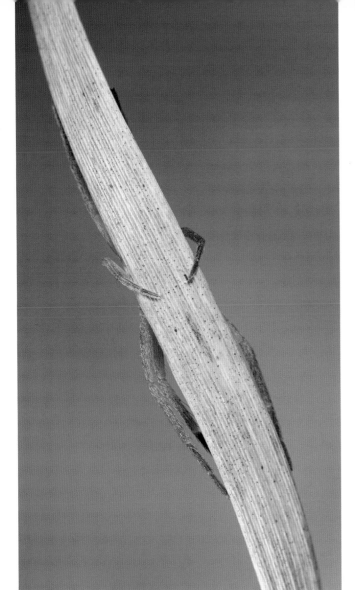
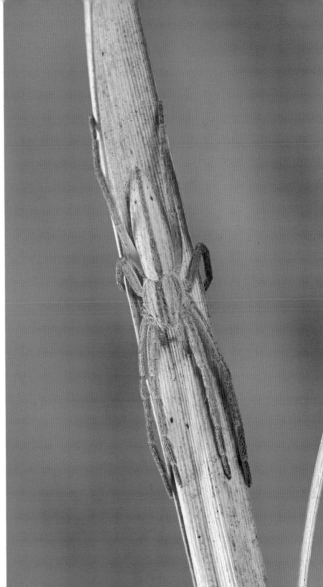

Dorsal and ventral views of the excellent camouflage and cryptic attitudes adopted by this active spider.

Grass-stem running crab spider
(*Tibellus oblongus*)

Tibellus from Latin "flute-shaped"; *oblongus* from Latin "oblong"

This long, nimble running crab spider has an impressive hunting strategy. *Tibellus* lives among the long grass of damp meadows, sand dunes and wet heathland, where it rests facing downward on a grass stem or sprig of heather waiting for some unsuspecting prey to make an appearance. With its straw-colored body and outstretched legs, the spider merges beautifully with the brown and green hues of the surrounding grass.

As soon as any suitable creature comes within striking distance, this spider flings itself onto its quarry with astonishing speed, giving chase in the unlikely event of a misjudged strike. It will even take on other spiders if the chance presents itself, pursuing them through the grass-blade jungle at speeds that can be difficult to follow.

This philodromid spider is an early summer species, during which season it can sometimes be very common. It is widespread throughout Britain and northern Europe and occurs in some areas of North America.

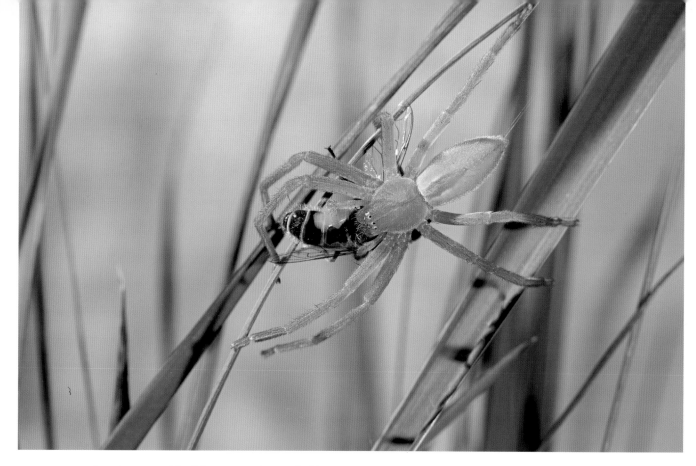

Female green spider (*Micrommata virescens*) with prey.

Green spider (*Micrommata virescens*)

Micrommata from Greek "small eye"; *virescens* from Latin meaning "turning green"

This splendid vivid green spider from the Sparassidae family is one of my favorites, and one that I found for the first time only a year or two ago. As with many spiders, the sexes exhibit conspicuous sexual dimorphism—the male and female appear very different, although in this case both are equally striking. Whereas the female is an overall bright green with a yellow-outlined cardiac mark, the smaller male has a yellowish abdomen with bold red stripes. In their youth the spiders are hay-colored, but they are difficult to spot in their grassy surroundings whatever their age.

The green spider has other attributes. Like the preceding species, *Tibellus,* it moves at the speed of lightning, being capable of darting up or down tussocks of moor grass seemingly in a fraction of a second. In spite of this ability to give any potential prey a run for its money, the green spider is more ambusher than agile hunter. It hides camouflaged in long grass, waiting to spring on some hapless grasshopper or other insect that wanders within range.

Probably the easiest way to find the green spider is during July, by examining oak saplings growing amid the grass. Here the female fastens several leaves together to form a silk-lined chamber that serves to protect her eggs.

Although by no means common, this species can be found throughout much of Europe, where it frequents damp woodland clearings, often within heathland habitats. Closely related to the running crab spider, it is the only representative of the Sparassidae family to be found in northern Europe. It is absent from North America.

➤ Male green spider camouflaged in long grass.

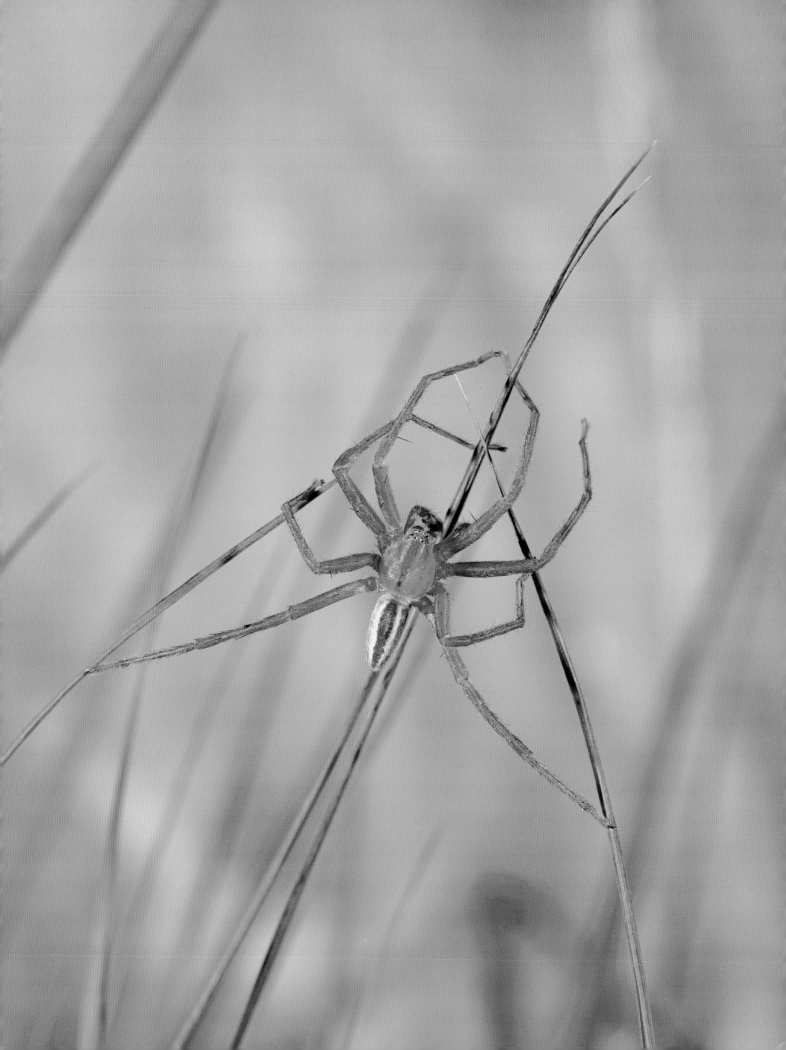

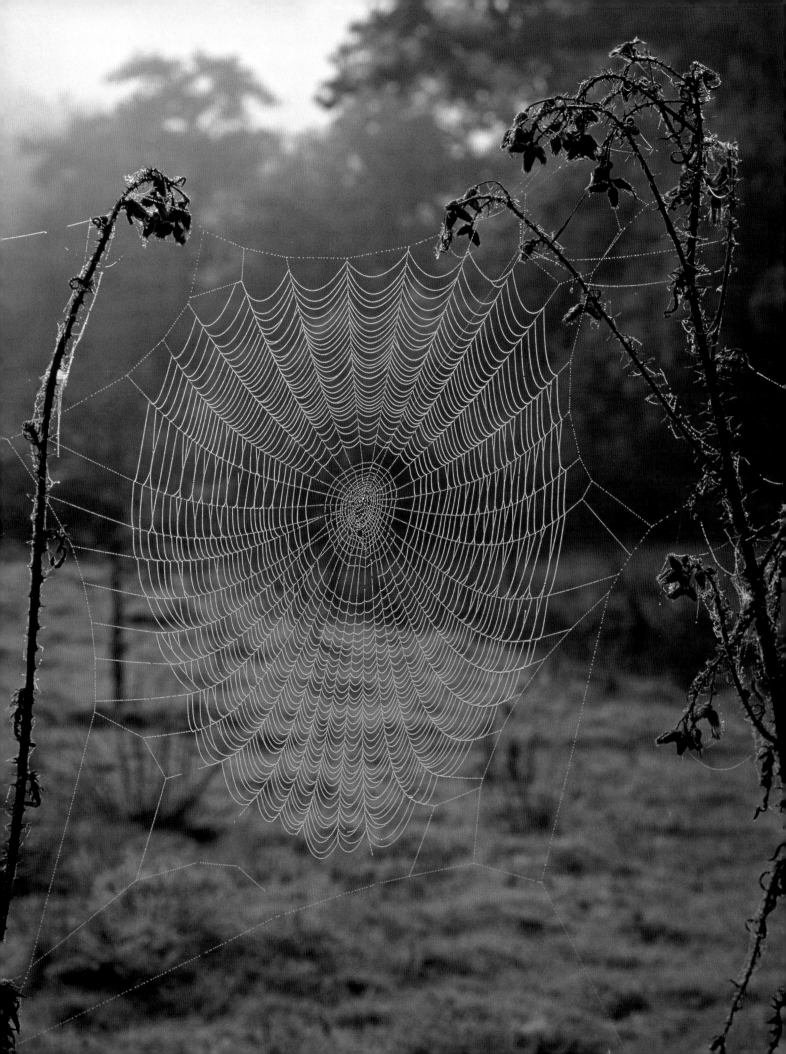

6 Trappers: Orderly Webs

Whenever we think of spiders, the orb web springs to mind. It is the symbol of the spider, representing the pinnacle of its achievement in design and construction. The orb web evolved to create the maximum prey-capturing area while minimizing the amount of silk, but what is perhaps more remarkable is that the spider constructs this web in less than an hour. Only about 10 percent of spiders capture prey by means of orb webs or, in a few species, a section of an orb. Each web will exhibit subtle differences in design: there may be variations in size, orientation, number and distribution of radii or spirals, and ornamentation—the design of the stabilimentum, when present (see orb weavers). Such differences provide very useful clues to identification of the spider.

These intricate web designs are of course not learned but under strict genetic control—orb weaver spiderlings spin perfect orb webs soon after hatching, and the web remains fundamentally the same throughout the spider's life. The only differences that occur are those necessary to suit the size of the spider and the position of attachment points. Most webs are suspended vertically, but some are angled at 45 degrees or occasionally positioned strategically on a horizontal plane, depending on the type of prey they are intended to trap.

Orb webs often go unnoticed unless moisture condenses on their fine threads or they are backlit by the slanting rays of a low sun. Indeed, a dew-laden early autumn morning is the best time to enjoy their radial perfection. In these conditions the enormous number and diversity of spider webs that swathe almost every twig and leaf of hedge and meadow are quite breathtaking, and a reminder of the vast number of spiders that share our world—a very good reason for rising early on such days.

Once insects learned to fly—about 350 million years ago—it gave them a massive advantage in avoiding their enemies. Many spiders had no option, therefore, but to find a way of trapping prey in mid-flight. Thus, over the eons, spiders perfected the orb web, a device that captures flying insects with super efficiency. It was

◄ Orb web on autumn morning.

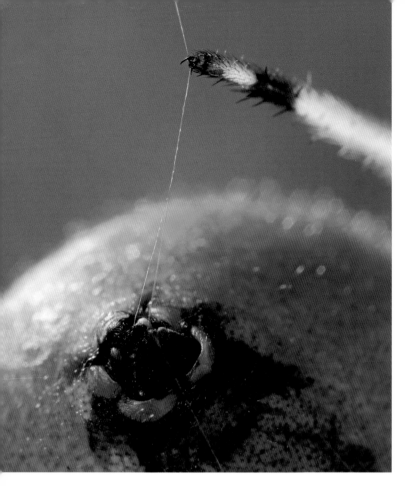

Web being extruded from spinnerets with aid of the rear claws.

no doubt a far simpler solution than evolving wings themselves.

The web itself is made from one of the strongest substances known. Although only a few microns in diameter, spider silk can stretch to many times its length before finally snapping. In this way the web absorbs the impact of rapidly flying insects with minimum risk of penetration. A further refinement in the construction reduces "bounce" so that the prey is not catapulted out of the web again. The insect's impact is confined largely to six radial spokes, which provide most of the forces that bring the web back to its original position. Recently it has been discovered that these spokes contain microscopic coils of web within the sticky drops along their length. These act as springs that help to stabilize the web, limiting bounce when prey hits it. There are also micro-

aerodynamic forces at work, based on wind resistance, that help the web to return quickly to its original position.

Different species position webs according to their favorite prey. The web's height, its angle and the type of habitat in which it is deployed are all crucial in providing the spider with as much food as possible. For example, some webs are installed near water to catch insects such as mosquitoes or midges, others may be angled low down in open meadow to trap leaping grasshoppers or leafhoppers, and others still are designed to catch larger flying insects such as butterflies and moths, so they are strung between shrubs and trees.

Only three spider families create orb webs. Most common are the webs made by Araneidae such as the garden spider. The other two families of orb weavers are the Tetragnathidae, or long-jawed spiders, and the Uloboridae. It is worth noting that a few spiders make orderly webs that are not at all based on the orb configuration—*Episinus* is a notable example. This genus belongs to the Theridiidae family, the scaffold-web spiders, which characteristically construct a web with threads that go in all directions. *Episinus* makes a much simpler web in the form of an H, with the two lower threads attached to the ground and the whole arrangement being held together by the spider (see page 139).

Orderly web-weaver families

Most spiders that build orb webs belong to the **Araneidae** family. The structure of their webs is subject to huge variations depending on species. Most are large in comparison with other orb-web spiders, almost all have a closed hub, and most of the webs are spun vertically. Whereas diurnal spiders dismantle and eat their webs in the morning, remaking them for daytime use, nocturnal species remake their webs in the evening.

Many orb weavers have colorful bodies marked with patterns of greens, yellows and reds, while others are drab brown. Most have rather short, spiny legs, which can help to distinguish araneid spiders from other families. As eyesight plays only a minor role in their daily life, araneid eyes are small. Their sense of touch provides most of the information they need about the outside world, particularly through contact with the web. Body size varies from 0.06 to 1.2 inch (1.5–30 mm). The Araneidae are a large family; 160 of them are found in the United States and 50 in northern Europe.

The **Tetragnathidae**, or long-jawed orb weavers, are closely related to the Araneidae, but most species have long bodies rather than round ones, sometimes up to two or three times longer than their width. Many species have enlarged chelicerae, particularly in the males.

Tetragnatha species constructs open-hub orb webs that are frequently oriented at an angle or in the horizontal plane. *Nephila*, on the other hand, makes a vertical bright yellow web, while *Meta* generally builds its web in dark places. Members of the *Pachygnatha* species construct webs only in the early stages of their lives, subsequently becoming vagrant hunters as they mature. When not in their webs, many species lie motionless, stretched out along a stem in a characteristic manner, where they are difficult to spot. This family has about 40 species in North America and 16 in northern Europe.

Uloboridae, the venom-free or cribellate orb-web spiders, are unique among spiders in two ways. First, they possess no poison glands; second, the various genera within the family construct entirely different webs. Some make complete orbs and others just triangular sections of an orb, while in some cases merely a few lines of silk are used. Also, unlike the Araneidae, rather than using sticky threads they make the capture area from fine cribellate silk.

The spiders themselves are generally smallish and have an unusual appearance, often with lumps or feathery tufts of hair. They can easily be mistaken for twigs or fragments of dead leaves. There are 240 species worldwide, 16 of which occur in North America and three in northern Europe. The generic name *Uloborus*, which comes from "lethal" in Greek, seems to be very inappropriate, as Uloboridae are the only family of spiders that do not possess venom!

The gold silk of the golden orb spider's web.

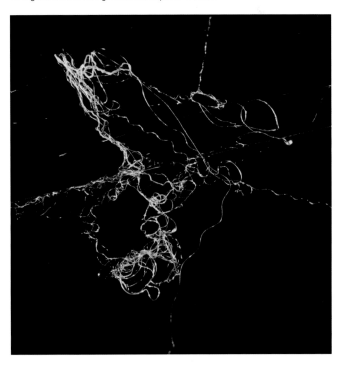

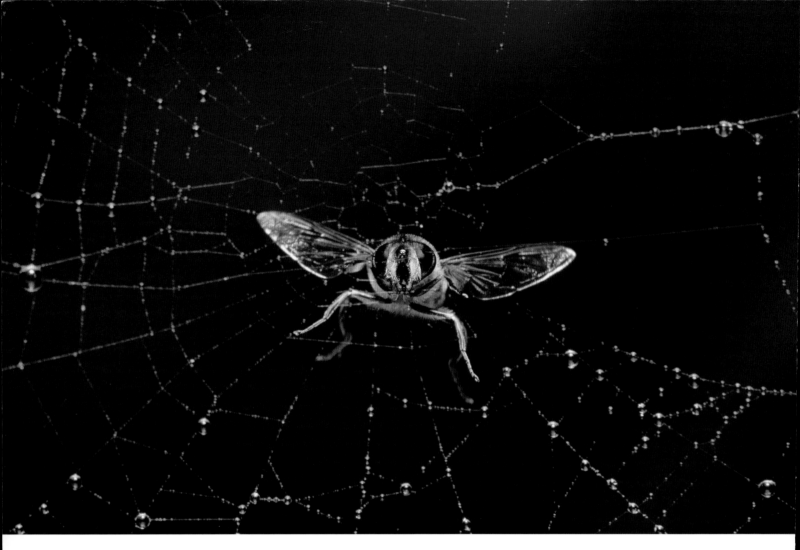

Hoverfly pictured a split second before flying into garden spider's web.

Garden spider; cross spider
(*Araneus diadematus*)

Araneus from Latin "spider"; *diadematus* from Latin "with a crown or diadem" (referring to the abdominal cross pattern)

The aptly named and ubiquitous garden or cross spider is the best known of all spiders, although it is not the most common spider to be found in gardens. During the Middle Ages the white cross on its abdomen boosted this member of the large Araneidae family into a creature of religious veneration, making it the paradigm of spiders. Sometimes it is extremely common in town and suburban gardens, among shrubs or on man-made objects such as window frames, where it is difficult to overlook because of its large size and tendency to sit bang in the center of its large orb web. Yet this species can be found in almost any habitat from heathland and woods to mountainsides and cliff faces. It is also found throughout the eastern United States, where it was introduced.

It is the female that is most frequently encountered, perched head down in the center of her orb. She is much larger than her mate, particularly in the autumn, when her spherical abdomen is hugely distended with up to about 900 eggs.

The orb web of the garden spider is the archetypal insect trap, designed for capturing insects as they fly around, oblivious to the invisible snare that awaits. The web, which is built on a near-vertical plane, is often large in relation to

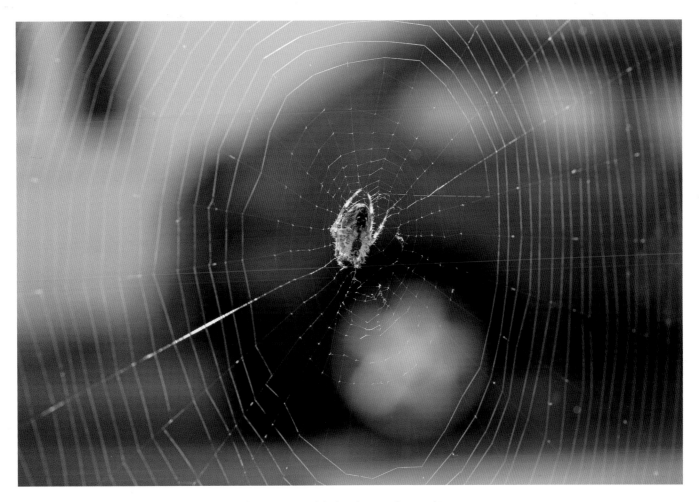

In the autumn the garden spider is a common sight in urban gardens and towns.

the spider and has between 25 and 35 radii and close-set spirals. The center of the hub consists of meshed threads surrounded by a small spiral, beyond which is a free zone before the main spirals begin. It is these main spirals that have sticky droplets along their length for entrapping flying insects. The spider will either sit in the center of the hub with her eight outstretched legs each in contact with a radial thread, or hide away in a nook among some leaves, holding a stout line that is connected to the hub center. The exact position of a struggling insect will be detected at the slightest movement, whereupon she will be galvanized into activity, biting the victim before wrapping it up ready for her next meal.

The unrestrained ease with which spiders move around their webs without getting trapped themselves can be clearly observed by watching this large spider. This astonishing ability is accomplished in a number of ways. To begin with, she tends to sit facing outward with her body clear of the sticky spirals, so if the web is slightly inclined to the vertical she will settle on the underside. She will also move around by grasping the dry radial threads with her tiny claws, as only the spirals are sticky. Orb builders have special tarsi, with an extra third claw and opposing serrated hairs between which the silk thread is grasped. By twisting her feet at an angle to tension the thread, the spider will be held securely in position (see page 25). Additional immunity from entanglement is assured by an oily covering on her legs that further impedes adhesion.

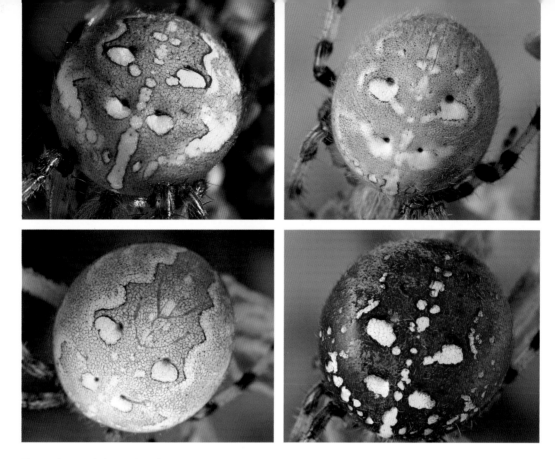

Four colour variations of the four-spotted orb weaver.

Four-spotted orb weaver
(*Araneus quadratus*)

Araneus from Latin "spider"; *quadratus* from Latin "square"

The four-spotted orb weaver, along with the wasp spider (*Argiope bruennichi*), is the largest orb weaver found in northern Europe; an egg-laden female often attains as much as 0.6 inch (15 mm) in length. The male, though, like so many spiders, is much smaller. *Quadratus* is the only spider that might be confused with the garden spider, but when viewed from above, the circular abdomen with its square of four bold white spots should separate the two. It is also one of the most attractive species, with a color varying from rust red or dark brown to subtle pale shades of greenish yellow (see above).

A. quadratus is common and widespread throughout Europe. It lives in heather, tall grasses and low bushes such as gorse, where it builds a large orb web of about 16 inches

(40 cm) in diameter at heights between 3.3 and 5 feet (1–1.5 m) off the ground. Most of the day is spent hidden away in a sizeable retreat of plant material held together with tough, papery silk. Although this araneid is absent from the Western Hemisphere, North America has an almost identical species: the shamrock spider, *Araneus trifolium*.

To those who are tuned in to the grassroot jungle, a familiar sight in spring is the balls of little spiderlings of this species (as well as of the closely related garden spider and others). These remain intact for several days after hatching, making no attempt to move away or feed until disturbed by a jolt, a shadow or the warm breath of an enthusiastic observer, whereupon the little creatures scramble off in all directions. When danger has passed they gradually coalesce once again into a tight golden ball. Over a few days the ball expands until the spiderlings eventually wander off to seek their fortunes.

➤ A ball of freshly hatched spiderlings.

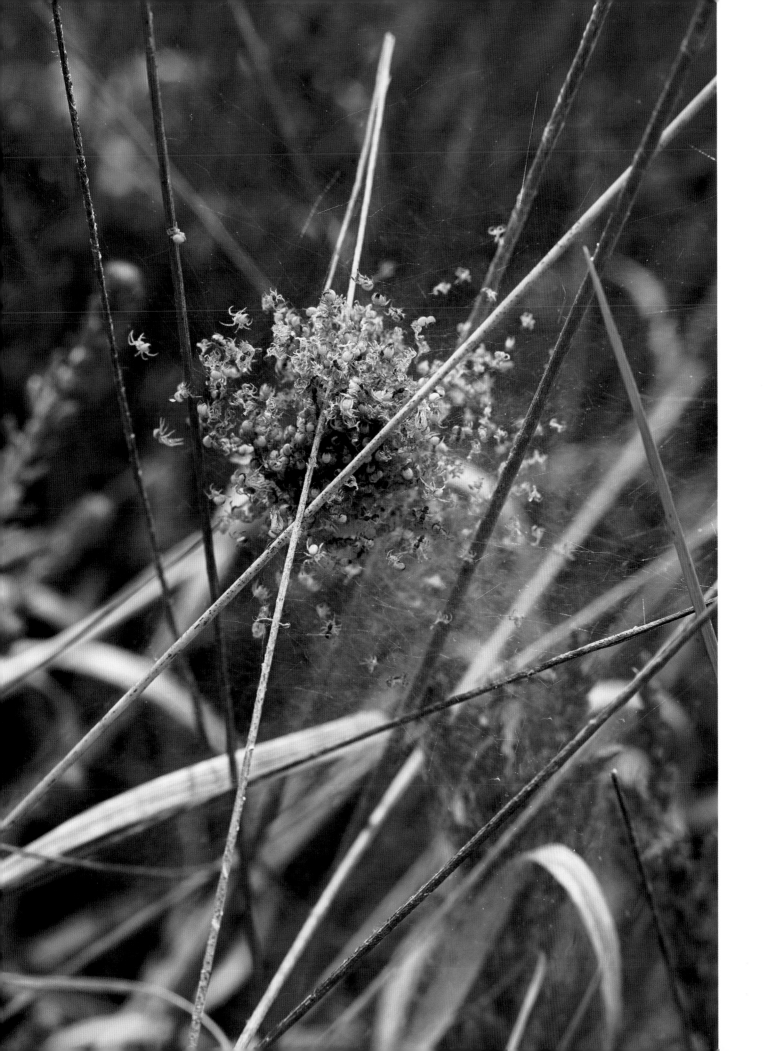

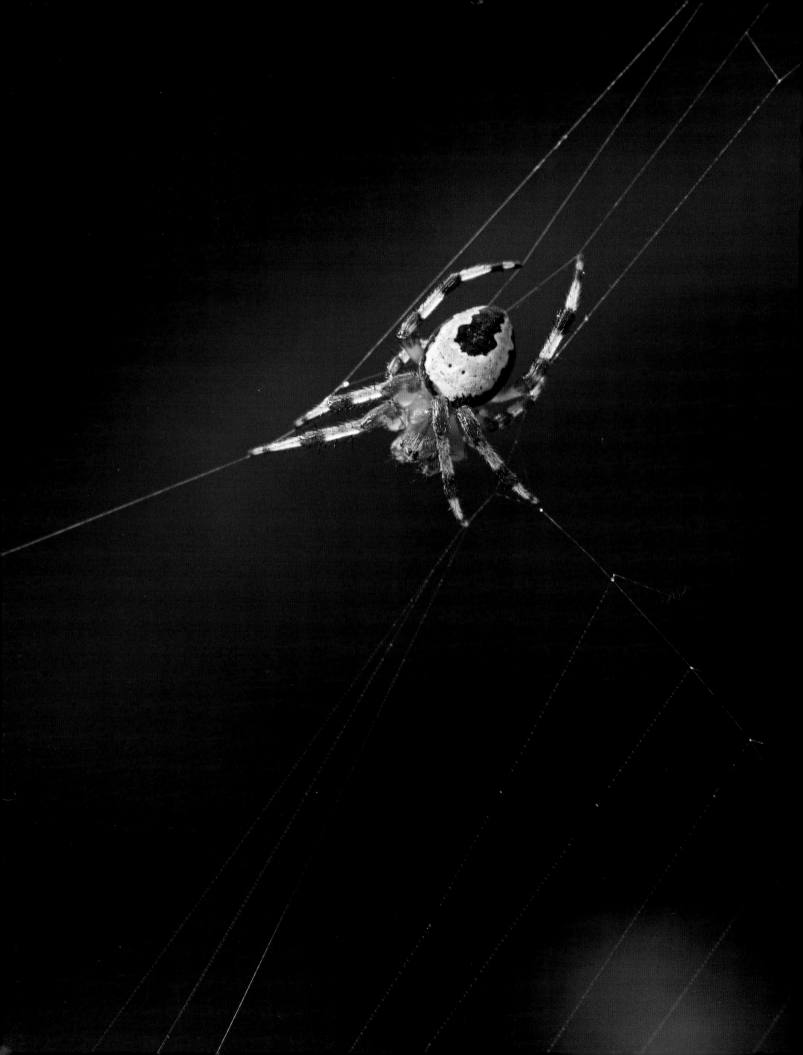

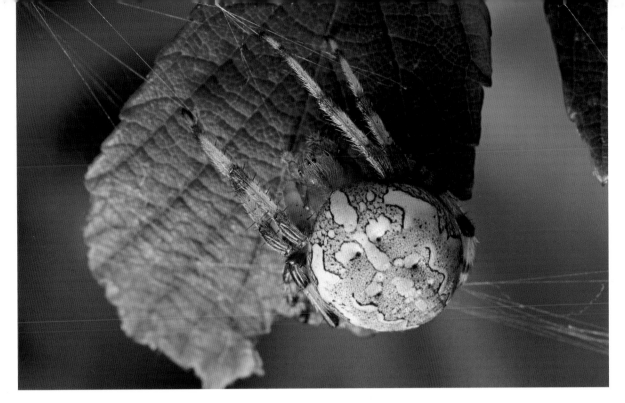

Marbled form of the spider.

Marbled or pyramid orb weaver

(*Araneus marmoreus*)

Araneus from Latin "spider"; *marmoreus* from Latin "like marble"

Another large orb weaver—and a particularly striking one—is *Araneus marmoreus*. This araneid is far less common than the preceding species, being very locally distributed in Britain, although widespread throughout Europe. The spider comes in two distinct color forms. The more handsome one (*pyramidatus*), as illustrated, with a bold brown mark toward the rear of its abdomen, is the most frequently encountered of the two. The other form is so different that it could easily be mistaken for a separate species altogether, perhaps a faded four-spotted orb weaver (see image on page 100). The spider's species name *marmoreus* refers to the marbled appearance of this less common form; indeed in North America, where this spider is also found, it is known as the marbled spider. For

◄ "Pyramidal" form of marbled orb weaver.

some reason this New World form has much bolder marbling, and could easily be mistaken for another species entirely.

However uncommon they may be elsewhere, my home village of Ardingly, Sussex, appears to be their headquarters. During late summer and autumn I frequently bump into these spiders in my garden and around the local woods. W.S. Bristowe, in his classic 1958 book *The World of Spiders,* noted that he found over 160 specimens in Ardingly. Not so long ago I even had an unfortunate encounter with *marmoreus* in my bedroom, when a large female somehow managed to find her way into my shirt. A little nip under my arm reminded me that some of our larger spiders can retaliate if severely provoked.

A. marmoreus builds its large orb web around brambles, tall grasses and the lower branches of shrubs and trees, where it hides under a silk-lined curled leaf. The best way to find this well-camouflaged and retiring spider is to look for an orb web and then follow the signal thread to its nearby hideaway.

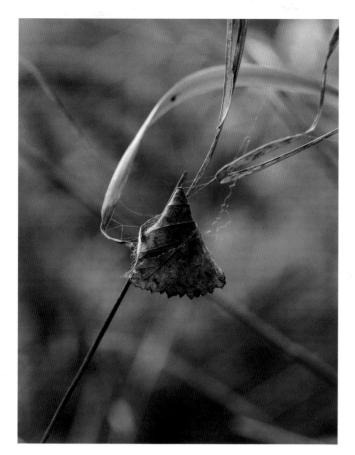 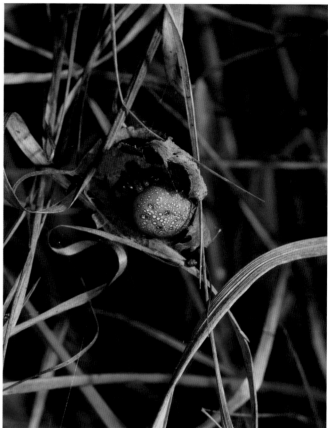

The strawberry spider's conical retreat made from a dead leaf, and right looking up at the spider inside the cone.

Strawberry orb weaver (*Araneus alsine*)

Araneus from Latin "spider"; *alsine* from Greek *alsos*, "wood" or "thicket"

In common with the vast majority of spiders, *Araneus alsine* has no English name, although "strawberry spider" has been proposed to reflect its likeness to a ripening strawberry. The cream-spotted pale orange to deep red-purple of the abdomen makes it almost impossible to confuse this splendid araneid with any other.

In spite of *A. alsine*'s bright appearance, only a fortunate few have had the pleasure of seeing it. I spent many hours almost upside down hunting about in its favored habitat before finally setting eyes on this shiny red spider. These photographs, taken in a boggy ditch, serve as a reminder of that memorable occasion.

A. alsine is not only very rare but also locally distributed; the female is found almost at ground level in the shade of rank growth amid damp wasteland, heaths and bogs. To compound her elusiveness, she spends her time out of sight in a silk-lined curled leaf in the form of an inverted cone, so to find her you have to look up into the cone or use a mirror. Perhaps the best way of finding this spider, having first located a known habitat, is to examine every inverted cone of curled leaves—if you have the patience! (The strawberry spider is absent from North America.)

The web is built low down and usually has about five strengthening spirals, which are particularly sparse around the signal line, similar to that of the window spider, *Zygiella x-notata*.

➤ Strawberry spider as it is rarely seen, running up a grass stem.

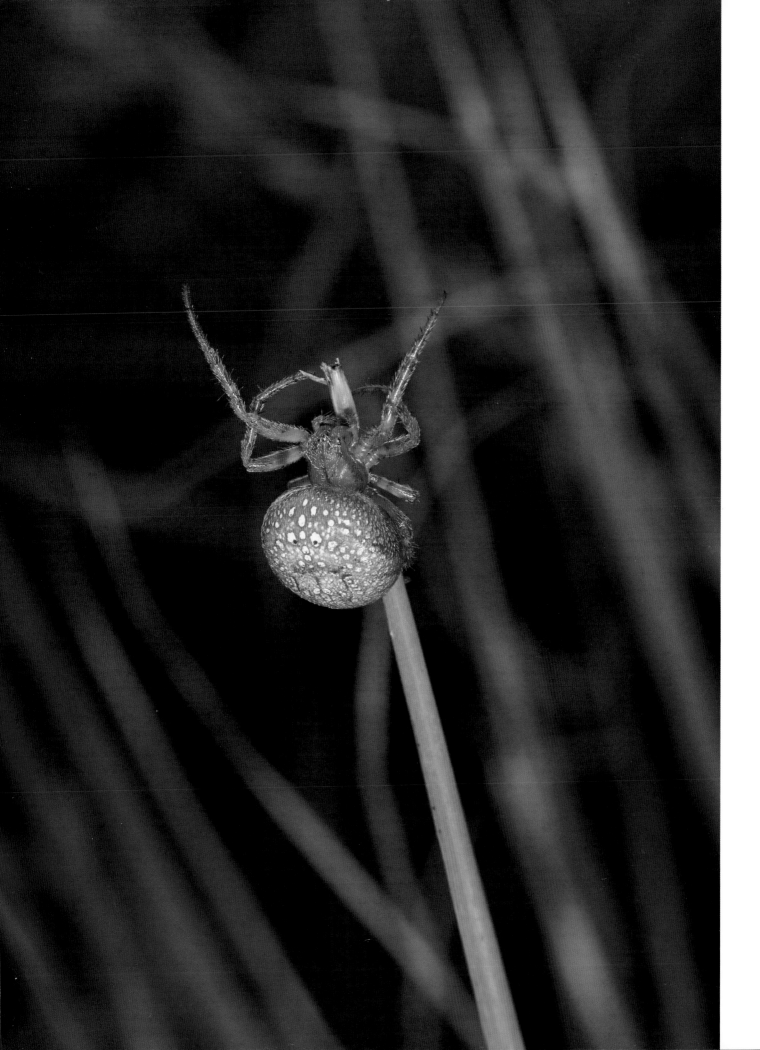

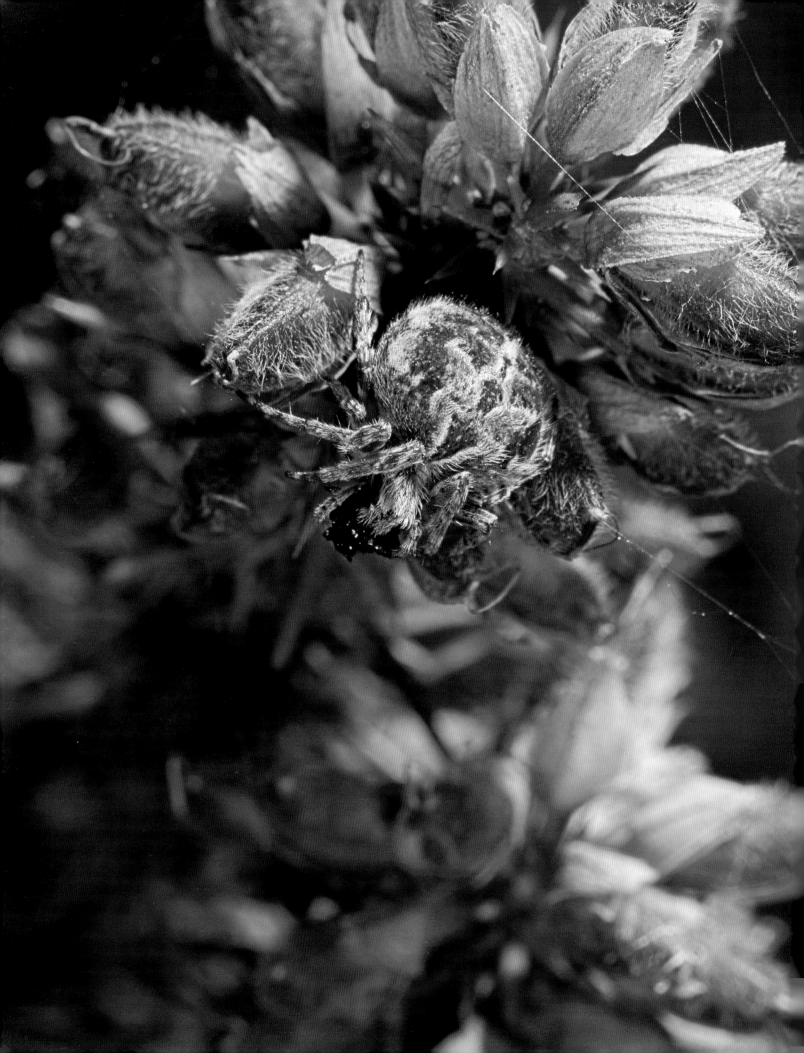

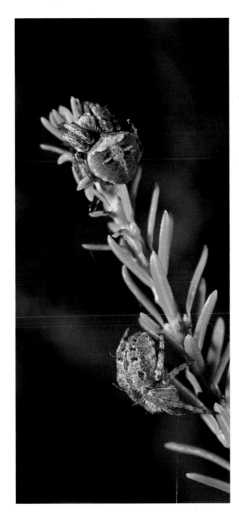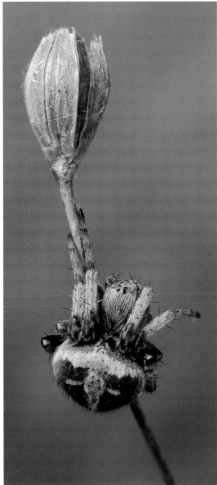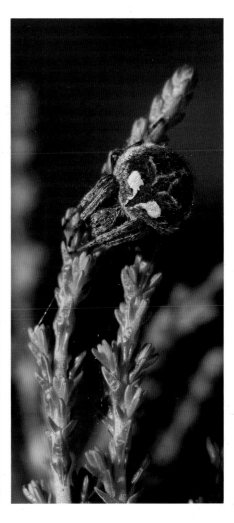

Four color forms of *Agalenatea redii*.

Orb weaver spider (*Agalenatea redii*)

Agalenatea from Greek "slowly"; *redii* possibly from Greek

Identification of spiders is often not easy; even spiders of the same species can show wide variation in color, pattern and sometimes form, as is clearly demonstrated in these photographs. Variation is especially typical of araneids. Because these spiders sit still in the open, it could be a strategy to avoid predators' learning and locking onto a search image. Like many of the world's Araneidae species, *Agalenatea redii* has leaf-like patterns on its abdomen; as it spends most of the day fully exposed on dead or brown seed heads of heather, gorse or similar plants, the spider is so well camouflaged that it becomes almost impossible to spot, for predators and arachnophiles alike. The orb web of *A. redii* has a dense lattice at the hub, but it waits for prey at the edge on a platform of fine silk.

Although this modestly sized spider may not be one of the most impressive of araneids, it has the distinction of being the single European member of its genus. The genus is absent from North America; in northern Europe *A. redii* is widespread throughout, although distribution is very local.

◄ Orb weaver (*A. redii*) camouflaged on its open retreat in gorse.

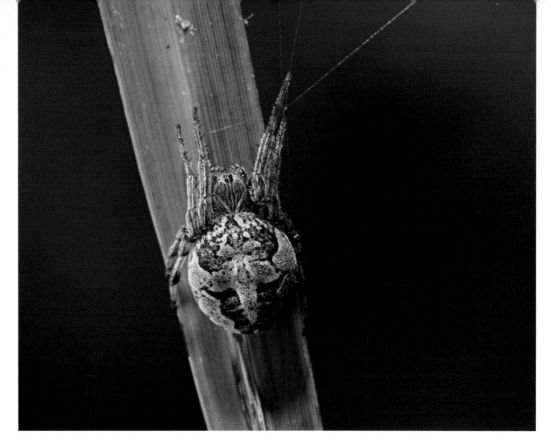

A furrow spider prefers to live near water.

Furrow spider (*Larinioides cornutus*)

Larinioides from Larino, Italy; *cornutus* from Latin "horned"

These next two species of orb weavers were at one time included in the *Araneus* genus alongside the garden spider, but because of structural differences in their reproductive organs they have now been transferred into the genus *Larinioides*.

Experts can separate *L. cornutus* from *L. sclopetarius* (right) by closely examining their palps and epigynes, but they can also be identified by more general characteristics—habitat being one of them. *L. cornutus* is nearly always found close to water, on reeds, tall grasses and other vegetation around the water's edge, where it catches mayflies, damselflies and sometimes even larger dragonflies. Color is often an unreliable guide to identification of spiders, and this species is particularly prone to variation. However, there is a difference in the size of adults: *L. cornutus,* at between 0.2 and 0.4 inch (5–9 mm), is smaller than its relation *L. sclopetarius.* This spider also rarely rests in its web, preferring to hide away in a retreat of papery silk in the head of a plant. Like many spiders it is nocturnal, typically building its web after dark; it stays there at night but monitors the web from its daytime retreat.

If danger threatens, *L. cornutus* will often leave the security of its refuge and rapidly drop to the ground on a thread to vanish among the debris, or it will even deliberately climb down a plant stem into the water. The spider may remain submerged for a minute or so before climbing hand over hand back up its safety thread. Other spiders sometimes behave the same way; for instance, I have seen *A. marmoreus* drop into water if its retreat happens to overhang the water's edge.

L. cornutus is common and widespread in Britain and Europe, as well as North America, where it is called the furrow spider.

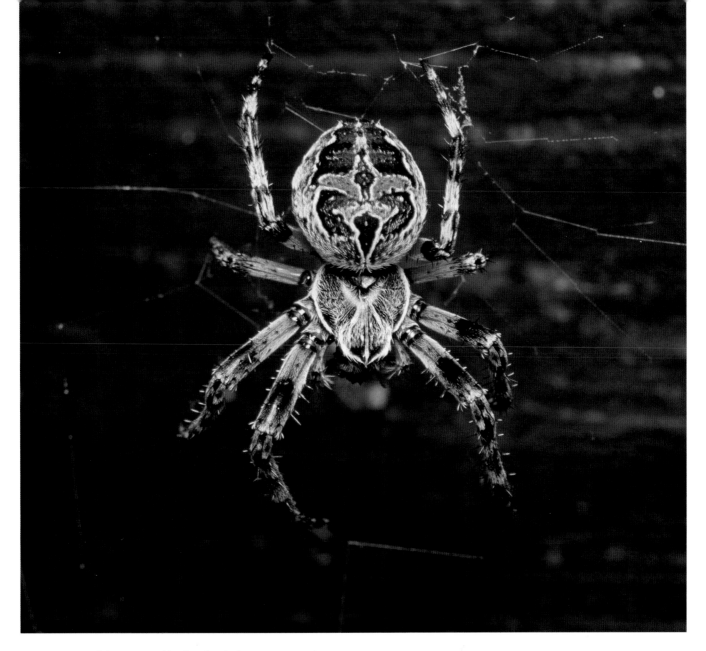

Orb weaver spider *L. sclopetarius*.

Orb weaver spider (*Larinioides sclopetarius*)

Larinioides from Larino, Italy; *sclopetarius* possibly from Latin

As well as being larger than the previous species—between 0.4 and 0.6 inch (9–14 mm)—*L. sclopetarius* is seldom found living among vegetation, preferring fences, buildings and bridges, although often also in the vicinity of water. A great many spiders thrive around aquatic habitats, as water acts like a magnet for flying insects as well as for other wildlife.

L. sclopetarius can also be identified by its distinctly velvety appearance: the head region of the carapace and the darker markings of the abdomen are outlined with white hairs. In England and Wales it is far more locally distributed and less common than *L. cornutus*, although widespread throughout most of northern Europe and North America. It can best be found by searching the cracks and crevices of gates and fences in the neighborhood of watery places.

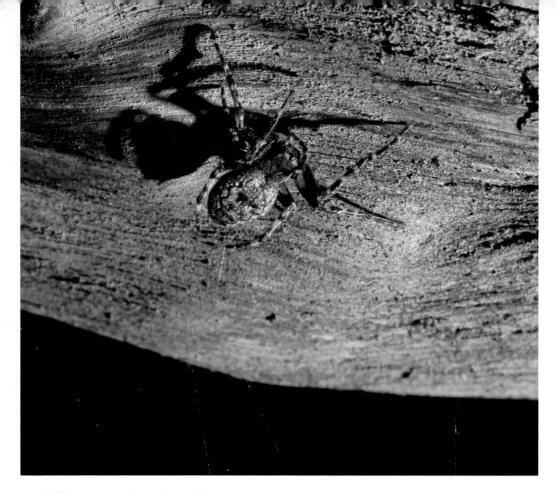

A strictly nocturnal moth-catching spider.

Walnut orb weaver (*Nuctenea umbratica*)

Nuctenea from Greek *nukta*, "night"; *umbratica* from Latin *umbra*, "shade" or "shadow"

Despite being widespread and common throughout Britain and Europe, this araneid spider is not often seen during the day unless disturbed from its daytime retreat. One way of finding N. *umbratica* is to look around old trees, sheds, gates or fences for signs of its characteristic web, which has many more spirals above the hub than below it. There is no signal thread and therefore no clue as to the whereabouts of the owner, whose flattened dark brown body is adapted to squeeze into narrow cracks and crevices. In spite of considerable variation in the depth of its color, N. *umbratica* cannot easily be mistaken for any other orb weaver, by virtue of its size, its flattened appearance and the brown scalloped folium on the back of its abdomen.

As the web of the adult is strong, large and highly elastic, it is capable of trapping and holding large moths and other nocturnal insects. Nevertheless, with such hefty prey the orb is easily damaged, so, as the light begins to fade each evening, this large spider emerges from its retreat to build a fresh web ready for the night's harvest. When it's complete, she sits in the center of the hub to await further action.

When disturbed this spider is particularly adept at feigning death (this is called a cataleptic reflex), dropping from its web like a stone onto the ground. Here it will lie motionless for perhaps several minutes with its legs tucked in, waiting for the danger to pass. The females may be found throughout the year, whereas the males die off at the onset of winter.

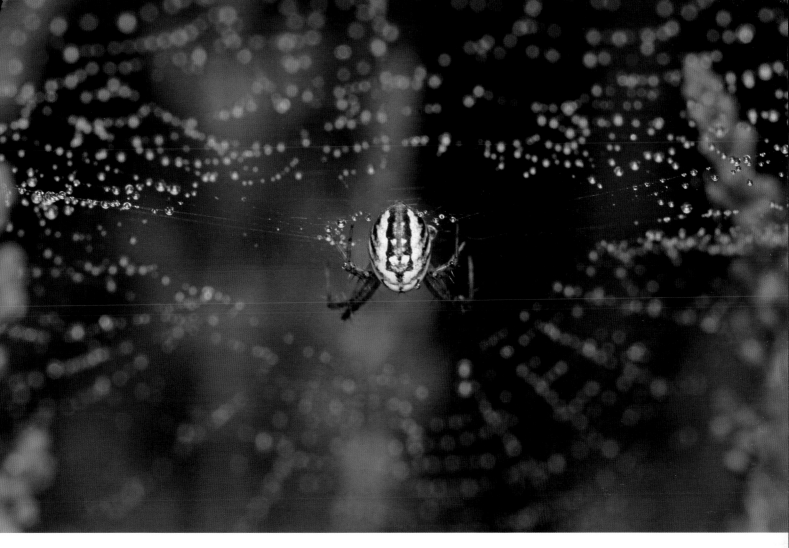

The cricket bat shape is clearly visible on the abdomen of this attractive orb weaver.

"Cricket-bat" orb weaver (*Mangora acalypha*)

Mangora from Greek "slave dealer"; *acalypha* from Greek "nettle"

Mangora acalypha is the only European species in its genus, and its distinctive markings make it impossible to confuse with anything else. Indeed, if this attractive orb weaver had to be given an English name—which it certainly needs in view of its obscure scientific name— then a suitable one would be cricket-bat spider, for it has a distinctive tawny brown and black cricket-bat pattern on the rear half of its abdomen, as well as a series of chevrons.

Mangora builds its web among low vegetation such as grasses or heather; unlike the majority of orb webs, it is inclined at a low angle, sometimes almost horizontal. Here the spider resides, brazenly positioned in the center without any apparent need for a retreat. The web is also unusual in that it has a larger number of radii (about 50) and strengthening spirals than those of the majority of other species.

This member of the Araneidae family is fairly common, especially in southern England, where it can sometimes be abundant, although it becomes increasingly scarce in the north. The spider is widespread in northern Europe, but again it becomes rarer as the climate becomes colder, being absent in Finland. In North America this spider is replaced by several similar *Mangora* species.

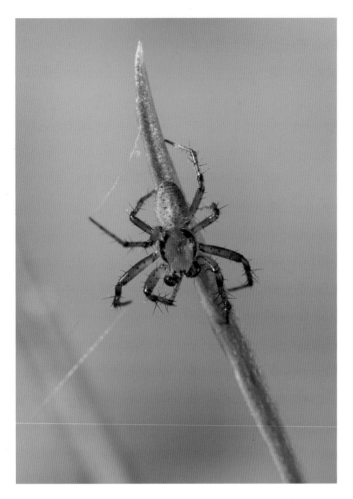

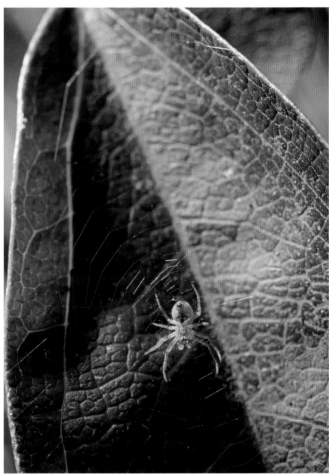

Male cucumber spider cleaning its foot.

The spider in its orb web spun within the confines of a small leaf.

Cucumber or green orb weaver
(*Araniella* species)

Araniella from Greek "diminutive"; *cucurbitina* from Latin *cucurbita*, "gourd"; *opisthographa* from Greek "writing behind"

There are several similar species of *Araniella* in this araneid genus, all of which can be recognized in the field by the attractive bright green abdomen with small paired black spots and a red spot just above the spinnerets. The abdomen of the male is smaller and has a well-marked reddish cephalothorax. The two most common species are *A. cucurbitina* and *A. opisthographa*, both of which are widespread throughout Britain and northern Europe, but they are not easy to tell apart without a microscope. Like most

spiders they reach maturity by late summer and autumn. The other Old World species are much scarcer in Europe; one of them, *Araniella dispicata*, occurs commonly in North America, where *A. cucurbitina* is rare.

The webs of all *Araniella* spiders are small and constructed at about head height or lower on bushes and trees. Sometimes they are spun within the confines of a small concave leaf, in which case the web may sometimes be a rather haphazard affair, hardly resembling an orb at all.

➤ Cucumber spider on its pollen-covered web.

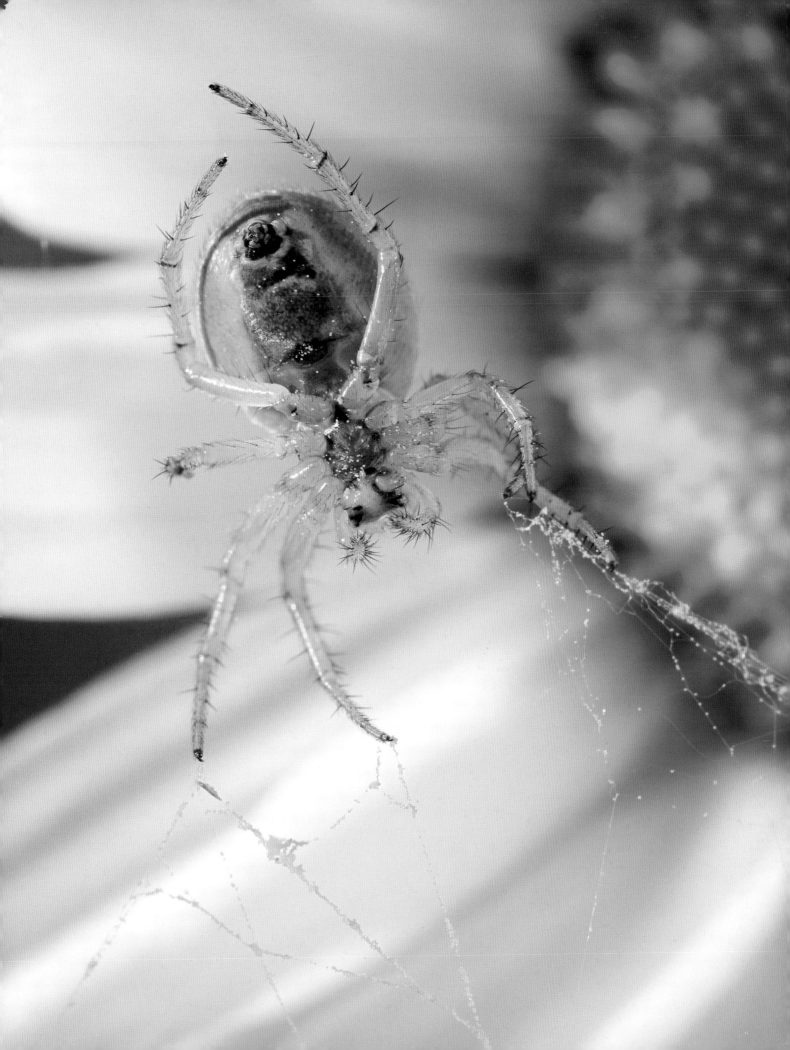

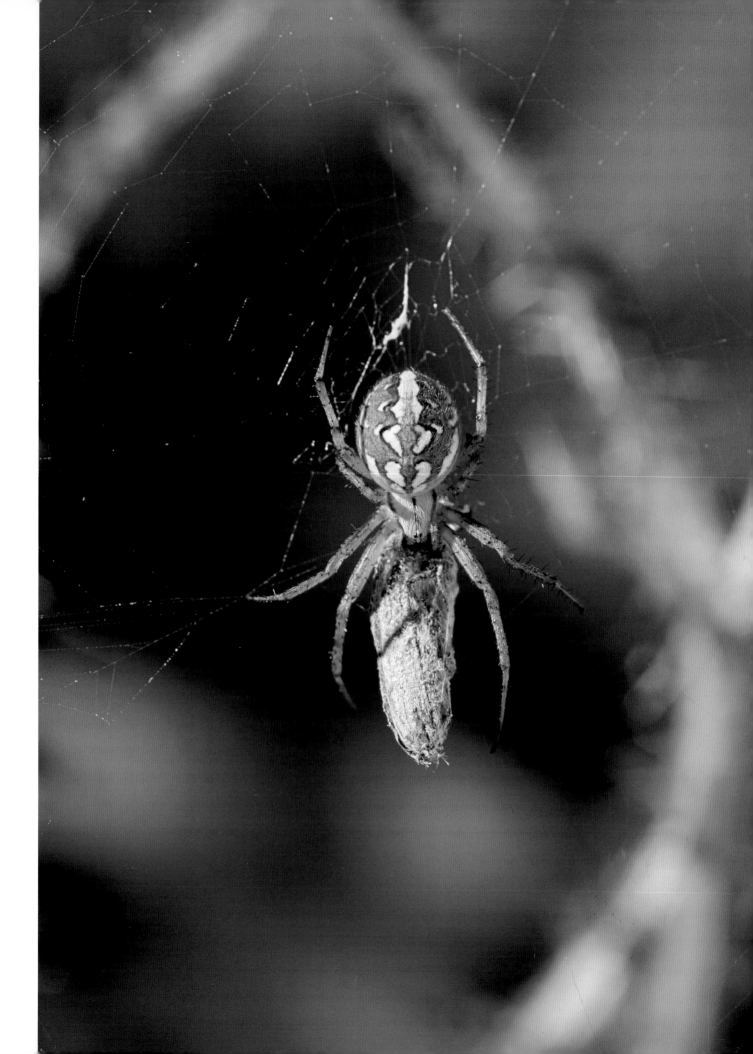

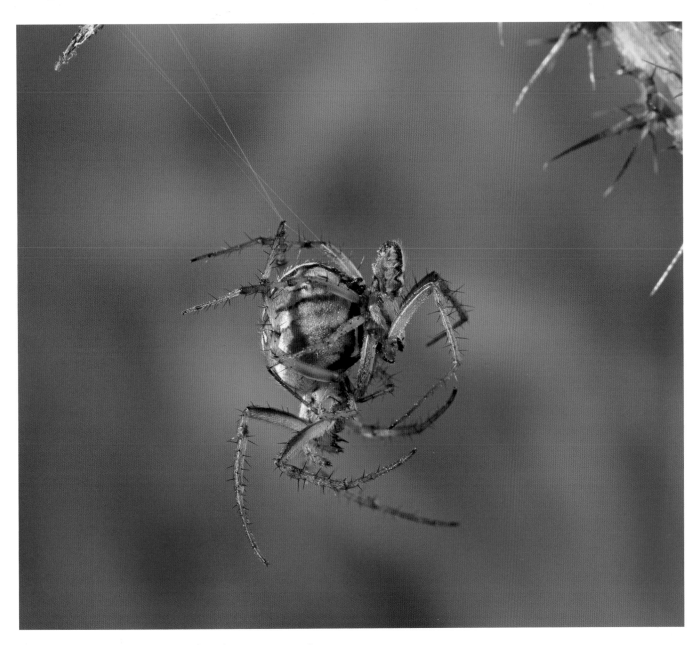

Orb weaver spiders mating (*Neoscona adianta*).

Bordered orb weaver (*Neoscona adianta*)

Neoscona from Greek "new dust"; *adianta* from Greek "dry places"

This attractive araneid is difficult to confuse with any other spider found in Britain. The female is about 0.4 inch (9 mm) long and has a series of

◄ *Neoscona* with captured prey.

black-bordered cream triangles on her abdomen set against a brownish or rusty background. The triangles become progressively smaller toward the posterior end (see also pages 30 and 31).

The female sits in full view on a silk platform beside the web, which is built in lowish plants such as thistle, gorse or heather. *Neoscona* is absent from North America and generally uncommon in Britain.

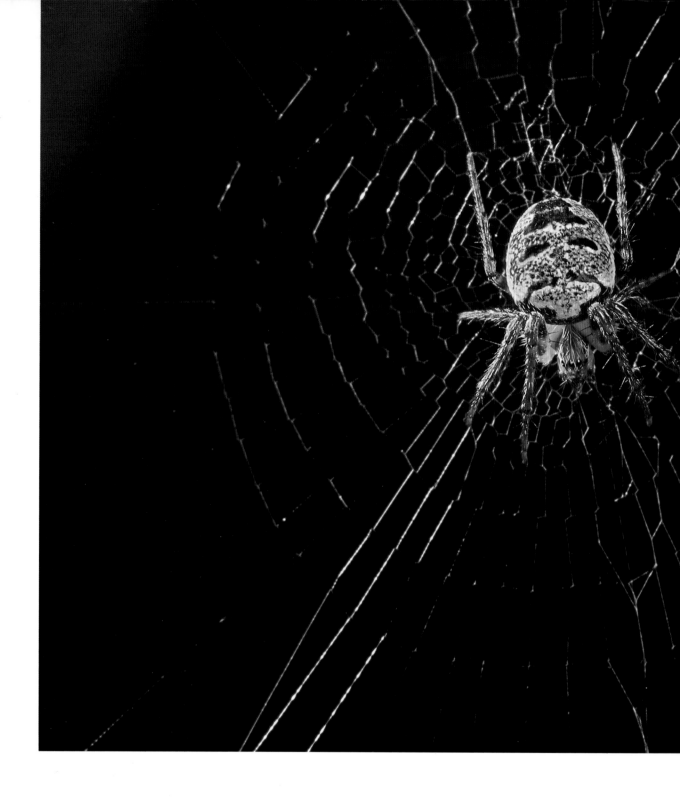

Orb weaver spider (*Zilla diodia*)

Zilla from a plant name; *diodia* from Greek "passageway"

Zilla is a small but distinctively marked orb-weaving spider that usually builds its perfectly concentric web in dark, shady situations at about waist level, where the spider tends to be quite conspicuous. Adding to its visibility is its habit of waiting for prey sitting bang in the center of the hub on an extensive latticed area of threads. The web can also be identified by

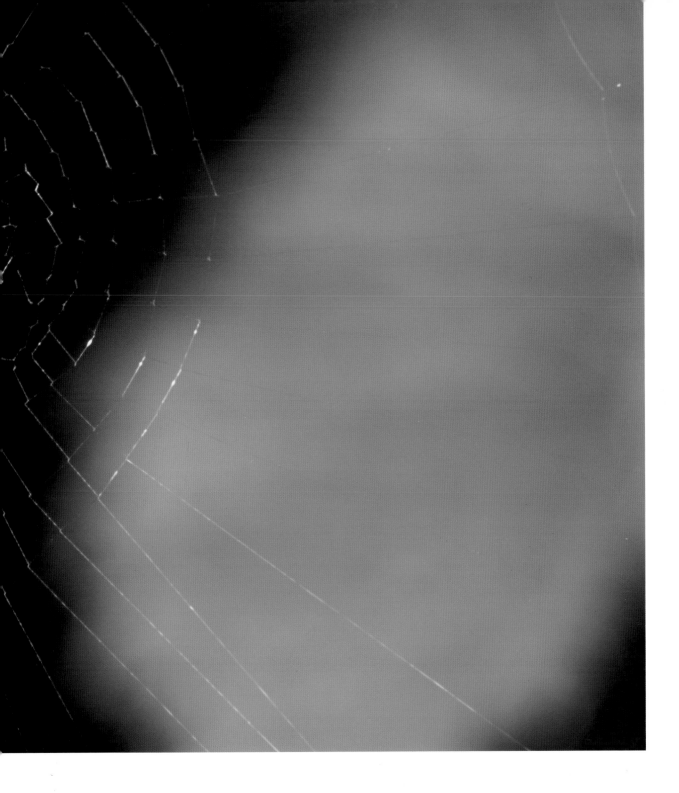

the unusually large number of strengthening spirals and radii and the absence of a retreat or signal line.

Z. *diodia* is the single European member of this araneid genus, while North America has none. Although widespread in Europe (apart from Scandinavia), in England this spider is restricted to the southern counties.

▲ *Zilla* on the central platform of its web.

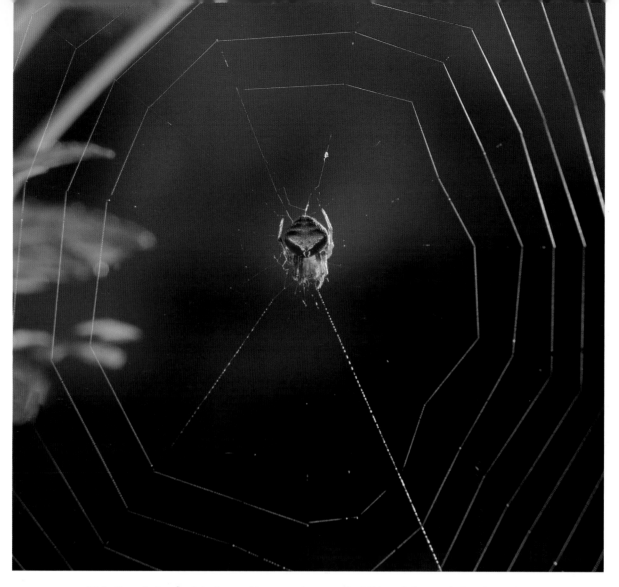

While the spirals are sticky for catching prey, the scarcely visible radials remain free for walking on.

Orb weaver spider *(Atea triguttata)*

Atea from Greek "horse"; *triguttata* from Latin "three spots"

Unfortunately this small but attractively marked orange-tinged araneid is rather rare in England, being confined largely to a few favored locations in southern counties. *Atea* makes its small, delicate orb web in deciduous bushes and trees. As is clear in the photograph, a large area in the center of the orb is kept free from spirals. Like *Zilla* (see page 116), this spider waits in the center for small insects to fly into the sticky spirals. The microscopic sticky droplets on the spirals are clearly visible in the picture; as with most orb weavers, the radials are not treated with this tacky substance and as a result are almost invisible. This allows *Atea* to move around its web with alacrity without itself becoming stuck. As soon as the web becomes damaged this spider recycles the remains without delay, eating its way through it in less than two minutes. Like many orb weavers it renews the web each day.

There are two similar species of *Atea*; the other one, *A. sturmi*, prefers to live in evergreen trees and is slightly smaller and less rare. Although absent from Scandinavia, both species of *Atea* are widespread through most of northern Europe. They are absent from North America.

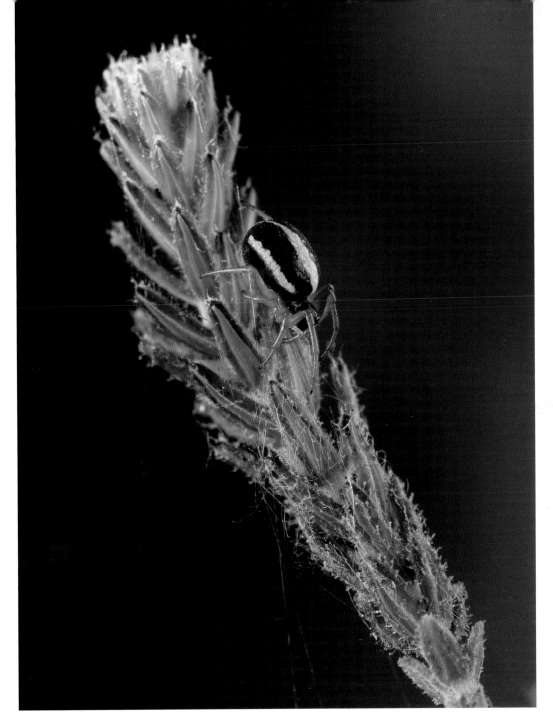

Hypsosinga spiders are small, round and glossy.

Striped orb weaver *(Hypsosinga species)*

Hyposinga from Greek "high"; *sanguinea* from Latin "blood-red"

Four species of this tiny, 0.098 inch (2.5 mm), but natty orb weaver are found in northern Europe, the genus generally being identified by its shiny, oval dark brown abdomen and longitudinal white or pale yellow bands. In North America the genus is represented by several other species.

The little orb webs are spun close to the ground among low vegetation, often near water or in damp situations. The species shown, *Hypsosinga sanguinea,* is rather rare and locally distributed in Europe and southern England; it prefers to live among heather.

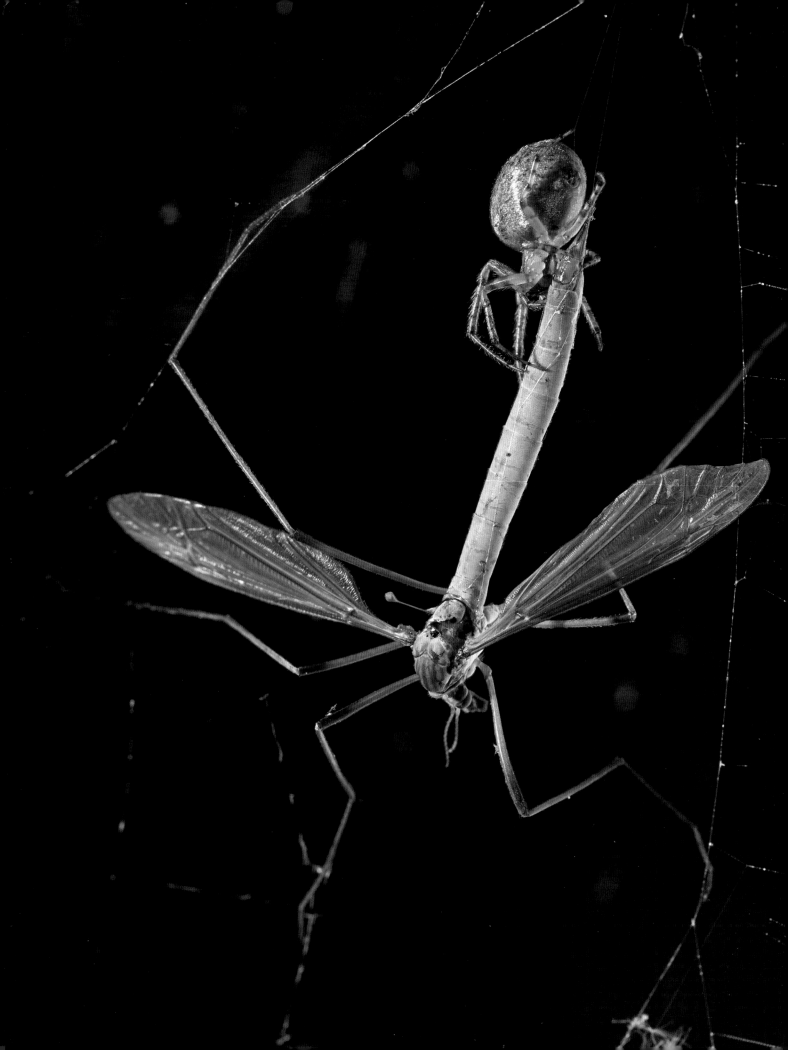

Window spider *(Zygiella x-notata)*

Zygiella from Greek "join together"; *x-notata* from Latin "marked with an X"

The window spider is one of the most abundant European spiders, and it also occurs in North America. It can be seen almost anywhere there are window frames, at any time, day or night, summer or winter. My house has at least one of these spiders on every windowpane, sometimes one at each of the four corners.

Although this araneid can be readily identified by the gray leaf pattern on its back, it is the web and its position that give the game away. The webs of all *Zygiella* species are easily recognized because the upper part of the orb is free of spirals. When making the web, rather than moving round in a spiral, the spider reverses direction each time it reaches this segment. Directly behind the vacant sector is a tough strand of thread, the signal line that leads up to the spider's tubular retreat at the edge or corner of the frame. Here the spider bides its time with the tips of its front legs on the signal line, waiting for some insect to make contact. Sometimes spirals bridge the missing sector—the orbs of young ones, for instance, are complete—and in late summer the webs made by some adults may have the complete segment intact. However, there is something about the signal thread and the stretched oval hub that makes these webs unmistakable.

Window spiders are particularly active at night, when nocturnal insects such as moths are attracted to the light inside the house. Crane fly season, in late summer, seems a profitable time for these spiders, although the clumsy insects quite often manage to break

away before the spider has time to administer its subduing bite.

The eggs are laid in a silken cocoon that is often covered with a dense tangle of threads at the edge or corner of the window frame; it holds about 50 eggs.

Web of window spider. Note the vacant sector with signal line.

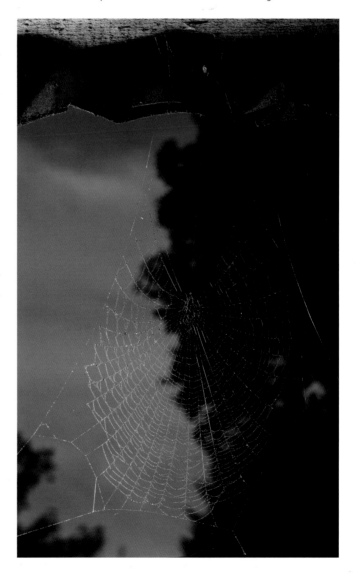

◄ Window spider with crane fly.

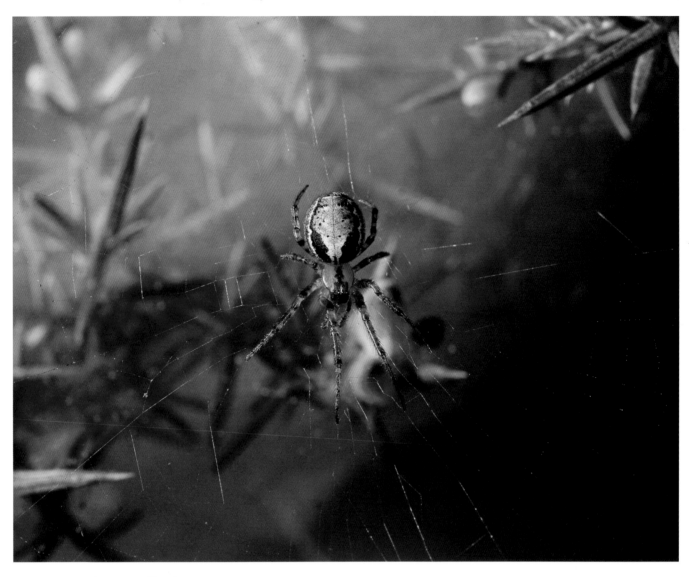

Orb weaver *Z. atrica*.

Orb weaver spider (*Zygiella atrica*)

Zygiella from Greek "join together"; *atrica* from Latin "of the house"

Almost identical in general appearance to the window spider is its close relative *Zygiella atrica*. The chief difference between the two lies in habitat: whereas the former chooses window frames around human habitations, *Z. atrica* prefers to build its web on heather, gorse and other bushes, often on open fields far from houses. This spider also thrives on rocks and breakwaters close to the ocean. The species name *atrica*

seems rather inappropriate, as it rarely lives around houses; the name is perhaps better suited to its relative.

Unlike the window spider, which remains in its retreat when disturbed, *Z. atrica* will drop from its web like a stone, trailing a dragline that enables it to easily find its way back home. Although the two species are similar in appearance, they can be told apart, as *Z. atrica* has a more silvery folium and reddish marks on the front of its abdomen. This araneid is widespread throughout Europe but less common than its relative. It is also found in North America.

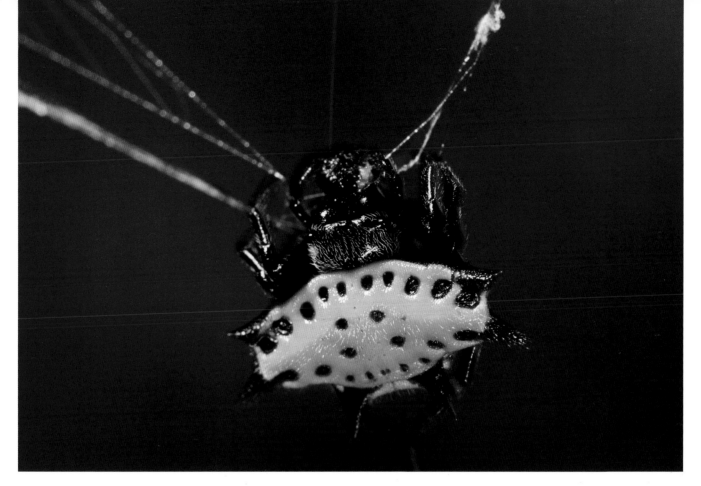

Bright warning coloration and spiny bodies deter predators.

Spiny-backed orb weaver

(*Gasteracantha cancriformis*)

Gasteracantha possibly from Greek "stomach"
or "belly"; *cancriformis* from Latin "crab-
shaped"

This odd-looking spider may not be a particularly
large orb weaver but its combination of shape,
color and "enamelized" abdomen makes it one of
the most conspicuous spiders found in warmer
regions of North America. Superficially it may
resemble a crab spider, but *Gasteracantha* spiders
have no relationship with the Thomisidae, being members of the Araneidae family.

The spiny-backed orb weaver—also known
as the crab-like spiny orb weaver, among a
range of English names—is the only species in
its genus in the Western Hemisphere, where it
can be found from the southern United States
down to Argentina. Because of variations in

its color pattern, over the years this spider has
been described by numerous biologists under
a plethora of names. It varies from whitish in
Florida to orange-yellow in Central and South
America, while the spurs can vary from black
to red. Now it is considered a single species.

The female is wider than she is long, varying
from 0.2 to 0.4 inch (5–9 mm) in length and 0.4
to 0.5 inch (10–13 mm) in width. The males are
much smaller, longer than wider, and lacking
the conspicuous abdominal spines. *Gasteracantha*
is found in woodlands and citrus groves, where
the webs are normally made between 3 and 20
feet (1–6 m) above the ground. It rests head down
in the central disc, which is separated by an
open zone from the sticky spirals beyond. When
an insect is ensnared, the spider snaps the web
around the capture area and rushes in to wrap
the prey, then carries the victim to its headquarters on the central disc to be consumed.

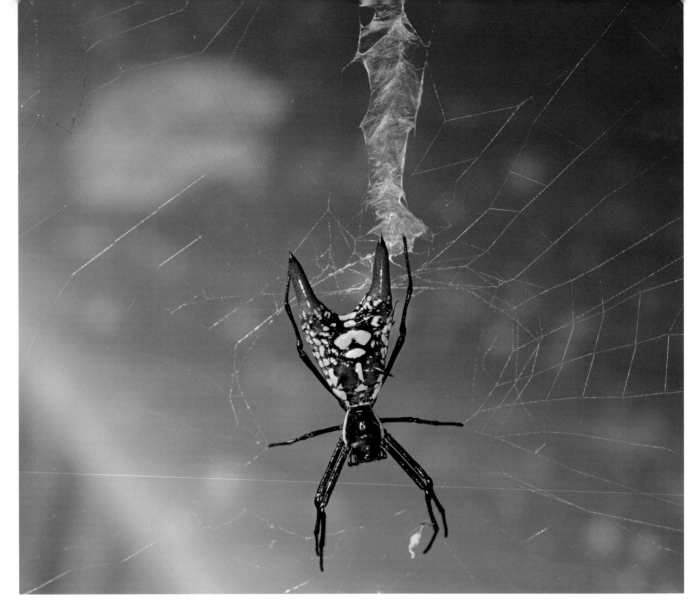

Micrathena in its web showing stabilimentum.

Arrow-shaped thorn spider

(*Micrathena sagittata*)

Sagitta from Latin "arrow"; *micr* from the Latin "small" and *Athena* from the armor-wearing goddess who spun

Another enamelized araneid spider is *Micrathena*, of which several species are found in the Western Hemisphere. The one shown here is a female arrow-shaped *Micrathena sagittata*, being one of the species that thrives in the eastern United States and Central and South America. The female is the more spectacular of the sexes with her long, diverging abdominal spines, but like the previous species, *Gasteracantha,* she is prone to considerable variation.

The slightly slanted 12-inch (30 cm) orb web of *Micrathena* is constructed on low bushes around woodland edges, shrubby meadows and gardens, and is made with many radii and closely spaced spirals. Sometimes there is a small stabilimentum above the hub. Here the spider rests upside down on the web's downward slope. Like many spiders it will drop out of its web onto the ground when disturbed or when an intruder gets too close. It is reputed to prey largely on leafhoppers.

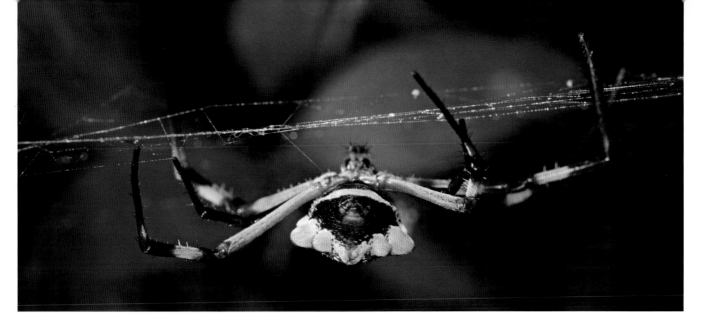

Rear view of a silver argiopid.

Silver argiope (*Argiope argentata*)

Argiope from the Greek name of a mythological nymph; *argentata* from Latin "silvery"

Argiopes are large, conspicuous araneids that hang head down in the center of their orb web. The web normally has a zigzag stabilimentum running through it that can come in a variety of forms; sometimes up to four are built in an X pattern, as is the case with this species. The purpose for these decorations is not certain. One reasonable theory is that the stabilimentum serves as camouflage, making the spider less conspicuous. This is supported by the fact that webs so endowed are made only by spiders that occupy the hub. An alternative explanation is that stabilimenta make the webs more visible so that birds are less likely to fly through them, saving the spider energy in repairs.

Argiopid spiders are largely tropical or semitropical species. The striking silver argiope, *A. argentata,* with its silvery cephalothorax, flared abdomen and yellow-and-black-banded legs, is found in the southern United States and Central and South America. Often several specimens may be found living in the same bush. Like a number of spiders, *A. argentata* does not necessarily bite its victim; its reaction to prey that become entangled in the web depends on the type of prey. The response to butterflies and moths is a long bite, whereas most other insects are first wrapped in silk. Presumably large insects, particularly those with loose scales, need to be rapidly subdued before they have a chance to escape.

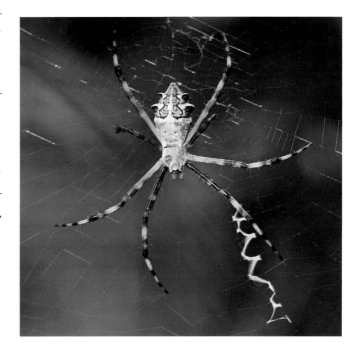

➤ Silver argiopid in its web, showing a single stabilimentum.

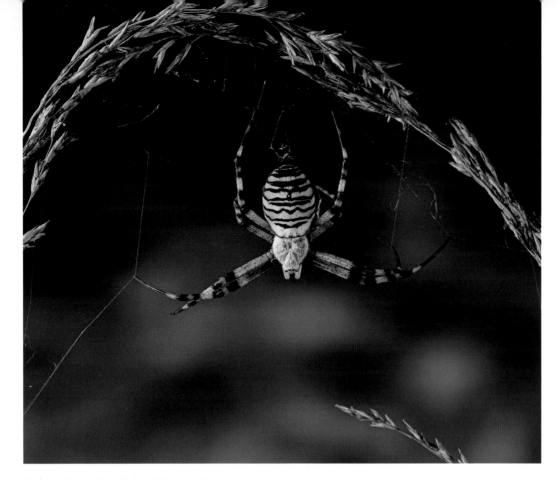

Wasp spider, with yellow and black stripes.

Wasp spider (*Argiope bruennichi*)

Argiope from the Greek name of a mythological
nymph; *bruennichi* after entomologist
M.T. Brunnich

This exotic-looking creature is the sort of spider
you would expect to find in a steamy rainforest
rather than a rough clearing on the south coast
of England. The female is not only large—especially in late summer, when full of eggs—but
also boldly colored with transverse black and
yellow wasp-like warning stripes. In contrast,
the male is an insignificant little brown dwarf;
indeed, it is difficult to imagine that the two
are even related. Hardly surprising, therefore,
that the female has little regard for her mate—
she usually eats her suitor, sometimes doing so
before mating has finished!

The large orb web, which is constructed
near ground level by the female, in common
with the rest of its argiopid kin, has stabilimenta running through it, one above and another below the hub. The webs of wasp spiders
are inclined at an angle, usually in long grass
around the edges of fields or wasteland, often
where there is a good supply of grasshoppers.

In warmer countries there are many species
of argiopid spiders, although the wasp spider,
which is locally distributed in Europe, did not
arrive in England till 1940, when it appeared on
wasteland in Hampshire. Since then the spider has become well established on the south
coast and is now extending its range northward. The one shown guarding her eggs in the
huge flask-shaped egg-sac was photographed
in Ashdown Forest in Sussex, well away from
the coast. A similar species found in North
America is the American garden spider, *Argiope
aurantia*. Argiopid spiders are well represented
in North America.

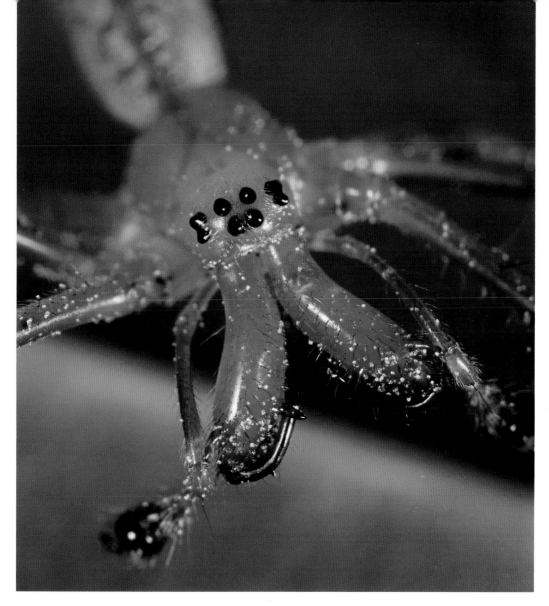

Close-up of long-jawed orb weaver showing its huge chelicerae.

Long-jawed orb-web weaver

(*Tetragnatha extensa*)

Tetragnatha from Greek "four-jawed"; *extensa* from Latin "stretched out"

Slim, tapering bodies, long, fine legs and outsized chelicerae usually distinguish the long-jawed Tetragnathidae spiders from other orb-weaving spiders, although not all species possess large jaws. They also have a habit of lying stretched out on a grass blade or twig, holding on with the third pair of legs and stretching the remaining three pairs in front and behind, parallel with their perch.

This cryptic pose, together with a body tinged with a light tracery of green and silver and dark veining, can make them very difficult to spot. The two commonest European species are *T. extensa* and *T. montana,* but they are tricky to tell apart in the field.

The webs of long-jawed spiders are delicate structures with few radii and widely spaced spirals; like *Meta*'s, they have a hole in the hub. The web is usually inclined at an angle or even horizontal. The name *Tetragnatha*—"four-jawed"—is fitting; in addition to the long, divergent chelicerae, their maxillae are similarly proportioned, giving the spider the appearance of having four jaws. These are used for mating, when the pair lock jaws in a wrestling posture, a precaution adopted by the male to prevent his being attacked by his mate.

The favorite haunt of long-jawed spiders is among reeds and rushes around the water's edge where there is a bounteous supply of flimsy, light-bodied insects such as gnats and mayflies to keep them happy. The webs are spun during the early evening before many of these insects become active. Long-jawed spiders, or grass spider species, as they are sometimes called, are common and widespread all over Europe as well as being found in North America.

➤ Long-jawed orb weaver with captured mayflies.

Long-jawed orb-web weaver in its web.

Long-jawed spider on grass blade.

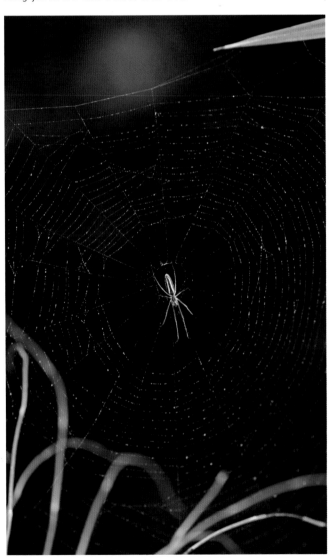

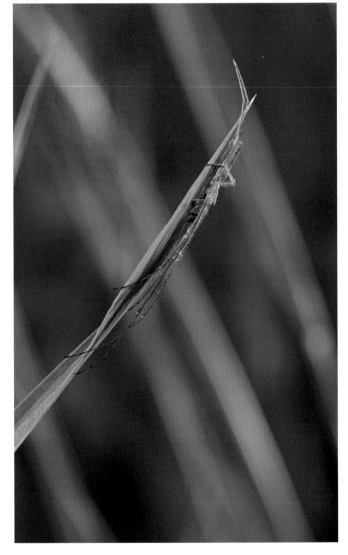

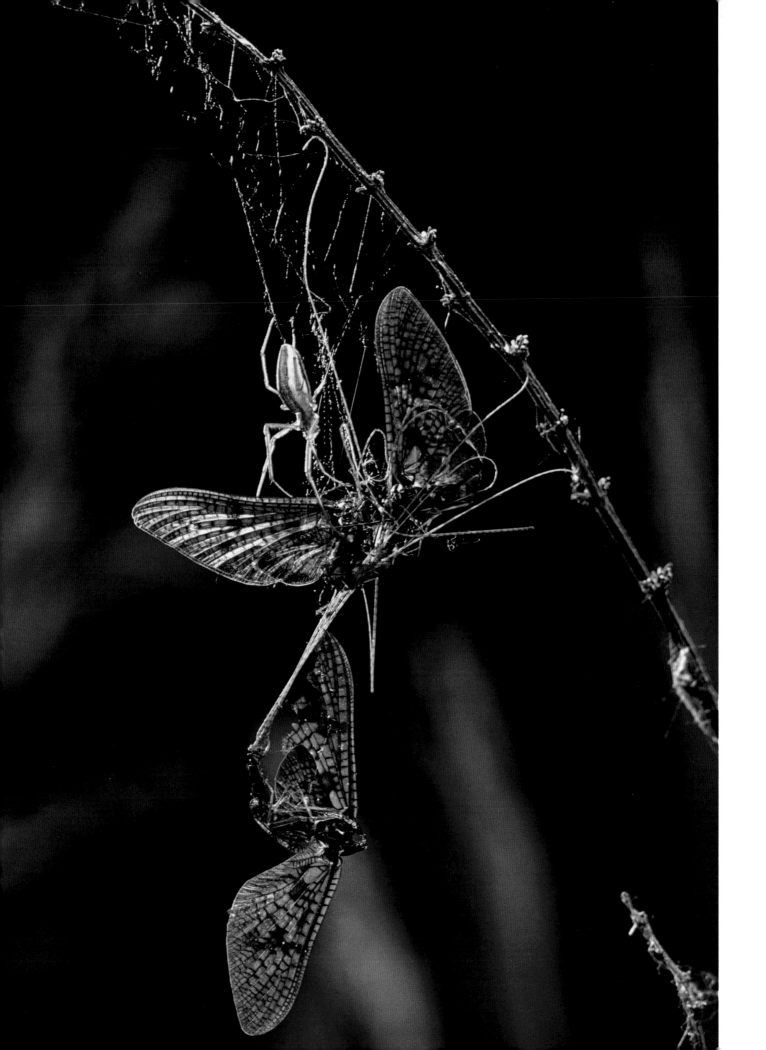

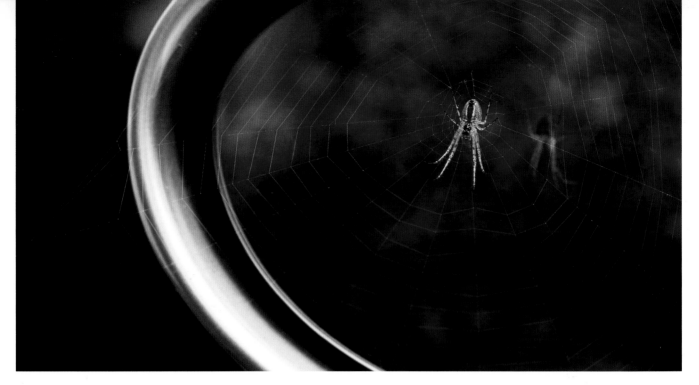

Lesser garden spider on car side mirror.

Lesser garden spider

(*Metallina segmentata*)

Metallina from Greek "made of metal";
segmentata from Latin "flounced"

The lesser garden spider is the most abundant orb weaver found in northern Europe, but it is absent in North America. In some years, you only have to wander outside in the autumn in suitable places (which are all around) to see that almost every shrub and patch of long grass has at least one *Metallina* orb attached to it, with a yellowish spider decorated with a brown or purplish leaf pattern posing in the center. The markings are subject to much variation in depth and color. In the male these are an attractive rusty brown, and he has longer legs.

There are five European species in this genus of the Tetragnathidae, and their webs are relatively small for spiders of this size. Distinguishing characteristics of the webs are a small hole in the middle of the hub, closely set spirals and a greater number of radii than those of the closely related long-jawed spiders. As the spider does not hide away in a retreat, there is no signal thread; instead it rests in the middle of the web, ready to dash out at the slightest vibration.

During the mating season, in late summer and autumn, the males of the lesser garden spider can often be found hovering around the edge of the females' webs; sometimes the two coexist quite amicably in the web before courtship begins. The female triggers the actual mating by catching prey. While her chelicerae are busily engaged in wrapping or feeding, the male can approach safely and mate. This apparently amicable relationship is probably possible only because the male is as big as his partner. He also possesses much longer legs, an advantage if any sparring should develop. Such a relationship seems more amicable than is the case with most *Araneus* species. Female garden spiders, for example, are twice the size and more fearsome, and the male is lucky to get away with his life.

Although the lesser garden spider depends on its web for catching the vast majority of its prey, it has been known to fall vertically on a thread from the inclined web to seize some insect moving below, suggesting that there can be little wrong with its eyesight.

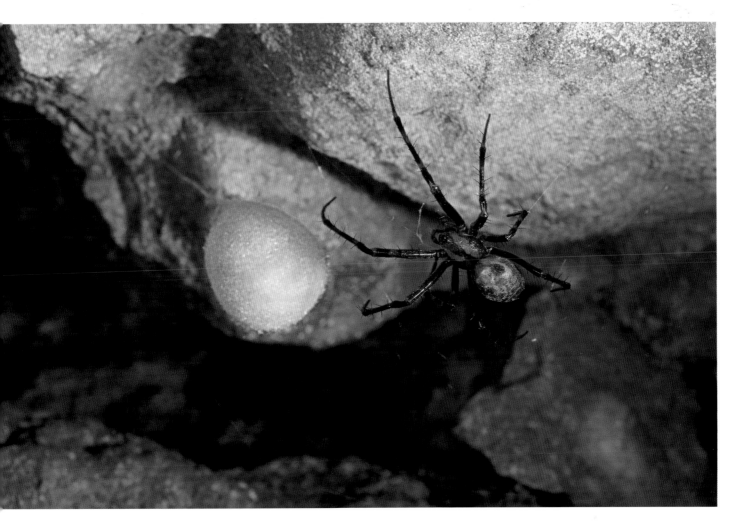

Cave spider with egg-sac.

Cave spider (*Meta menardi*)

Meta from Greek "cone"

The cave spider, *Meta menardi,* is a weird and rather large, creepy tetragnathid that spends its entire life in the pitch darkness (or near-darkness) of damp caves, sewers and the middle portions of long railway tunnels. As demonstrated by the female guarding her egg-sac in the photograph, the spider makes up for this with her subtle bronze and black markings, which are sometimes enhanced by a suffusion of yellowish patches, although these colors show up only when illuminated by a bright light.

Surprisingly, this spider is an orb weaver, but the web is difficult to discern in the gloom and is made even less visible by being constructed very close to the walls and roof of its drab habitat. Fortunately *M. menardi* is a very lethargic spider, which is just as well for arachnophobes who are able to pluck up sufficient courage to view this creature in its claustrophobia-inducing habitat!

M. menardi feeds on any invertebrates that venture into dark and damp places, such as woodlice, mosquitoes and hibernating butterflies and moths—I have found the remains of peacock butterflies and herald moths caught in their webs. Although by no means common, this spider is widespread throughout northern Europe and has also been recorded in some areas of North America. Be aware, though, that other species are also referred to as cave spiders, so it's best stick to scientific names whenever possible.

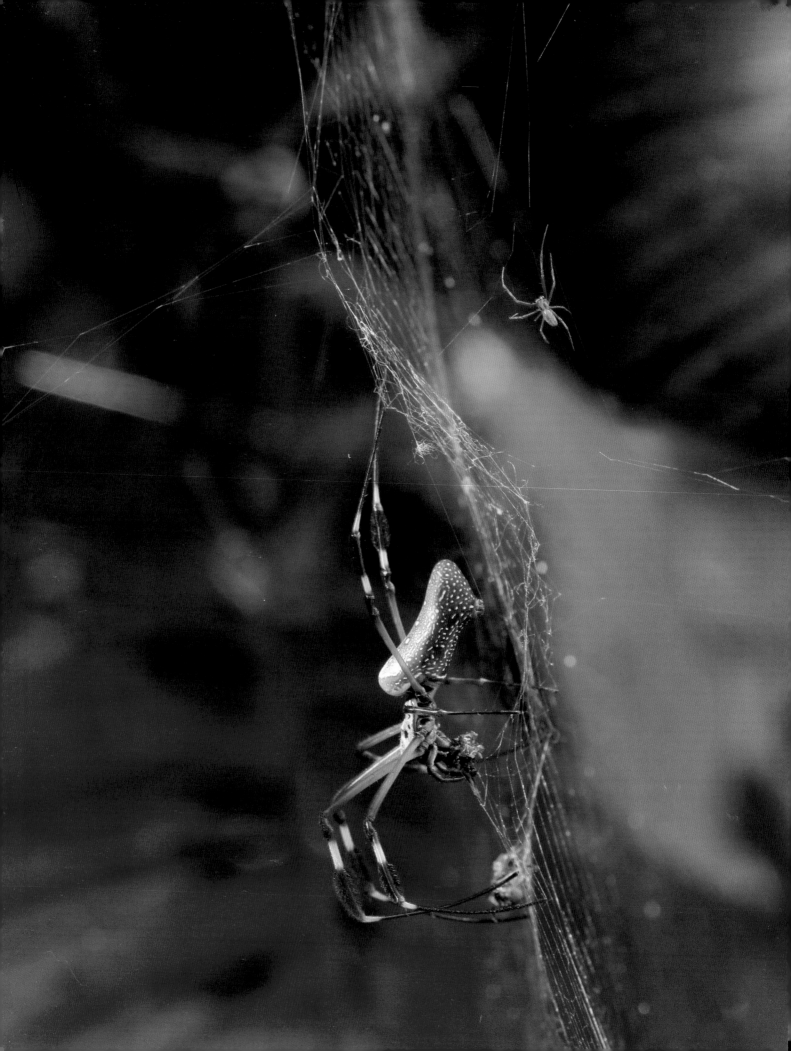

Golden orb spider (*Nephila clavipes*)

Nephila from Greek "fond of spinning"; *clavipes* from Latin "club-footed"

The largest araneomorph spider in the world is the golden orb spider, *Nephila clavipes,* a member of the Tetragnathidae. This impressive spider can be recognized not only by its size—the female has a body about 1.5 inch (3.75 cm) in length—but also by its long legs with conspicuous tufts of black hair on the femur and tibia of legs I, II and IV. The huge golden web, which can span gaps of up to 60 feet (18 m), also gives the game away. *Nephila* can be found in wooded areas from the southeastern United States through Central America and beyond. Unfortunately this spider does not grace the countryside of northern Europe.

I well remember the first time I ran into *Nephila,* during the early seventies, long before I had developed any particular interest in spiders. I was walking down a broad ride between pine trees in the Florida Everglades. I stopped in my tracks when I suddenly became aware of a sinister blurry form a few inches in front of my face, glinting in the late afternoon sun. Stepping back a few paces to focus, I became aware of the largest spider I had ever encountered, suspended in an orb web made from golden silk. The web was enormous—the orb itself was at least a yard (1 m) across and was held in place by thick silken strands that stretched across the 50-foot (15 m) wide track. Being a consummate arachnophobe at the time, I beat a hasty retreat.

Nephila sits in the center of her orb waiting for large insects—even the occasional hummingbird has been reported to have been taken. More often than not the male will be lurking close by in the web. In comparison with the female he is an insignificant creature that weighs about a hundred times less than his mate. Indeed, he is so small that the female ignores him as potential prey, even allowing him to crawl around her without fear of being eaten. He is also much more agile than she is, so he can easily escape from his relatively clumsy partner if the need should arise. It is interesting to note that whereas most male spiders have evolved a complex array of visual and tactile signals in order to herald their sexual intentions and avoid the disaster of becoming another meal, *Nephila* has developed this novel size-disparity approach to achieve the same end.

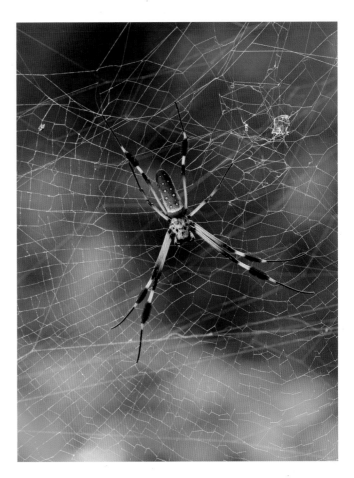

◄ Pair of golden orb spiders, the male is above.
➤ Golden orb spider showing femoral tufts.

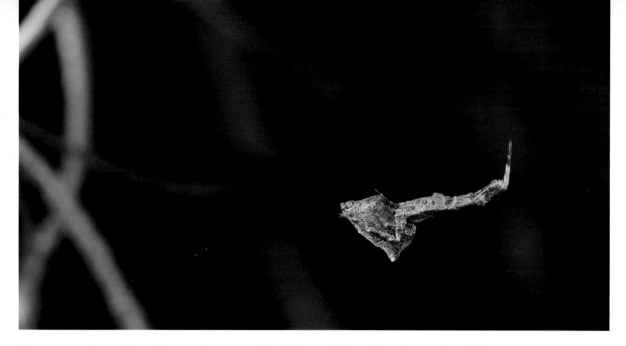

Lateral view of the garden center spider (*Uloborus plumipes*) showing cryptic attitude.

Garden center spider (*Uloborus plumipes*)

Uloborus from Greek "lethal"; *plumipes* from Latin "feathered feet"

The so-called garden center spider is a very recent addition to the fauna of Britain, where it can be found in increasing numbers in garden centers throughout the country. This member of the Uloboridae family is particularly common in the tropical humid biome of the Eden Project in Cornwall. *U. plumipes* builds a large, fragile-looking orb web among the plants or fabric of garden centers and greenhouses, thriving on the little flies and bugs found in such places, where insecticides are not routinely used.

This spider is unmistakable in appearance and capable of adopting a variety of strange poses, most often resembling a dried leaf or some other bit of debris. The best distinguishing features are the body shape and the tufts of hair on the front legs, together with its habit of sitting motionless with legs stretched out.

It is clear that this spider has been imported along with plants coming into the country from the European continent, as it has a wide distribution throughout much of Europe, the Mediterranean, Africa and a few areas in North America, where there are also a number of similar species.

◄ Ventral view of spider in its web.

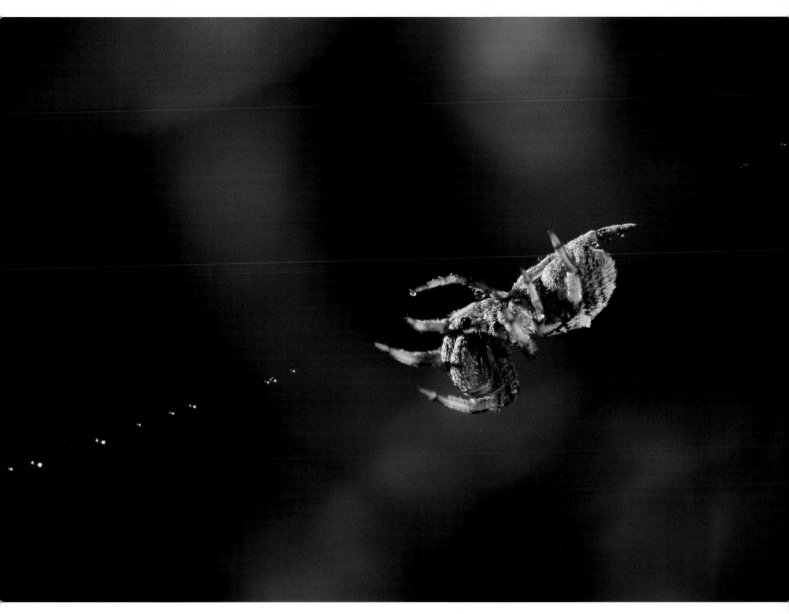

Sub-adult male triangle spider on web.

Triangle spider (*Hyptiotes paradoxus*)

Hyptiotes from Greek "supine"; *paradoxus* from Greek "strange" (possibly referring to the spider's peculiar attitude in its web)

This bewitching little uloborid—certainly one of my favorite spiders—is far from being a typical orb-web spinner. It is a rare species, 0.12 to 0.16 inch (3–4 mm) in length, found in a handful of locations in England. It spends its life in the middle and upper branches of yew and sometimes box trees. The combination of small size and a predilection for remaining motionless for much of its life in dark and obscure places may partly account for its apparent scarcity.

Adding to this spider's enigmatic qualities is its curious un-spider-like appearance, which resembles a fragment of leaf litter. It never spreads out its eight legs like a proper spider, preferring to keep them bundled up close to the body, giving it a hunchbacked look. As well as this strange form, *Hyptiotes* is blessed with enormous, balloon-like palps that are as large as the already bulky cephalothorax.

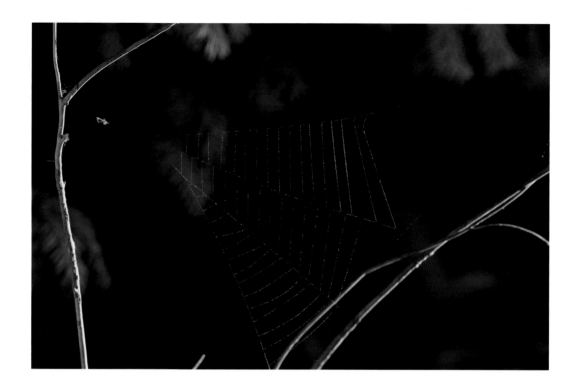

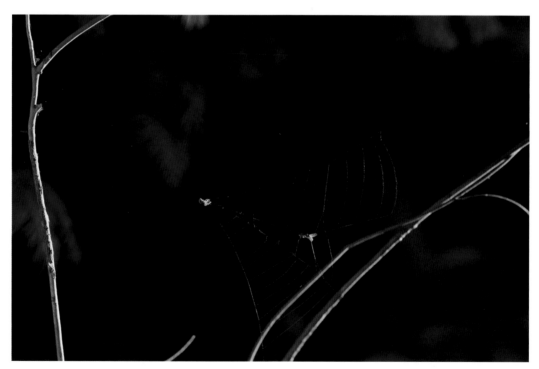

Four part sequence of *Hyptiotes* entrapping its prey (this page top to bottom, then opposite top to bottom).

Hyptiotes constructs about a sixth of an orb in the shape of a triangle. The web is tensioned by the spider, which sits at the apex with its front feet holding onto a loose loop of web that it has ratcheted in to increase the tension. When a fly strikes the web, *Hyptiotes* releases the loop, partially collapsing the web and so further entrapping the fly. This action is carried out several times, with the spider letting out more silk from its spinnerets while gradually advancing

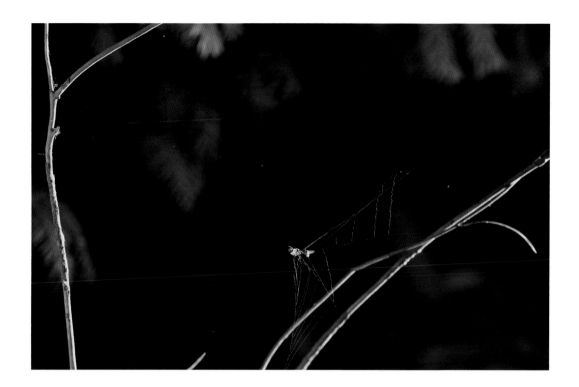

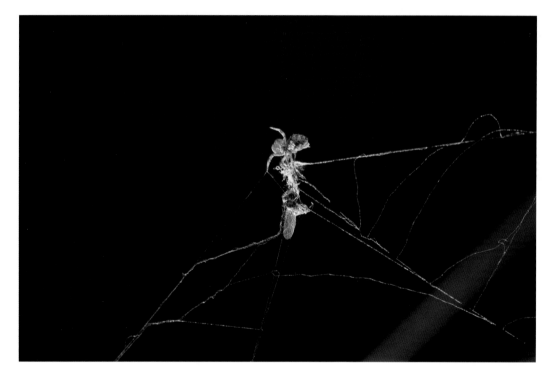

toward the struggling prey. The series of photographs here, the result of several weeks spent
trying to encourage the spider to spin its web in
a visible position, shows the operation clearly.

H. paradoxus has a local distribution in northern Europe but does not occur in North America,
where it is replaced by several other, similar
Hyptiotes species.

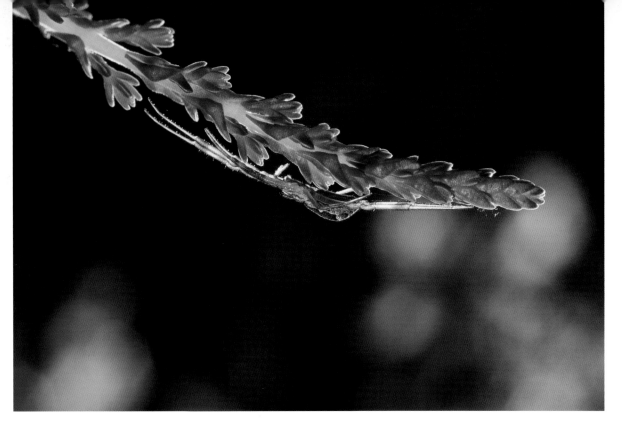

Episinus in cryptic position on heather stem. Sometimes these spiders are almost impossible to spot.

Scaffold-web spider (*Episinus angulatus*)

Episinus from Greek "injurious"; *angulatus* from Latin "angular"

This little spider is not related to the orb weavers at all, but is a member of the scaffold-web family Theridiidae, the next group of spiders to be described. Contrary to the normal behavior of theridiids, which make scruffy webs with threads running in all directions, *Episinus* constructs one of the simplest and most elegant webs of any spider. Thus the status of this species has been elevated here to that of the orderly web builders.

The web of *Episinus* consists basically of four threads in a sort of H shape, with the spider sitting at the center with another thread attached to it from its spinnerets. The two lower ends are fixed to the ground. While all eight legs are in contact with different sections of the web, the hind legs take most of the spider's weight. When crawling insects such as ants touch either of the two lower gummy threads (the sticky beads can be seen in the photograph),

the spider is galvanized into action and attacks the prey.

The physical appearance of *Episinus* is unlike other members of its family: the abdomen is narrow at the front and gradually widens to a broad, truncated end with two conical prominences at each corner. As can be imagined, this spider is extremely difficult to spot in its ground-level habitat, as it is not only small—0.12 to 0.16 inch (3–4 mm)—but also well camouflaged both in color and shape, resembling a small fragment of suspended leaf litter. The minimalist web is also next to impossible to discern unless it somehow manages to catch a glint of backlight (unlikely in its situation). Even in a semi-captive setup using controlled lighting, it proved difficult to show the complete web at one time.

Several species of *Episinus* are found in North America, while three are found in England and northern Europe, although they are not particularly common.

➤ *Episinus* in its simple H-shaped web.

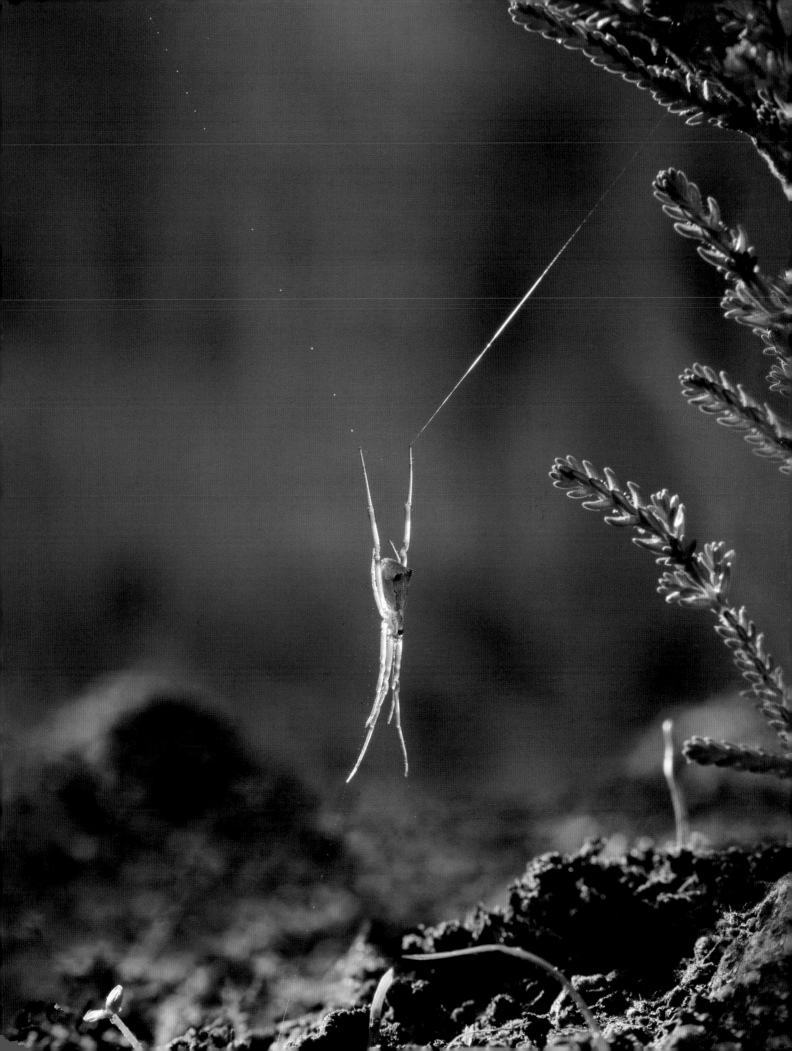

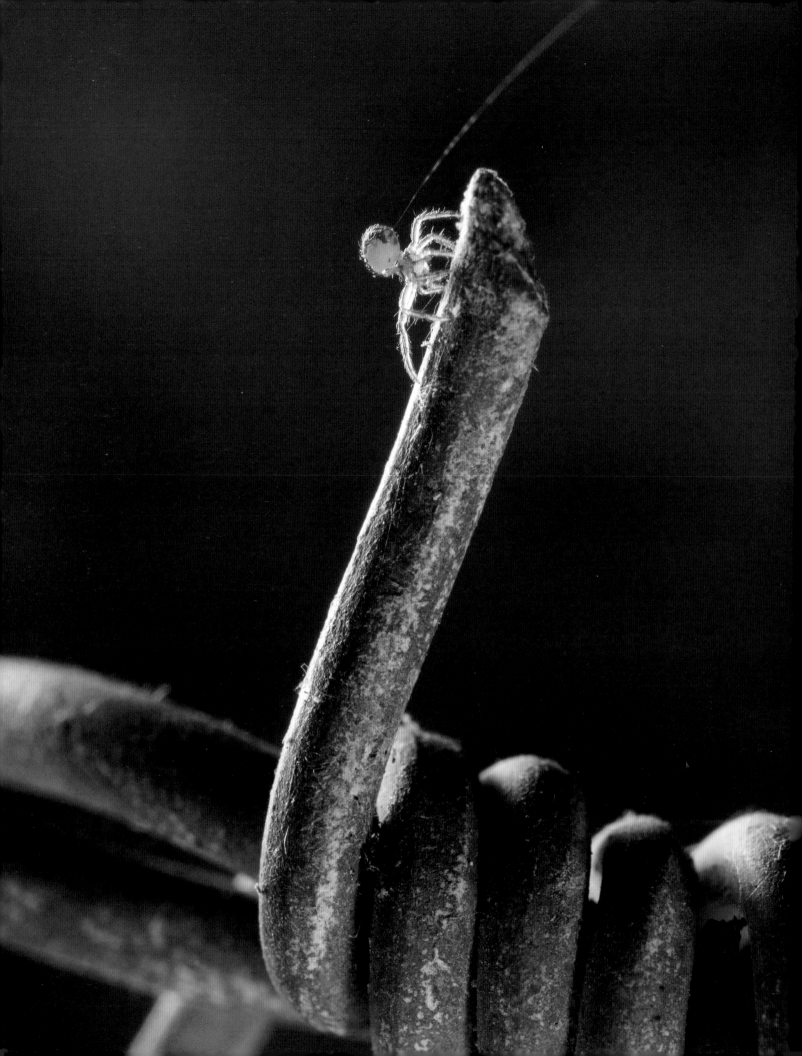

7 Trappers: Disorderly Webs

The grouping of disorderly webs here does not always follow scientific rules, nor are the webs confined to specific spider families. Sometimes orb weavers spin untidy webs with little or no pattern—young cucumber spiders (*Araniella*), for instance—while some of the linyphiid sheet webs are far from being disorderly. Indeed, few webs are as disorderly as they may appear to us; nature always has sound reasons for adopting a particular design.

One of the scruffiest webs is produced by *Pholcus*, the daddy longlegs spider, and its appearance is not improved by the dust and debris that usually cling to it. The webs of dictinid spiders also appear disorderly. They are often made on dead or dying vegetation and consist of a dense weave of cribellate silk that is added to daily. The spider lives in the center, protected from would-be predators by the increasingly dense web.

The cobweb spiders, Theridiidae—or comb-footed spiders, as they are known in Britain—construct webs of irregular structure, but their varied designs are more precise than casual observation suggests. These are often called scaffold webs for reasons that become clear in the photograph on page 143. The central area of the snare is often a maze of threads, sometimes in the form of six-sided meshes or sometimes an open platform of loosely woven trelliswork. Their trapping action works as follows: sticky drops are placed along strategically placed threads, with the distribution depending on whether the web is intended to catch crawling or flying insects. Crawling insects form the principal prey of many species, including *Steotoda nobilis*, which constructs its trap attached to a wall or window or near the ground. When an insect blunders into a sticky blob at its base, the line ruptures and the insect is lifted into the air as the elastic thread contracts. This allows the spider to haul up the victim hand over hand. When it's in reach but at a safe distance, sticky threads are flung over the prey. Once the insect is sufficiently trussed up it is finally bitten on the leg. Theridiids will

◄ A ballooning spider.

frequently tackle prey much larger than themselves, including potentially dangerous insects such as wasps.

Although theridiids have weak-looking chelicerae, they are compensated for by the powerful, rapidly acting venom. Unlike araneids, which chew their prey into pellets, the theridiids suck their victims dry, leaving a hollow husk behind.

When compared with orb webs, the sheet webs of linyphiids may seem disorderly, but those spun by many species are extremely clever, efficient and beautiful, especially when seen laden with fresh morning dew. Many have a scaffold-like superstructure and a platform beneath, shaped variously into concave or convex bows and domes. Insects knocked down by the trip wires above fall onto the web, while the spider lurking underneath strikes upward through the sheet.

Disorderly web-weaving families

The members of the **Theridiidae** family are commonly known as scaffold-web, cobweb or comb-footed spiders. Most spiders in this family are small to medium-sized and characterized by their glossy spherical abdomen and short legs. Although they have small chelicerae, their venom is potent, as evidenced by one of its members, the black widow (*Lactrodectus*).

Scaffold-web spiders are so named because of their web's scaffold-like structure (see page 138), while their alternative name, "comb-footed," stems from a row of curved serrated bristles on the tarsi of the hind pair of legs (which may be difficult or impossible to see unaided, particularly in adult males or the smaller

species). The comb plays a vital role in drawing out the viscous silk and flinging it over prey.

Some species are capable of producing audible mating calls by means of a stridulatory apparatus. This consists of a file on the rear of the carapace that is rubbed on a scraper equipped with teeth on the overhanging abdomen. North America has over 230 species, while northern Europe has 76.

The well-known **Pholcidae**, or daddy longlegs spiders, often construct their untidy or dome-shaped webs in houses. Others of the world's 870 species live in a wide variety of dark places, from inside caves to under logs. The typical pholcid can easily be recognized by its very long, slender legs and relatively small body, and its tendency to occupy dark corners. They also have an almost circular carapace with a characteristic eye arrangement. North America has 34 species, while northern Europe has three.

The **Dictynidae**, or mesh-web spiders, are a cribellate group of small spiders—they possess a cribellum and a calamistrum. The cribellum is a modified pair of spinnerets that produces thick, viscous silk that is combed out by a line of stiff hairs on the tarsus of the hind leg—the calamistrum—into a broad band of bluish silk. This traps prey by entanglement rather than by its adhesive properties. These organs are almost impossible to discern without considerable magnification.

The snares of dictynid spiders consist of an inconspicuous veil of threads radiating downward from the tops of low plants such as grass heads or bushes. Further lace-like cribellate threads are added to the radial ones, and it is these that catch the legs and wings of insects that are often considerably larger than the spider itself. The spider attacks its prey by

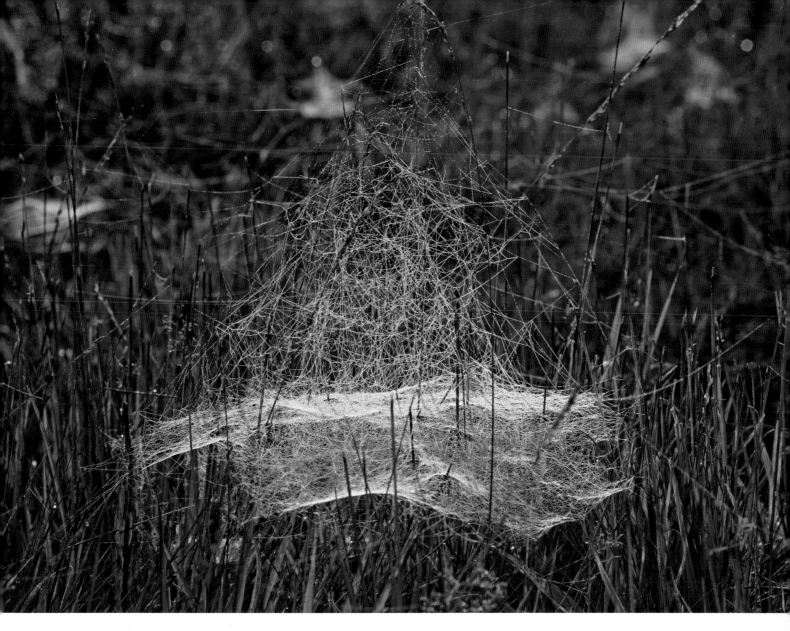

The web of this money spider is beautifully designed to catch low-flying insects.

inflicting multiple bites to the legs until the victim's struggles subside; the remnants of past victories can often be seen littered around the outside of the web. All these spiders are less than 0.16 inch (4 mm) in length, and many have an abdomen patterned with downy hairs.

The vast majority of species live in temperate regions of the Northern Hemisphere. Nearly 300 species occur in North America but only about 10 in northern Europe.

In the northern United States and Europe the **Linyphiidae**, hammock-web, dwarf or money spiders, are the most abundant family of spiders, with nearly a thousand named species in North America alone. Most are tiny, being between 0.04 and 0.16 inch (1–4 mm) long—in North America they are known as dwarf spiders. They are usually next to impossible to identify in the field; being so small, their positive identification requires exacting examination under the microscope. Thus only two of the larger species are described here, and a small unidentified species is illustrated on page 144.

Members of this family make delicate sheet webs, often with trap-lines above and below. The spiders hang upside down under the sheet,

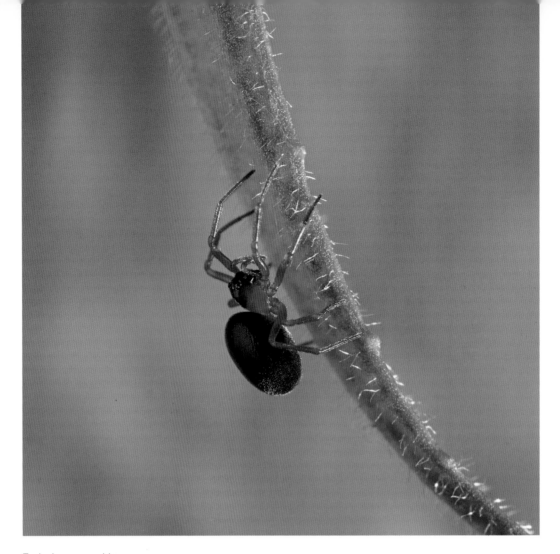

Typical money spider.

attacking prey from below. The head of many of the smaller linyphiid males is embellished with bizarre protuberances and turrets that play a part in courtship.

Being so small, this family goes unnoticed most of the time, but when conditions are suitable—usually on warm, sunny days in late autumn—the countryside becomes cloaked with exquisite dew-covered webs and intercrossing draglines of gossamer. It is at such times that we get some inkling of the vast numbers of normally invisible spiders around us, and it is the Linyphiidae more than any other family that are responsible for this.

The tiny linyphiids are often joined by spiderlings from other families in a unique method of aerial dispersal. Together they are impelled by a strange urge to climb upward to the pinnacle of some plant or fence. There they stand on tiptoe and throw silk out into the soft breeze (see page 140). As the current helps to draw more web outward, the spiders are lifted into the air and transported to wherever the breeze happens to take them. In this way small spiders can move hundreds of yards to fresh habitats or, if the wind is sufficiently strong, migrate huge distances surprisingly rapidly. Sometimes these aeronautical spiders may balloon upward to thousands of feet, enabling them to travel hundreds of miles over mountains and oceans and to far-off islands. During his voyage on the *Beagle*, Darwin recorded the arrival of thousands of spiders, 60 miles (100 km) from the nearest land.

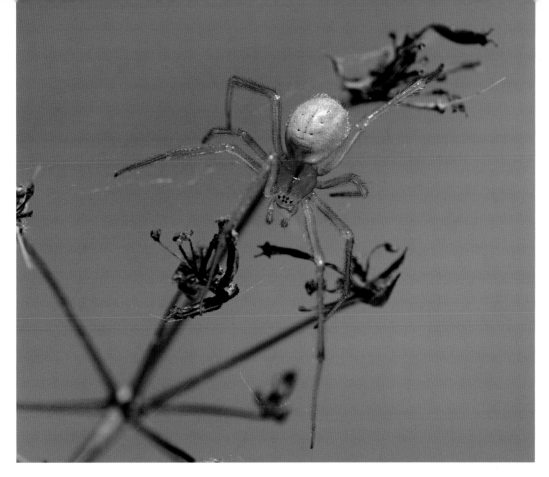

A female candy-stripe spider, here in the more common form without red stripes.

Candy-stripe spider (*Enoplagnatha ovata*)

Enoplagnatha from Greek "armed jaw"; *ovata* from Latin "egg-shaped"

This handsome and common light-colored theridiid can be found all over northern Europe, Britain and North America, where it was introduced. It comes in several forms, the pale yellow-green one here being the most frequent. Other, rather less common forms are even more attractive, with either a single broad red band down the center of the abdomen or two narrower bright red bands on each side. The several pairs of black spots are always present. Males have enlarged divergent chelicerae armed with teeth.

The web is a typically theridiid untidy three-dimensional affair consisting of an apparently disorganized crisscross of threads. It is usually set in low vegetation or bushes, sometimes around flowers, where the spider bides its time close by. In spite of its fragile appearance, *E. ovata* is a force to be reckoned with, capable of tackling large, violent prey that many larger spiders will hurriedly cast free. As soon as an insect touches one of the gummy threads, the spider emerges and flings sticky web all over the prey. Dangerous prey such as wasps and bumblebees are tackled with equal aplomb. Indeed, this belligerent spider is not averse to poaching prey caught by other spiders and has even been known to attack them in their own webs—all helped no doubt by the particularly potent venom for which this family is renowned.

In contrast to this rapacious hunting behavior, most theridiids have a more endearing aspect to their nature: their parental care for eggs and offspring. *E. ovata* stands guard over her bluish egg-sac until she dies at the onset of winter; the spiderlings emerge much later, in spring.

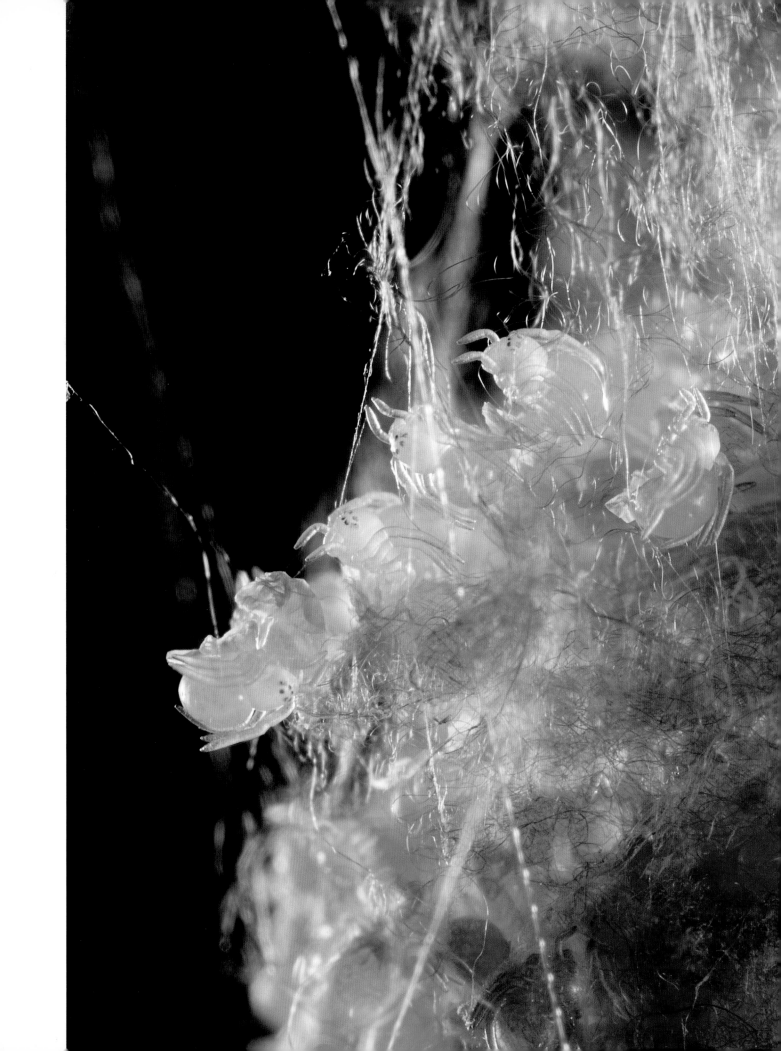

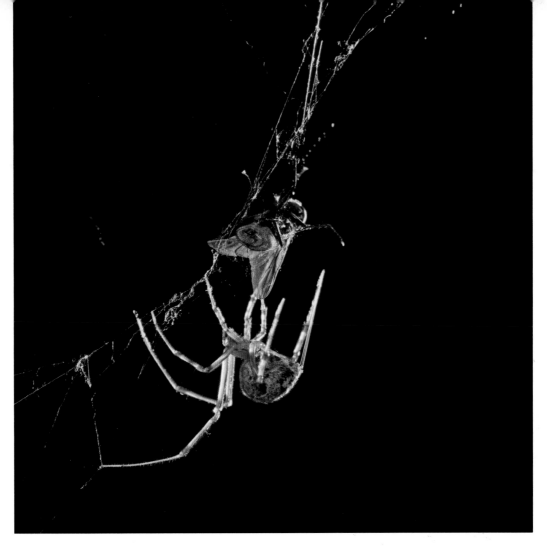

American house spider wrapping up house fly. Note web extruding from spinnerets.

American house spider

(*Achaearanea tepidariorum*)

Achaearanea from a place in Greece named after spiders; *tepidariorum* from Latin *tepidus*, "warm" (referring to its warm, dry habitat choice)

Experts are unsure where this spider originated, although the neotropics seems the most likely. What is certain is that this successful member of the Theridiidae has managed to spread all around the globe; in some places it has become extremely common. It generally thrives close to humans, living in dark corners of houses, under furniture and in sheds and fences. Although it is found throughout North America, in northern Europe it can survive only in warm places such as heated greenhouses and, less often, in houses. In southern regions it can occasionally be found outside.

Achaearanea is a somewhat nondescript and very variable dark brown or dirty orange spider. The female is 0.2 to 0.24 inch (5-6 mm) in body length, with front legs three times longer than the body. The scruffy web is often smothered with dust, and the spider sometimes hides under debris such as a feather or leaf fragment. The male and female frequently live together in harmony in the same web. These spiders feed on any insects, sometimes quite large ones such as crickets and cockroaches, or even other spiders that happen to become entangled in the sticky strands of their web.

◄ Embryo American house spiders on the point of hatching from egg-sac.

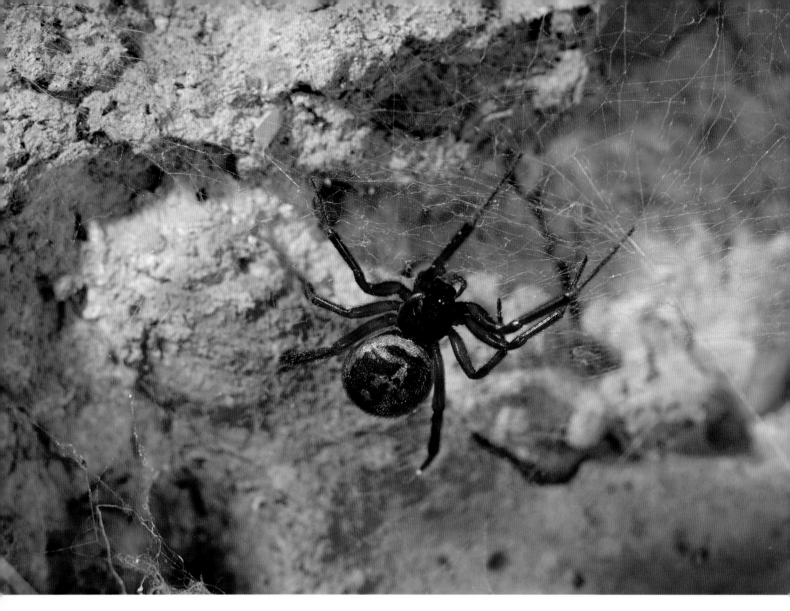

False black widow spider (*Steotoda*).

False black widow spider (*Steotoda nobilis*)

Steotoda from Greek "like"; *nobilis* from Latin "well-known"

Like the true widow spider, *Steotoda nobilis* has a round, bulbous dark abdomen, but the female is marked with a lighter goldish pattern with a cream-colored band. Fully grown females range in size from 0.3 to 0.6 inch (7–14 mm).

This large theridiid spider is gaining a dodgy reputation—not only is it aggressive if mishandled, but it has a mildly poisonous bite. This reputation is unfortunately being made worse by expanding distribution and a preference for living around human habitation. People who have been bitten by this spider report numbness and pain similar to a wasp or bee sting, with the effects lasting a day or two.

S. nobilis is an introduced species in England, having arrived in shipments from the Canary Islands and Madeira, and is spreading from dock areas around the south coast. It can now be found in many southern counties, and with global warming it is steadily advancing northward. It has not yet been reported in North America. The one illustrated here was found living in the exterior walls of Chichester Cathedral in southern England.

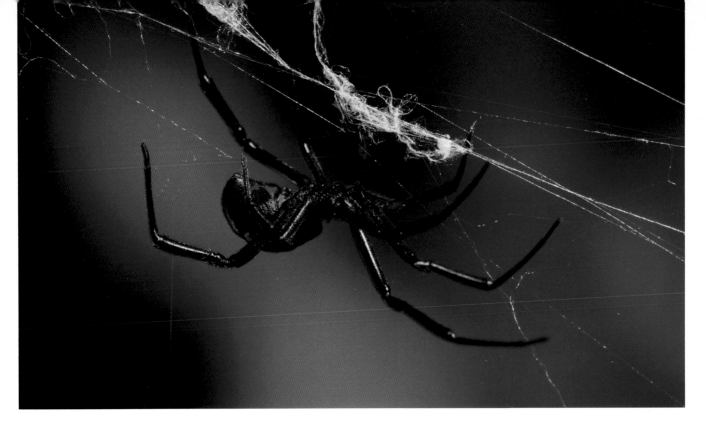

Black widow spider (*Lactrodectus*) showing red hourglass mark.

Black widow spider (*Lactrodectus mactans*)

Lactrodectus from Greek "biting"; *mactans* from Latin *macto,* "to kill"

Now we come to the spider that strikes fear into the hearts of so many people—the black widow. Even its scientific name has a sinister ring to it. Actually, like most spiders, the black widow is timid, preferring to escape or hide rather than attack. It just happens to choose to live where humans tend to put their fingers or other exposed parts of their body: in and around outbuildings, barns and outside toilets, or in dark, damp spaces between logs or stones, in holes for water meters and empty watering cans. To avoid being crushed, the spider defends itself by biting, injecting a virulent neurotoxin that can cause excruciating abdominal pain, severe muscle cramps, spasms, breathing difficulties, convulsions, paralysis and shock for those unfortunate enough to get bitten.

There are several species of widow spiders spread around the world, some of which have been given local names such as *malmignatte* in southern Europe, redback in Australia and *katipo* in New Zealand. It is the black widow from North America that is best known, although there is considerable variation in color and pattern depending on age and locality. Broadly there are two forms, a northern and a southern one. The females of both forms are between 0.3 and 0.5 inch (8–12 mm) long and have a shiny black globular abdomen with a characteristic hourglass mark on the underside and a red mark by the spinnerets. The northern form usually has an additional row of red spots down her back. The males are much smaller and are not dangerous to humans.

As this spider is a member of the Theridiidae, the web is a tangled affair that operates in the normal theridiid manner, but it has a characteristic conical area in an upper corner where the spider hides during the day or retreats when disturbed.

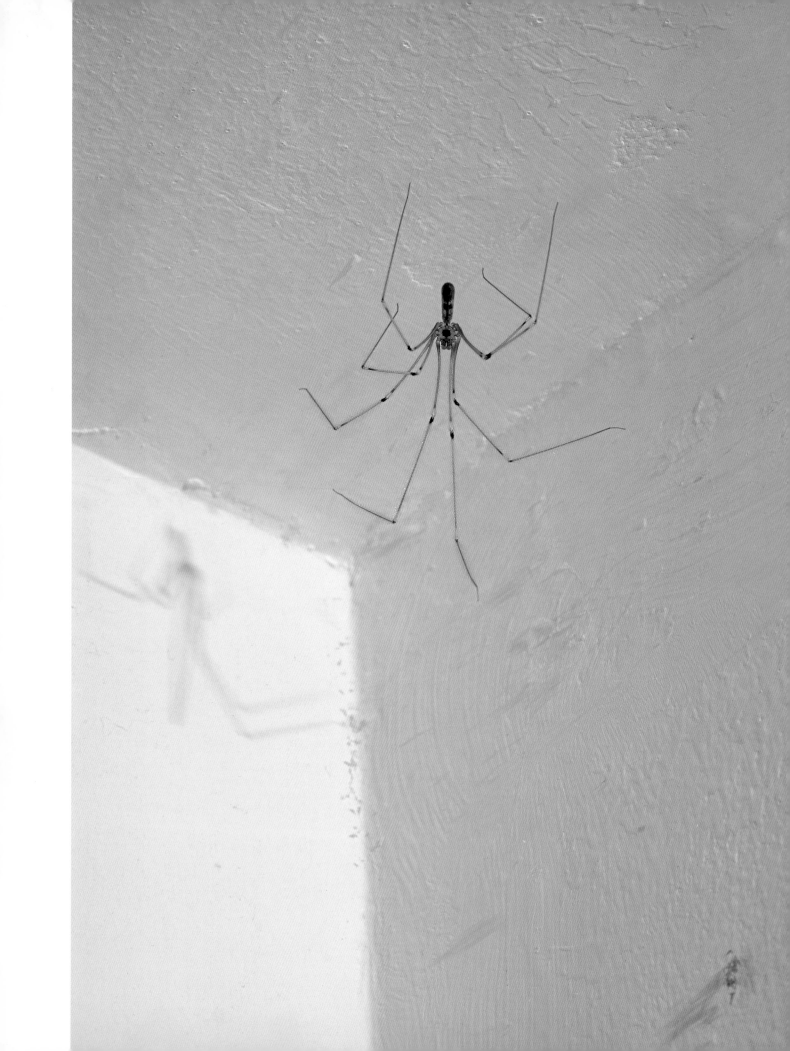

Daddy longlegs spider

(*Pholcus phalangioides*)

Pholcus from Greek "squint-eyed";
phalangioides from Greek "fingers"

If there is an international spider, then the daddy longlegs spider must be it. *Pholcus phalangioides* occurs all over the world, including Europe, North America and Australia—in fact, almost anywhere that is sufficiently warm for it to live and breed. Common and widespread it may be, but this spider is far from dull, as we will see.

Being a lover of warmth—it needs an average temperature of 50°F (10°C) to survive—the daddy longlegs spider is absent from northern England and northern Europe. Unfortunately its English name (which is too long to keep repeating) tends to cause confusion because this spider has a superficial resemblance to both the crane fly, an insect, and the harvestman, an opilionid. Further confusion can arise because its alternative name, cellar spider, is also used for another spider in a different family altogether. How lost we would be without scientific names!

Pholcus, as we shall call it, shares our homes, favoring undisturbed places such as cellars, little-used rooms and nooks and crannies, especially in the corners of ceilings, where it is less likely to be sucked up by a vacuum cleaner. Such places are often well away from water, so this spider is adapted to survive long periods without it.

Pholcus is a very discreet spider; as well as being anorexically thin, it rarely moves around, preferring to remain motionless in the corner of a room where it can go unnoticed. Unfortunately its web, which is normally a scruffy but unobtrusive scaffold of fine threads, eventually becomes visible because it collects dust, so it, together with the spider, is often destroyed by meticulous housekeepers. In contrast with *Pholcus'* usual languid state, it becomes highly animated when disturbed, oscillating so rapidly in its web that it effectively becomes invisible, a novel technique evolved to outwit predators.

The hunting strategy adopted by *Pholcus* is particularly intriguing. It remains motionless for perhaps days on end until prey passes by—the nature of which may come as a surprise.

◄ Daddy longlegs spider in typical domestic habitat.

► Daddy longlegs spider with captured house spider.

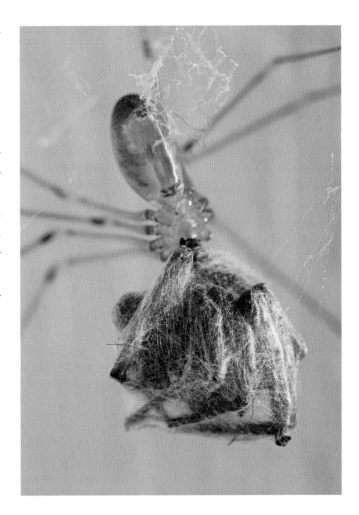

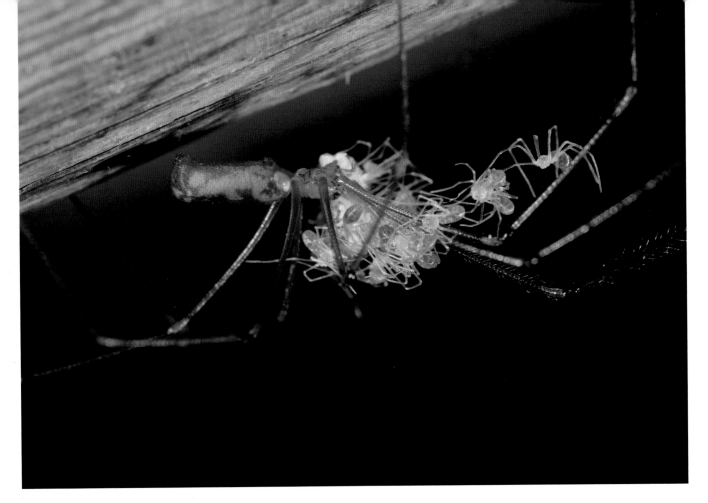

Daddy longlegs spider with newly hatched young.

This fragile-looking spider specializes in feeding on other spiders, even much larger ones such as the intimidating house spider *Tegenaria*. In North America it will even tackle the deadly black widow! Of course it is perfectly happy to take flies and other insects that invade our homes, so this is a guest to encourage rather than to eradicate. The advantage of long legs is not apparent until this spider encounters formidable prey. It draws threads from its spinnerets and flings them over the intruder from a distance, keeping well out of reach of potentially dangerous enemies or prey. Once the victim is incapacitated, *Pholcus* ventures sufficiently close to administer a bite with its very small chelicerae, injecting a tiny quantity of potent poison. In winter, when suitable food is sparse, this spider tends to become active, wandering around the house on hunting trips. If prey becomes very hard to find, these intrepid creatures are not averse to attacking their own kind.

The courtship and mating habits of all spiders may seem bewildering to us, and those of *Pholcus* are no less so. Like many spiders, before mating the male deposits a dollop of sperm on a little web that he then picks up with his chelicerae before sucking it into a special cavity in the palps. From there the sperm is transferred to the female's epygyne in the conventional spider manner, where it is stored until she is ready to lay.

The circular bundle of eggs, which is held together by strands of web, is carried around with the chelicerae before hatching two to three weeks later. The young then hang motionless for about 10 days, like laundry on a clothesline, before they venture out to lead their own lives.

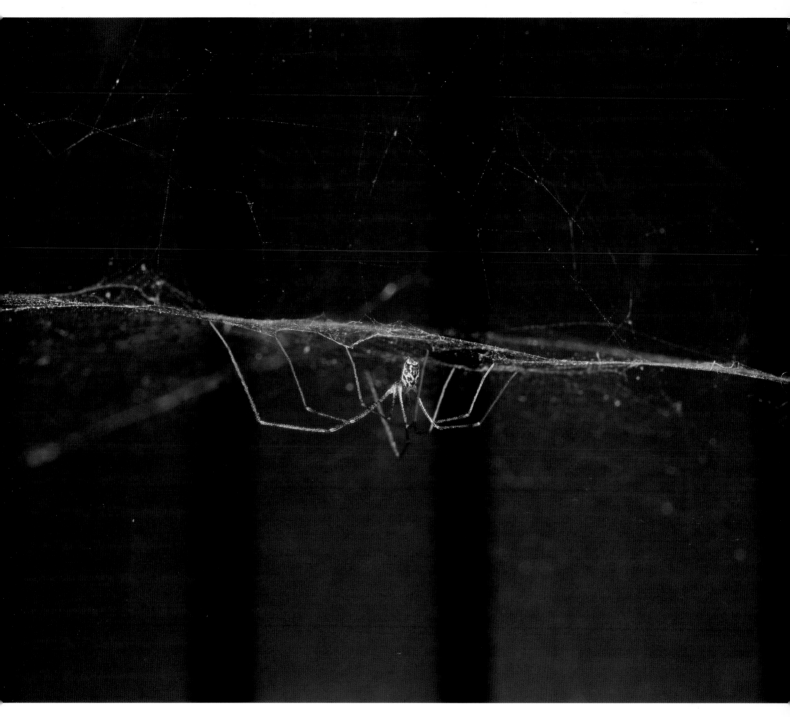

Wine cellar spider hanging from its platform within its scruffy web.

Wine cellar spider (*Psilochorus simoni*)

Psilochorus from Greek *psilo*, "smooth" and *choros*, "dance"

Another pholcid from a different genus, *Psilochorus simoni* was introduced to England recently. For a long time it was typically found in wine cellars but it now thrives happily in some greenhouses and garden centers. It is smaller than *P. phalangioides* and makes a much neater, dome-shaped web. North America sports many similar native species.

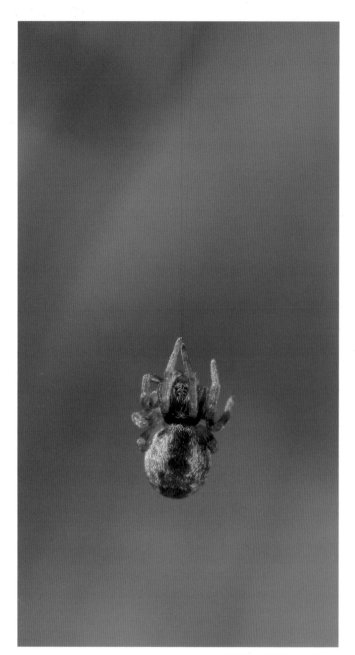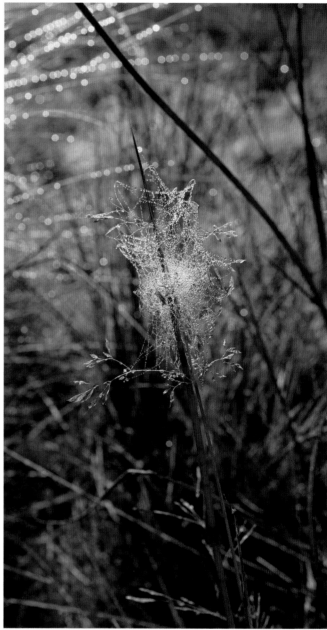

Mesh-web spider (left) and its characteristic tangled web (right).

Mesh-web spider (*Dictyna arundinacea*)

Dictyna from Greek *diktuon*, "hunting net"; *arundinacea* from Latin *harundo*, "reed"

This 0.14-inch (3.5 mm) spider is common in North America and throughout Europe, but not often noticed. A close examination using a hand lens reveals a rather cuddly velvety brown spider. Very often the male and female are found sharing their web and hunting together.

The best time to find evidence of dictynid activity is while ambling beside wide roadside borders or rough pastures in early morning during the fall, when the uninspiring webs really come to life. The combination of autumnal mists and low backlight makes every little web sparkle and glow like clusters of fairy lights.

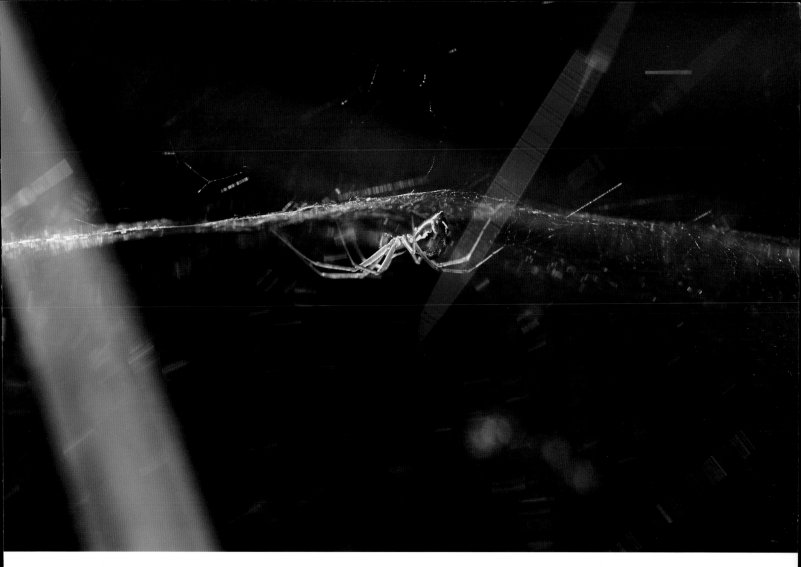

Linyphia triangularis in characteristic pose.

Sheet-web spider (*Linyphia triangularis*)

Linyphia from Greek "to weave"; *triangularis* from Latin *triangulus*, "triangular"

At around 0.24 inch (6 mm) long, *Linyphia triangularis* is one of the largest spiders in the huge Linyphiidae family. It is also one of the most abundant spiders in Britain during late summer and autumn, when it can be found on almost any plant or bush strong enough to support the large web.

L. *triangularis* is one of the few members of its family that can be readily identified in the field, as it possesses distinctive markings on the abdomen. Viewed from the side, which is the angle we usually see it at, this brownish spider has a humpbacked appearance and distinctive dark and white oblique streaks on the side of the abdomen. When the top of the carapace is in view, a characteristic dark tuning fork–like mark is revealed. The male has long, divergent chelicerae and frequently lurks in the background.

Like the majority of spiders in its family, L. *triangularis* sits upside down on the underside of its sheet web and waits for insects to tumble onto the sheet after hitting the superstructure of crisscross threads. The spider then dashes to the spot, bites through the sheet, and then drags its prey below. Although abundant throughout Europe, L. *triangularis* is not found in North America.

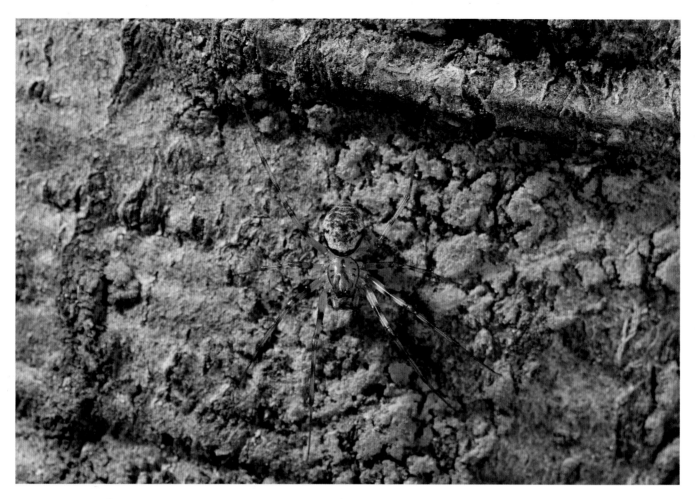

The "invisible" spider on a beech trunk.

Invisible or tree-trunk sheet-web spider
(*Drapetisca socialis*)

Drapetisca from Greek "small fugitive"; *socialis* from Latin "living together"

Another linyphiid spider, *Drapetisca socialis* is especially interesting because it spends its life in social groups, running around at great speed on the trunks of trees (usually beech) in a characteristic jerky manner as it hunts for aphids and other small insects that roam the bark. The spider is so well camouflaged that, unless moving, it is virtually invisible.

Although it's classified here as a sheet-web spider, not so long ago it was thought that this spider had abandoned web building altogether. Now we know that the web is so fine and close to the bark that it is invisible unless the light catches it at the right angle. Although the spider appears to be touching the tree surface, in fact all eight legs are in contact with the thin strands of its delicate web—this can just be discerned in one of the photographs.

To most eyes, linyphiid spiders seem small and dull, but *Drapetisca* is an exception with its subtle and variably colored abdomen, which only becomes evident when magnified. *Drapetisca* is widespread throughout Britain and northern Europe and has two counterparts in North America.

➤ The web supporting this small spider is just visible from a low viewpoint when backlit.

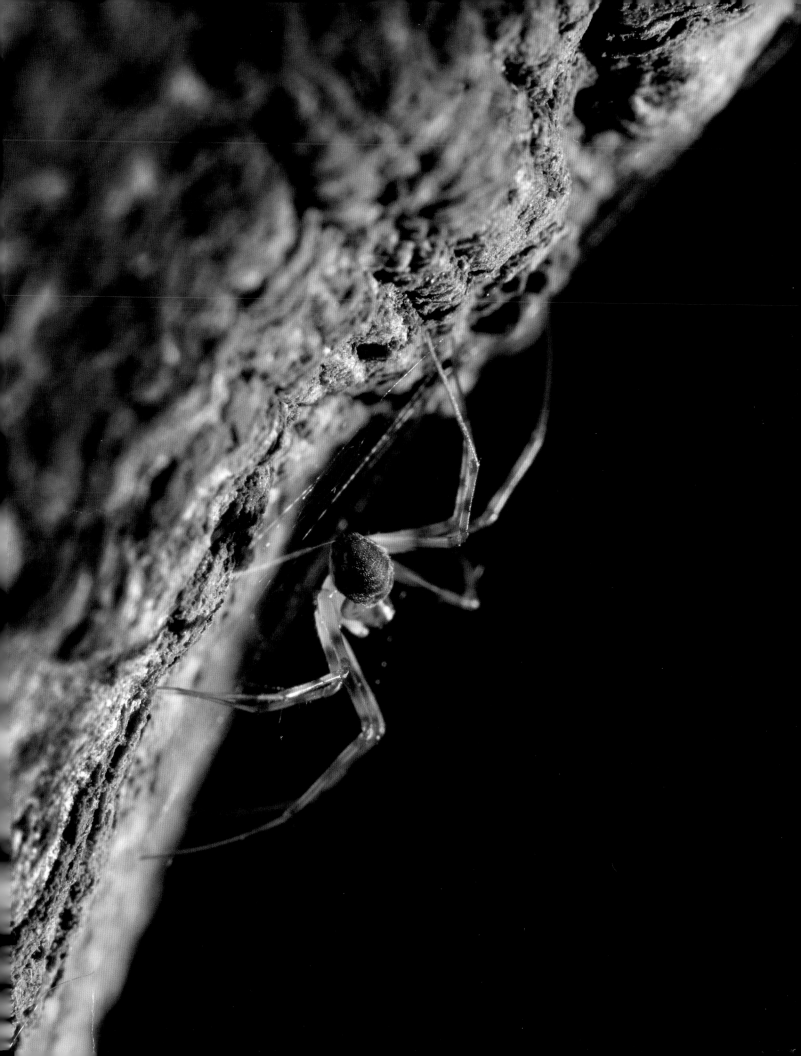

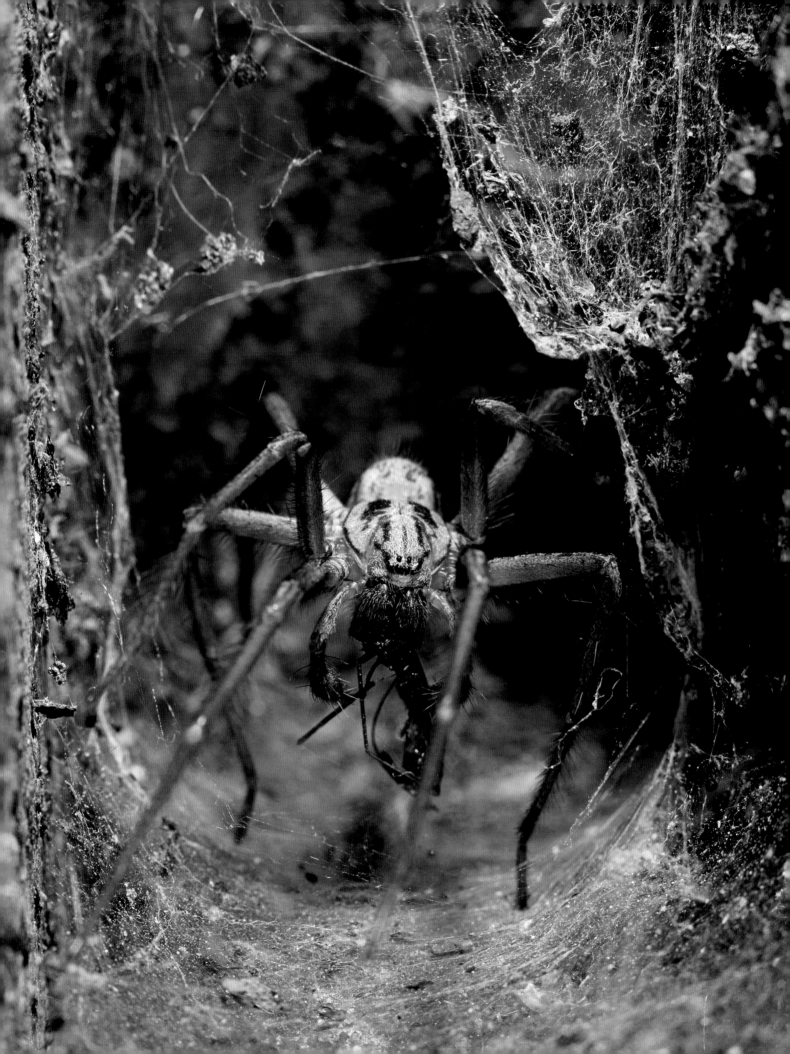

8

Tunnel-web Builders

Some families of spiders construct tubular retreats from which extends a collar or sheet of web—the house spider is a good example. Whereas house spiders, *Tegenaria,* build simple sheets that are usually slightly funneled, others such as the labyrinth spider, *Agelena,* create a platform of vertical threads above to entangle jumping or flying prey. As soon as the spider senses web vibration it darts out onto the upper surface and wraps the victim in silk before dragging it back to its tubular retreat. Spiders from other families, such as *Segestria* and *Amaurobius,* hide in a silk-lined hole in a wall or tree from which lines or a mesh of web extrude. Here they wait patiently for prey to make contact with the trap, then dash out in a flash. The majority of species are more active at night.

The world's most notorious spider, the funnel-web spider from Australia, also lies in wait, but in an underground silk-lined tunnel. It belongs to another group of spiders altogether from the mygalomorphs.

Tunnel web–building families

The **Agelenidae**, or funnel-web, spiders are typically characterized by their long, hairy legs and long spinnerets. They construct non-sticky funnel webs with a flat open sheet for prey capture and a tunnel retreat in one corner that is often out of view. When an insect blunders onto the sheet, the spider shoots out at lightning speed and drags it back into its lair. Several large species inhabit dark corners of houses, to the dismay of their occupants! Agelenids are primarily nocturnal but sometimes respond to and capture prey during daylight. There are 85 species in North America and 11 in northern Europe.

◄ European house spider (*Tegenaria domestica*) with prey.

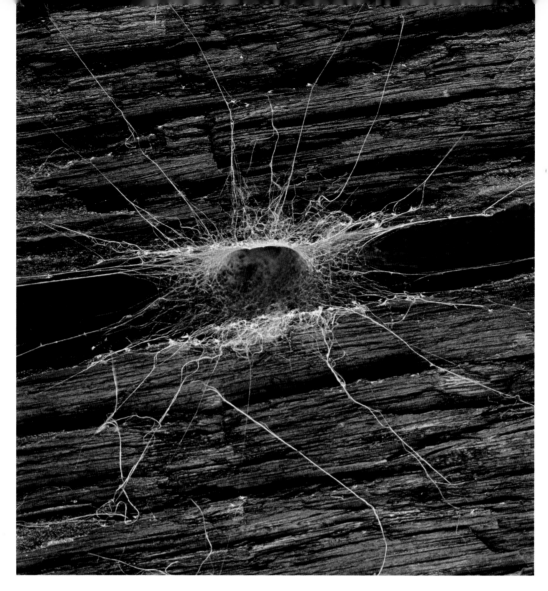

Entrance of tube web spider's tunnel with characteristic radiating "fishing" lines.

Amaurobidiidae, mesh or lace-web weavers, are ground- and crevice-dwelling spiders. They are most often found in crevices in buildings, under rocks, in the bark of trees or among decomposing logs. Most build blue-tinged fuzzy cribellate webs with a radiating tangle and tubular retreat. There are about 97 species in North America and a mere five in northern Europe.

The long, tubular bodies of **Segestriidae**, or tube-web spiders, are well adapted for a life in long, narrow silken tunnels. These tubular retreats have elaborate webbing around the entrance that is equipped with signal lines radiating outward. Because they spend their lives in narrow tubes, only one pair of legs points backwards; the other three pairs are directed forward. When waiting for prey, segestriids rest near the entrance with their front pair of legs extended forward, resting on the rim of the opening. As soon as some small animal makes contact with a line, two more pairs of legs are extended forward to rest on the web lines for a brief moment—to sense the direction of the prey—before the spider makes its final dash. So that the stings of potentially dangerous insects such as bees and wasps cannot harm it, this spider hauls prey backward into the retreat in a C-shape so that both the rear and front ends face away from it.

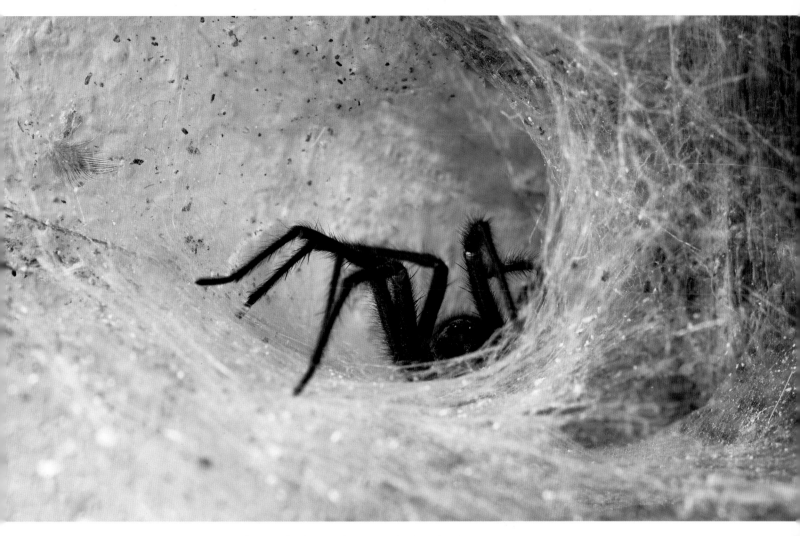

European house spider (*Tegenaria domestica*) lurking in its funnel-web.

Segestriids are closely related to the wood-louse spiders (Dysderidae); both families have only six eyes. Seven species live in North America and three in northern Europe.

Tarantulas—the big, robust, hairy ones—are largely tropical spiders of the **Theraphosidae** family, which are also known as bird-eating spiders; apart from one species from Spain, they are not found in Europe. However, several species occur in the warmer southern United States. Although the majority of the spiders in this family may appear impressive through sheer size, their prey-catching methods and diversity of lifestyles are not in the same league as their cousins the true spiders, or araneomorphs.

Theraphosids are the largest spiders in the world, and because of their huge size and hairiness are much feared. However, apart from a few that may be potentially dangerous, most tarantulas are relatively docile and bite only if severely provoked. Even then, the effects are unlikely to be worse than a bee sting.

Tarantulas inhabit silk-lined burrows during the day, appearing in the entrance at night to wait for prey to pass close by. They rarely stray far from their tubes, although males do wander in search of females. Many of them have trip lines radiating out from the burrow to detect any creature that wanders too close. This is considered to be the earliest technique that employed silk for catching prey.

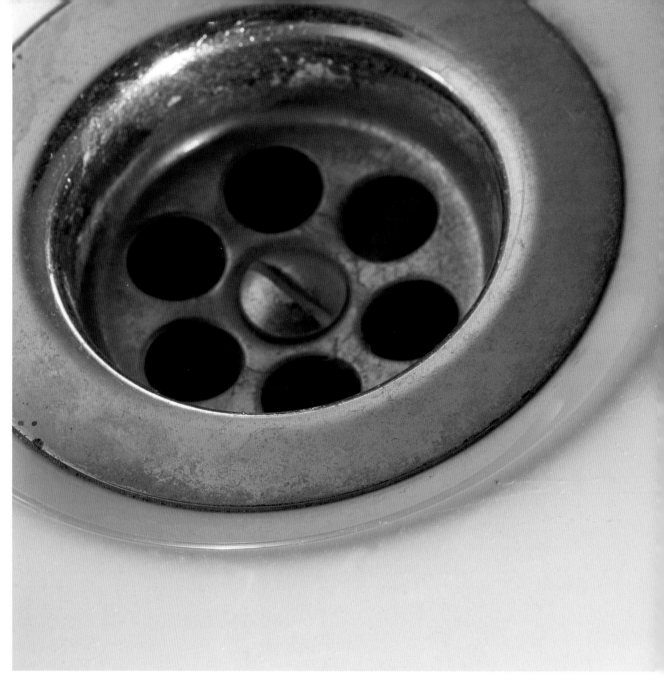

A male European house spider trapped in a bathtub.

European house spider

(*Tegenaria domestica*)

Tegenaria from Latin *teges*, "mat"; *domestica* from Latin "of the house" (referring to sheets of web in the house)

Of all the spiders found in northern Europe and North America, the house spider must be the most reviled by arachnophobes. This member of the Agelenidae family is large, it is dark, it is hairy, and it moves like greased lightning. I know three renowned spider experts who are terrified of these creatures, and I too, having been bitten by one at the age of four (a mere pinprick), share their horror.

Interestingly, the larger the spider, the less stamina it has—a fully grown *Tegenaria* can run at top speed for only about 20 seconds before almost collapsing in a state of exhaustion. By comparison, very small spiders can keep going for hours. This is because it is difficult to get sufficient oxygen to all the tissues when using

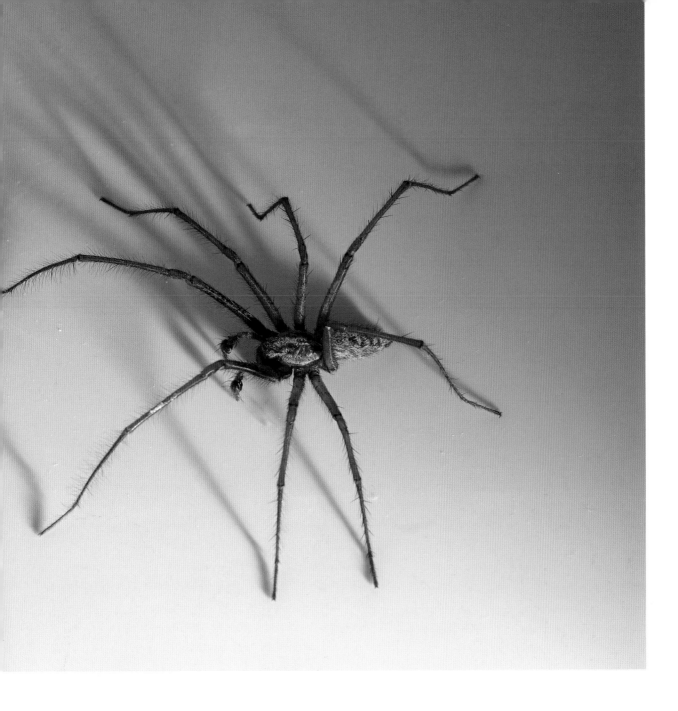

a breathing and circulatory apparatus that become less efficient with bulk.

Eleven similar species of so-called house spiders are found in northern Europe, but only two or three generally share people's homes, where they spend most of the time unobtrusively in their webs. Come autumn they may be spotted sprinting toward you across the carpet—these are most likely to be males of *Tegenaria domestica* looking for mates. Most other species live outside under stones, in tree trunks or amid thick vegetation. They are all generally smaller than *T. domestica*.

There is an exception to this size rule: an even scarier species, *T. parietina*. The female can grow up to 0.8 inch (20 mm), with exceptionally hairy legs spanning nearly 4 inches (10 cm). Not nice, but fortunately it rarely comes indoors, preferring to live outside in old buildings. Like most of its family, this spider builds large sheet webs extending from tubular retreats, usually in dark, dusty corners, where they lie in wait for prey.

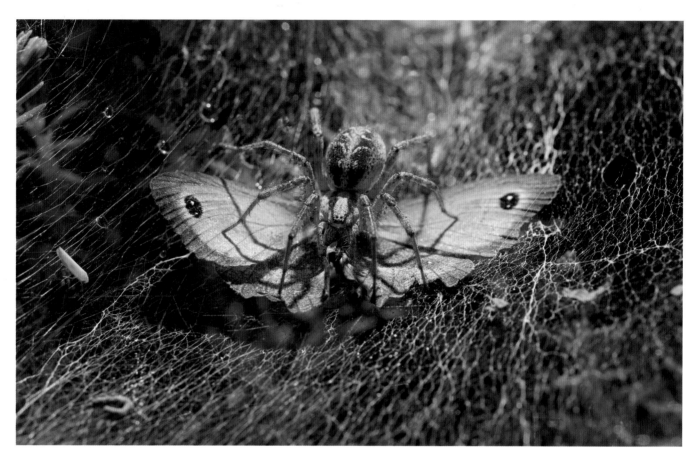

Labyrinth spider immobilizing a butterfly.

Labyrinth spider (*Agelena labyrinthica*)

Agelena from Greek "gregarious"; *labyrinthica* from Greek "maze" (referring to the maze-like webs)

The labyrinth spider, like its close relative the European house spider, spends most of its life in or at the entrance of its tubular retreat, emerging onto the large expanse of sheet only to tackle prey or to mate.

The conspicuous webs are spun among low vegetation, usually grass or small shrubs, and are often present in large numbers during July and August. The web is a lot subtler than would appear at first sight. Although not sticky, the superstructure of scaffolding threads is very efficient at arresting flying or jumping insects and knocking them down onto the sheet below. The sheet's edges slope upward like a hammock, directing the prey into the center. What is extraordinary

is the way the spider itself can navigate through the maze of trip wires at lightning speed to deal with a captured insect, which staggers through them as though wading through molasses. After administering a few bites, *Agelena* drags the prey into the retreat to be eaten.

Mating takes place on the web, after which the male is allowed to remain with the female until he dies. Finally, in August, when ready to lay her eggs, she leaves her web to construct another home close by, which consists of a complex labyrinth of chambers. Here she lays her eggs and remains with the spiderlings until she too dies.

This spider is widespread in northern Europe, common in the south of England, but absent from Scotland. The ecological equivalent in North America is *Agelenopsis,* the grass spider.

➤ Web of labyrinth spider.

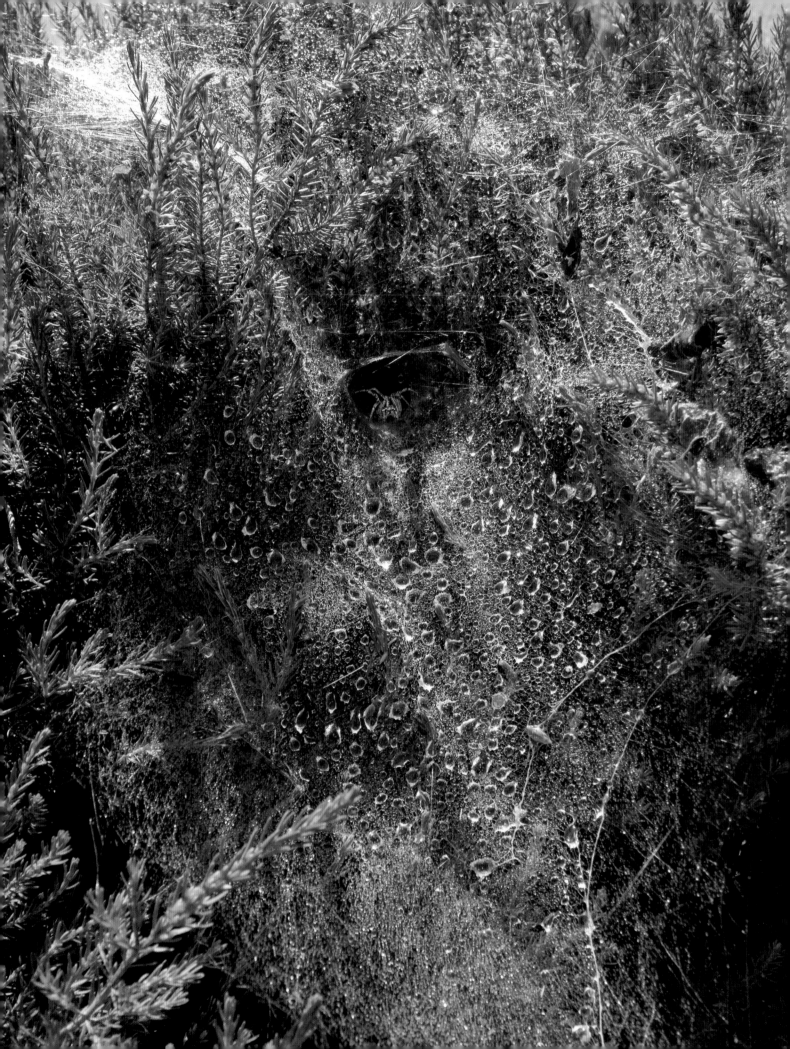

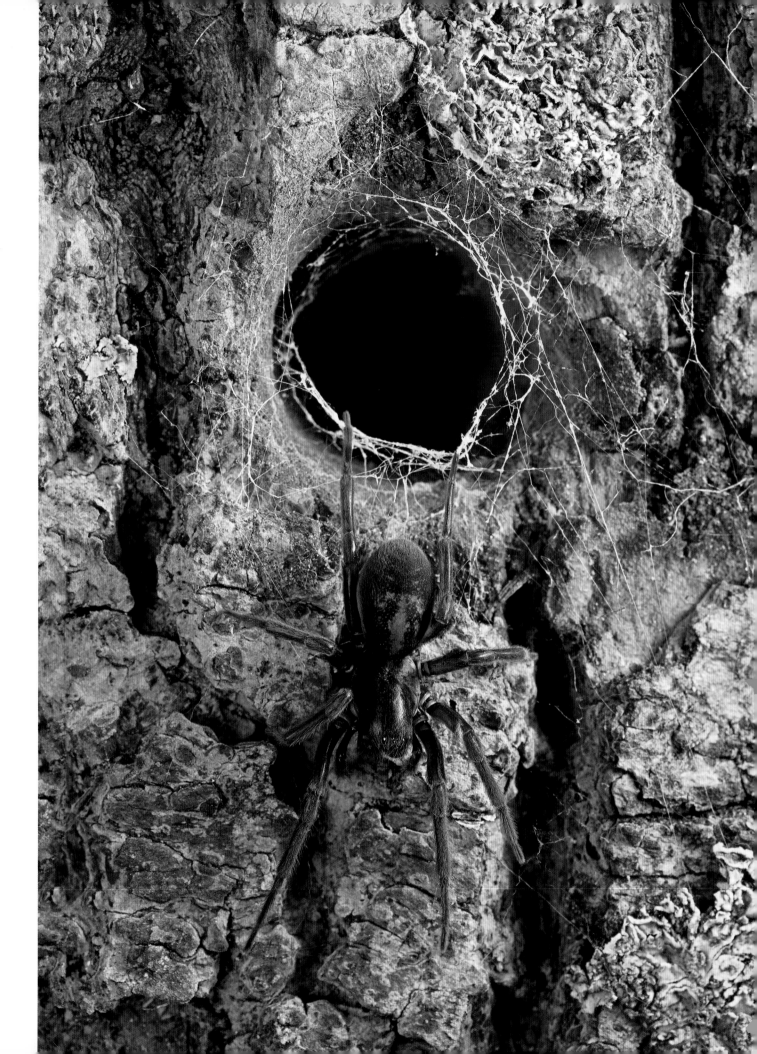

Lace-web spider

(*Amaurobius similis; A. ferox*)

Amaurobius from Greek "dark"; *similis* from Latin "similar"; *ferox* from Latin "warlike"

For those who have not made the acquaintance of *Amaurobius*, search around the nearest fence or old wall and look for the characteristic untidy meshed web that surrounds its circular retreat. When fresh, the web has a bluish, lace-like appearance. Other favorite habitats include gloomy places such as cellars, sheds, crevices in bark and under stones and logs.

The best way of glimpsing this amaurobidiid spider or observing its hunting technique is to venture out at night with a flashlight and a tuning fork. Just touching the web with the vibrating fork should initiate a rapid response from the animal lurking within, which will shoot out to investigate the intruder and maybe grab onto the fork with its fangs. The large, thickset spider that emerges often has dull, skull-like markings on the abdomen that give the creature a rather sinister demeanor.

Although essentially nocturnal, this spider will take prey at any time of the day or night, hauling the victim into its den. The prey could be any insect unfortunate enough to stumble across the web, including flies, earwigs and moths. I happened upon this one only because I heard a wasp buzzing in its frantic efforts to escape.

Besides their general appearance, *Amaurobius* species can usually be identified by the cephalothorax, the dark head-end of which is raised and shiny in contrast with the pale hind region. More specifically, if you are brave enough

◄ A large lace-web spider (*A. ferox*) ventures out of its lair at night.

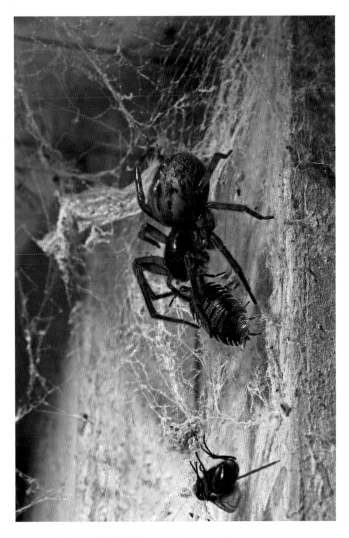

Lace-web spider (*A.similis*) retrieving a woodlouse.

to examine a specimen in your hand with the aid of a magnifier, you will see that *Amaurobius* possesses a cribellum just above the spinnerets and a double-rowed calamistrum on the metatarsus of the hind leg.

Males are mature by late summer, when, like the house spider, they may sometimes be seen wandering away from their webs looking for mates. There are five species of *Amaurobius* in northern Europe, all broadly similar in appearance. *A. similis* is common, widespread and found in North America, where there are also a number of like species. *A. ferox* is a little larger and darker than its relative and tends to prefer living under logs and stones near walls and fences.

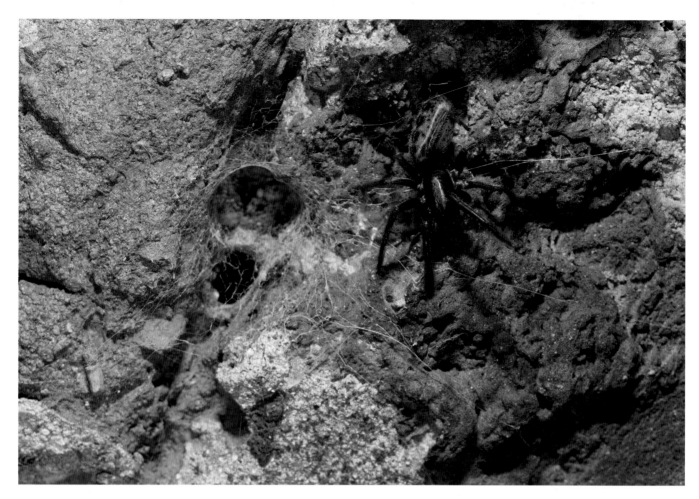

This tube-web spider is returning to its lair so rapidly that its body has twisted in two planes.

Tube-web spider (*Segestria florentina*)

Segestria from Latin *seges*, "cornfield"; *florentina* from Latin "from the city of Florence"

One of the most intimidating spiders likely to be encountered in northern Europe is a nocturnal member of the Segestriidae family, *Segestria florentina*. To start with, it's huge, having a body length of up to 1 inch (24 mm), several millimeters longer than the largest house spider.

S. *florentina* is the most impressive of three European species in this six-eyed genus of spiders. It lives in silk-lined tubes made in holes and crevices in old walls and trees; radiating from the entrance are about a dozen strong "fishing lines," as seen on page 160. One way to catch a glimpse of this formidable creature is to gently brush one of these lines with a blade of grass, upon which the occupant will dart out at awesome speed, flashing its green jaws, and bolt down its hole again. The action is so rapid that it is almost impossible to see exactly what the spider looks like. A fast flash photograph is one way to view it, but even the photo here—taken at one three-thousandth of a second—was not quite fast enough to arrest all movement.

A way to view this spider a little longer is to block the entrance hole with a stick before it returns, but extremely rapid reactions and strong nerves are needed to achieve this. If you are successful, this fierce spider will bite violently at the obstacle in its efforts to get back in. I don't mind admitting that my nerves

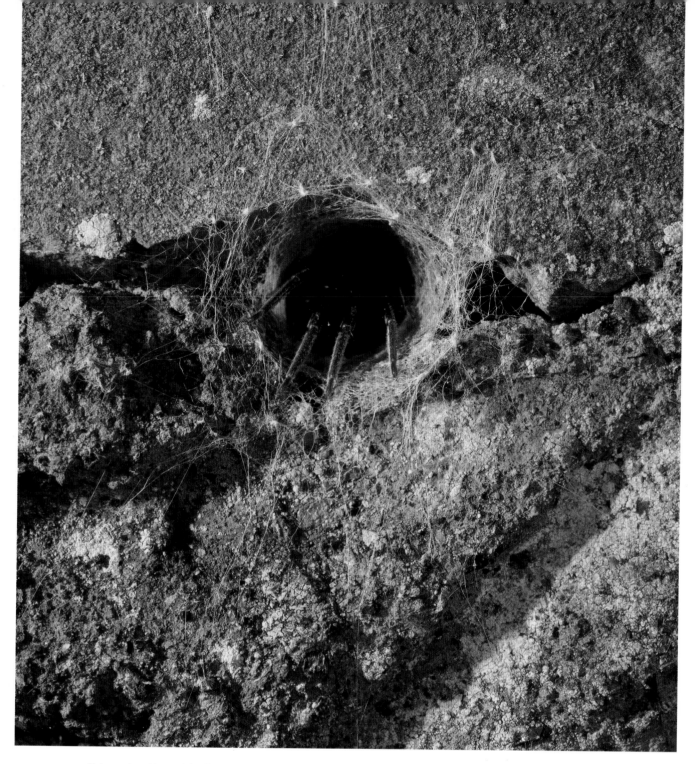

Tube-web spider waiting for prey at tube entrance.

found it difficult enough to stand the strain of obtaining this picture, let alone of blocking its entrance! Certainly any prey that touches one of those fishing lines is in for a shock.

This spider was probably inadvertently imported into England with ships' cargoes from southern Europe, possibly many hundreds of years ago. It is found around ancient ports such as Bristol, Exeter and the City of London. *S. florentina* is widespread throughout southern Europe; in North America, *Ariadna* and other *Segestria* species replace it.

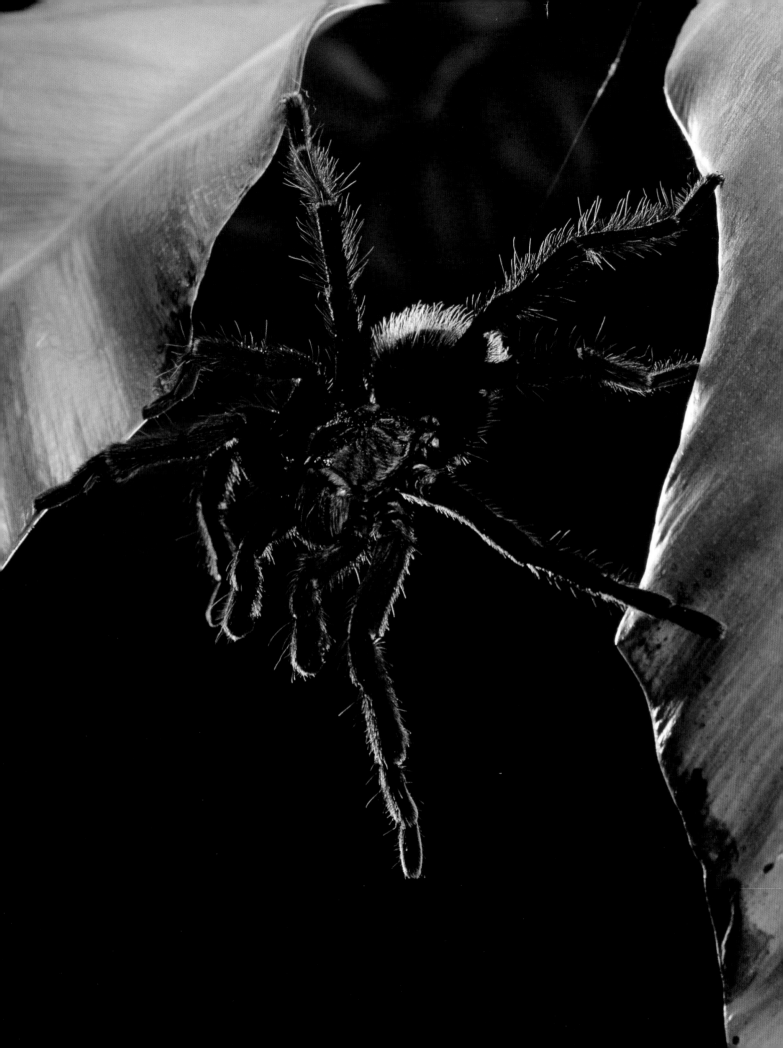

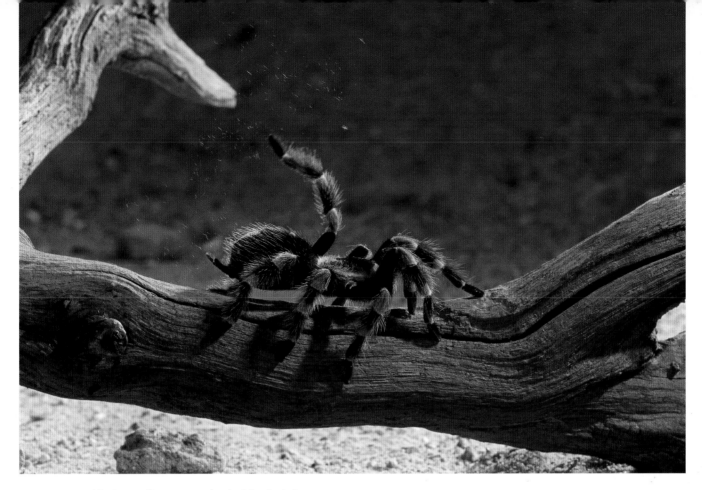

Mexican redknee tarantula shedding its hairs.

Red-rumped tarantula (*Brachypelma vagans*); Mexican redknee (*B. smithi*)

Brachypelma from Greek "short scopula"; *vagans* from Latin "wandering"

The red-rumped tarantula, *Brachypelma vagans,* belongs to the suborder Mygalomorphae, which includes the trap-door and purse-web spiders as well as the larger theraphosids. It attains a size of about 3 inches (75 mm) and is black in color overall, with long reddish hairs on its abdomen. It is fairly catholic in its choice of habitat, which ranges from the tropical rainforests of Central and South America to the semi-arid rock and scrub of Florida, where it has been introduced. Like most mygalomorphs the red-rumped is nocturnal, spending the day in an underground burrow and appearing at night to feed on ground-dwelling arthropods and the occasional small vertebrate.

Many New World tarantulas, the red-rumped included, can defend themselves from enemies by kicking off urticating barbed hairs from the rear of the abdomen, using the hind legs. This is clearly shown in the photograph of a similar but even larger species, the Mexican redknee, *Brachypelma smithi,* which shows the hairs flying through the air in all directions. These hairs are irritating to the skin, particularly to mucous membranes; if they get into the eyes they may cause temporary or even permanent blindness in its attackers. The redknee does not occur in the United States, having a more restricted range close by in Mexico, where it lives in burrows at the base of cacti and rocky outcrops in dry areas. Unfortunately this spider is threatened by over-collection for the pet trade, so if you have a need to keep tarantulas, ensure that they are captive-bred.

◄ Red-rumped tarantula.

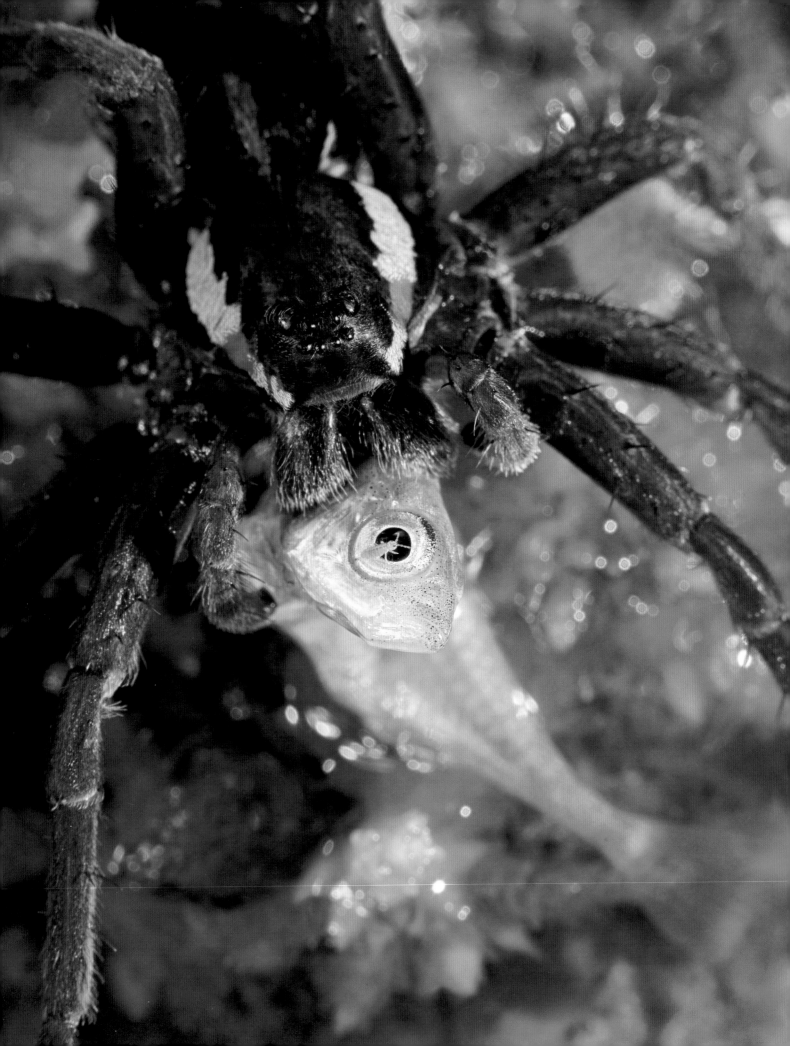

9

The Nonconformists

There is nothing scientific about the way these nonconforming spiders are grouped. They're merely a motley collection of especially unusual spiders from various families that do not fit neatly into any of the preceding hunting divisions. One characteristic they do share is a particularly unconventional approach to finding and capturing prey.

Many of these spiders utilize webs in some form, while others don't, but whatever their technique, the evolutionary paths that led to their current way of life would be fascinating to have witnessed.

Nonconformist families

Few spiders have a more macabre way of ambushing prey than the **Atypidae**, or purse-web spiders. They are large, thickset mygalomorph spiders related to the tarantulas. They all live in burrows from which they extend a long, sock-like tube that is closed at the end. Some species extend the tube up the base of a tree trunk or shrub, but all rely on vibrations transmitted by the web to detect prey. Only two species occur in northern Europe, but eight live in North America.

The velvety, tarantula-like spiders, **Eresidae**, typically construct a burrow in the ground, sometimes with a coarse cribellate sheet of web extending from it, but little is known about these secretive spiders. The Eresidae are strictly an Old World family, and so are not found in North America. Only one species is found in northern Europe.

The **Pisauridae** are known as the wetland nursery-web spiders. *Dolomedes* spiders are usually found around water, each species being adapted to a particular wetland type. They are unusual in that they have adopted a semi-aquatic lifestyle, hunting in and on the water as well as the surrounding vegetation. Known as raft or fishing

◄   Raft spider with stickleback.

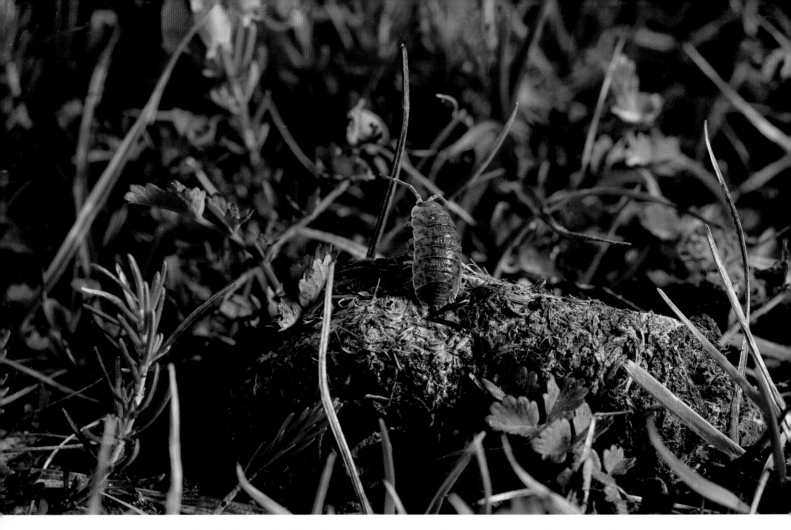

Purse-web spider (*Atypis affinis*) impaling a woodlouse. Its two fangs can be seen striking through the purse.

spiders, they are among the largest, most handsome and impressive spiders likely to be found in northern Europe and North America. More details about this family can be found in chapter 2.

Apart from one extraordinary species that has evolved into a totally aquatic existence, **Argyronetidae**, the water or soft spiders, comprise a little-known family. They are related to the sheet web-building Agelenidae, but only a single species lives in water.

Few spiders are more bizarre in their lifestyle and appearance than the spitting spiders, or **Scytodidae**. With their huge marbled domed carapace, thin, groping legs and six eyes arranged in three groups of two, the family cannot be mistaken for any other spiders. Scytodids are unique among spiders in that they capture prey by spitting jets of venomous glue from their specially adapted fangs. The best known is the cosmopolitan species *S. thoracica,* but North America supports a further six species.

If there is a family of spiders that can be described as sheep in wolves' clothing, the pirate or cannibal spiders, **Mimetidae**, must be it. Who would imagine that this group of superficially undistinguished little spiders leads a cannibalistic lifestyle? Neither are they the drab nobodies of the spider world—a magnifier reveals a pale yellow body delicately patterned with brown or black. The chief distinguishing feature of pirate spiders is the unique and conspicuous arrangement of spines on the front legs, consisting of rows of long erect bristles with shorter ones between. Many species, particularly those in the *Ero* genus, also have one or two pairs of tubercles on the abdomen.

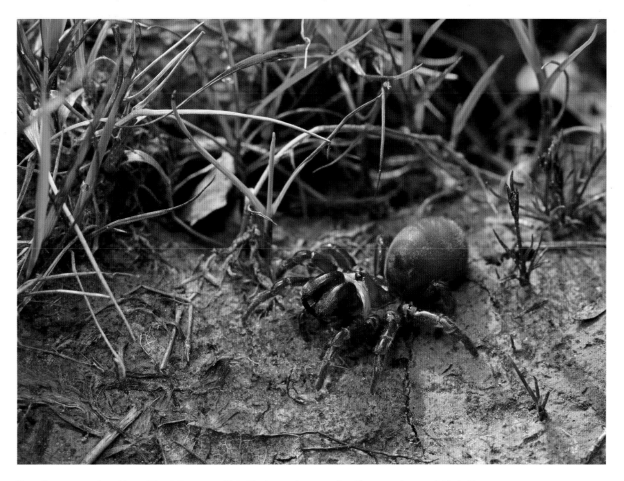

Female purse-web spider without its purse. Note the large downward-acting mygalomorphid chelicerae.

Purse-web spider (*Atypus affinis*)

Atypus from Greek "misshapen"; *affinis* from Latin adfinis, "relation"

This member of the Atypidae family is rare and very fussy about where it lives. It can survive in only a few ideal grassy habitats, usually unshaded south-facing chalky downland in southern England and northern Europe. Here it spends all its life in a burrow 6 to 10 inches (15–25 cm) underground. The male appears in the open only when looking for a mate. In order to be photographed, the female illustrated was carefully removed from her underground tube (and, of course, reinstated after the photography).

Atypus ensnares its prey in the following intriguing manner. The spider lines its underground tube with web, but the top few inches lie above ground like a filled sock. The web is camouflaged by plant debris and soil—indeed, it is so well concealed that locating its home is extremely difficult, possibly one reason why this spider appears to be so rare. Here it patiently waits for some insect to wander by and walk over the sock. As soon as *Atypus* senses a footstep or any vibration, it runs up the tube (if not already there) and strikes through the sock with its massive fangs, impaling the hapless intruder—as can clearly be seen in the photographs. The attack is shark-like, with the spider striking through the web from underneath. As soon as the victim becomes immobile, it cuts a hole in the sock using the serrated teeth on its chelicerae and drags the prey into the interior to be consumed. In due course the sock is repaired, ready for the next potential meal.

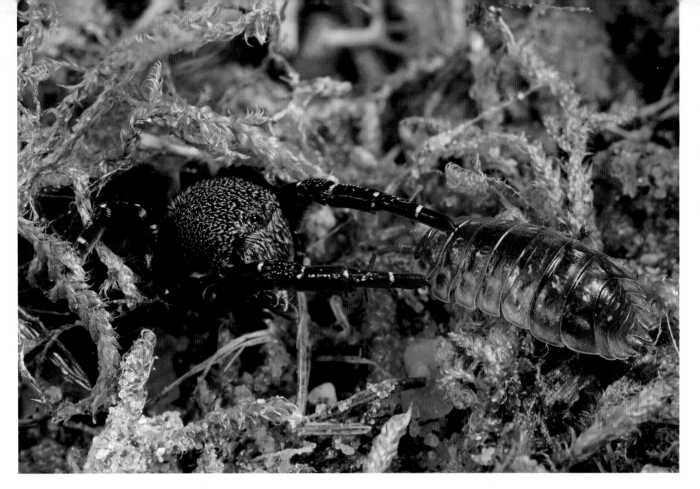

Female ladybird spider using front claws as grappling hooks to haul in prey. The other three pairs of thick strong legs help pull both the spider and its prey into its underground refuge.

Ladybird spider (*Eresus cinnaberinus*)

Eresus from Greek "spring" (the season); *cinnaberinus* from Latin *cinnabaris*, "vermilion"

This large, velvety, thickset black spider is the rarest and perhaps the most impressive spider to be found in Britain and Europe. At one time it was considered extinct, until two males were discovered in 1979. In Britain this eresid spider is now confined to a "secret" half-acre patch of south-facing Dorset heathland, where this female was photographed. It is the only spider in Britain listed in the *Red Data Book* of endangered species, and so is protected by law.

The ladybird spider ("ladybird" is the British term for ladybug) is so named because the extraordinarily handsome male has a scarlet body embellished with four black spots, and dark red legs further ornamented with white bands. Unfortunately the male appears above the surface only for a few days during spring in his search for a female.

The large and totally black female excavates a burrow about 3 inches (7.5 cm) deep that she lines with silk. One side of the burrow forms a roof by extending upward and over, while further strands of tough cribellate threads branch out to attach to the surrounding heather, forming a sheet. The female lurks underneath the sheet waiting to attack beetles and other large insects that get caught in or blunder over the web, usually striking upward through the sheet and eventually pulling her prey down into the burrow. She rarely if ever leaves the protection of the web, but may partly emerge to attack insects walking nearby.

➤ Male ladybird spider searching for a female among the heather.

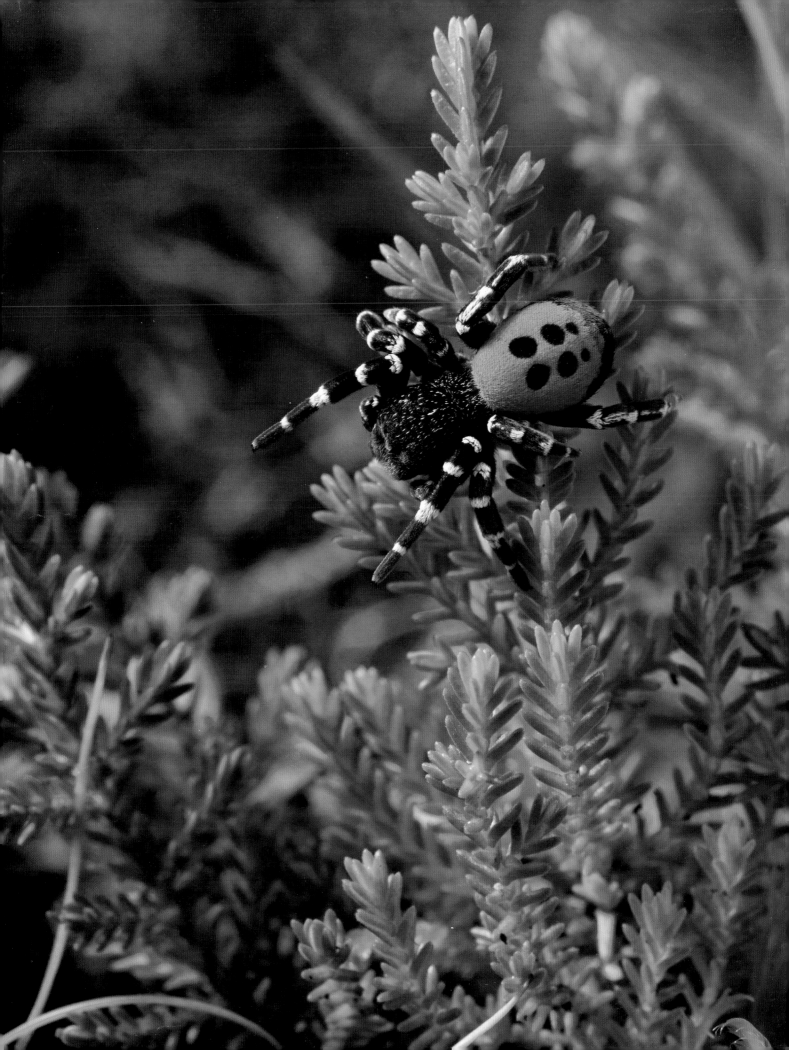

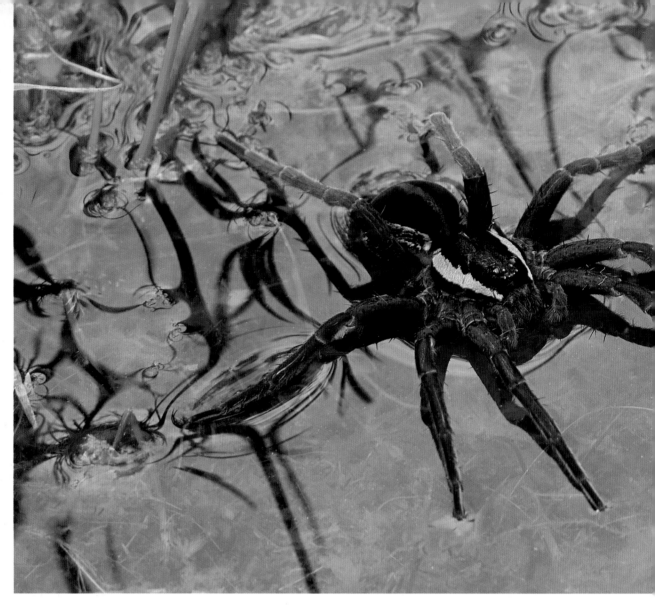

Fishing spider waiting on the surface of a pool, among sphagnum moss.

Raft or fishing spider (*Dolomedes fimbriatus*)

Dolomedes from Latin *dolo*, "pointed staff"; *fimbriatus* from Latin "fringed" (referring to the abdominal pattern)

A spider named *Dolomedes* must be an impressive one, and indeed this worldwide genus contains some species that are spectacular in both appearance and lifestyle. North America hosts several species, the best known being *Dolomedes triton*, while a very similar species, *D. fimbriatus*, is the European version. Like its relatives *Pisaura* and *Pisaurina* (page 56), *Dolomedes* is, along with other daylight hunting spiders, a nursery-web spider (Pisauridae family), but in view of its intriguing hunting methods it has been given special attention here.

Dolomedes is found in wet areas of acid bogs and heaths where there are permanent pools of water. With its cream-striped, dark chocolate-colored bulky body and thick legs, *D. fimbriatus* can appear quite awesome. The female specimen illustrated measured 1.04 inch (26 mm) in body length—probably one of the largest specimens ever recorded in England! It hunts by waiting motionless on the surface of the water, or on a natural raft consisting

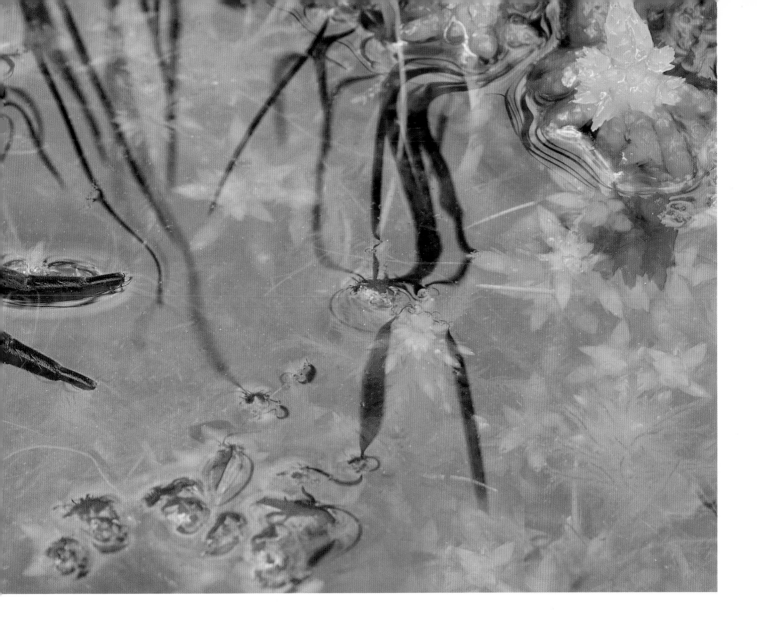

of moss or a leaf at the water's edge, with its front legs resting on the water. By so doing it can detect the slightest ripple or vibration from an insect, tadpole or small fish moving beneath the surface; prey are then dragged out of the water and devoured. The spider has also been recorded tapping the water's surface with its toe to attract fish from beneath, and will often run across the water for some distance to pounce on an insect that has accidentally fallen in. When alarmed the spider will sometimes vanish by climbing down the stem of a water plant, where it can remain submerged for up to an hour.

Like her land-dwelling cousins, *Dolomedes* weaves a large silken tent around her egg-sac that she protects from nearby. On hatching, the spiderlings disperse, often moving away from the water to exploit higher, dryer places in surrounding shrubs.

There are two species of raft spiders in Europe, *D. fimbriatus* and *D. plantarius,* the latter being very rare and legally protected in the United Kingdom. Although widespread in Europe, raft spiders are very local in their distribution. In North America the genus occurs mainly in the east.

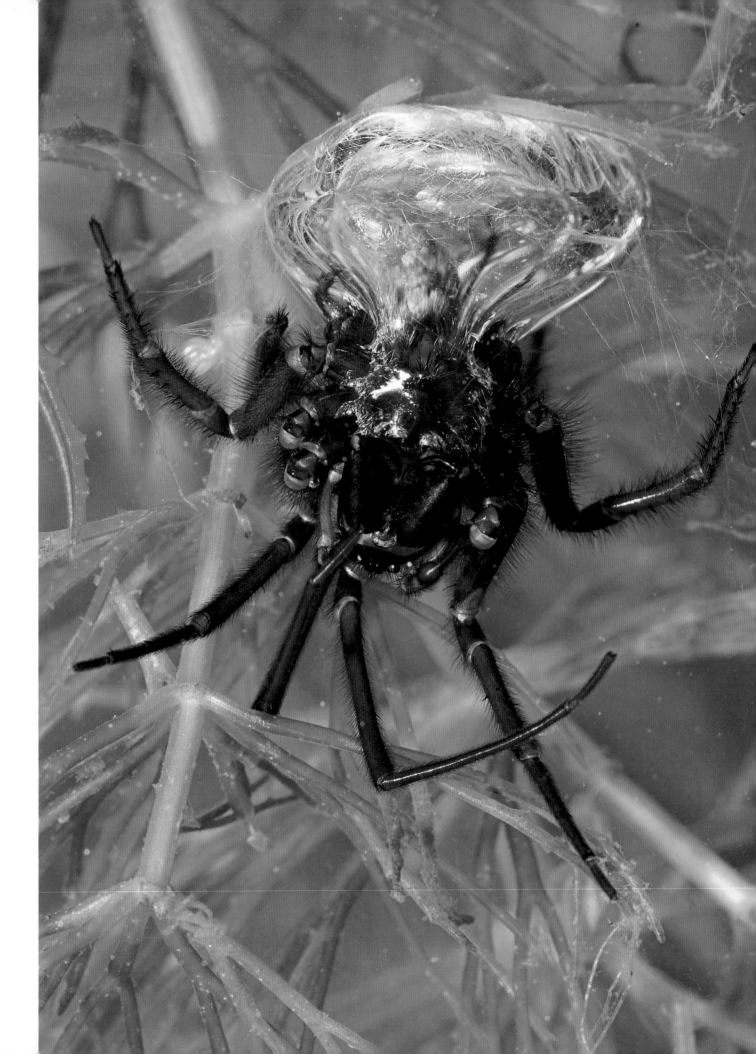

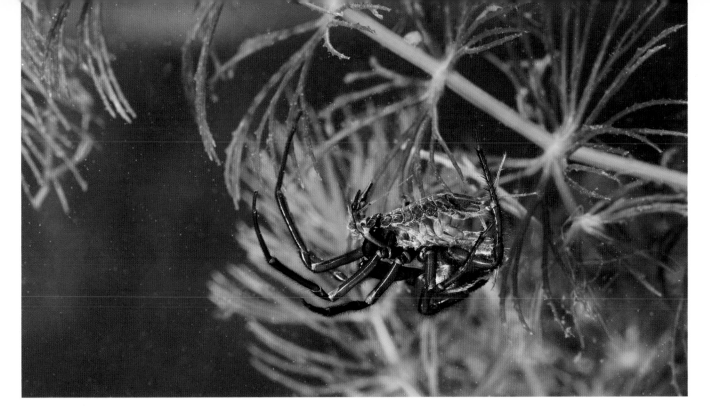

Water spider feeding on a waterlouse.

Water spider (*Argyroneta aquatica*)

Argyroneta from Greek "silver net"; *aquatica* from Latin "living in water"

The well-known water spider of the Argyronetidae family is the only spider in the world that spends almost its entire life underwater. Here, if you are lucky, you may see the spider pursuing aquatic creatures among the weeds, glittering like a ball of quicksilver.

All hunting takes place underwater, the spider deriving its oxygen from a bubble of air trapped among the hairs of its abdomen. To improve mobility the two pairs of hind legs are furnished with long, fine hairs so they act as paddles, a characteristic that makes it possible to identify even small, immature specimens.

◄ Water spider with bell.

This is a large species: males grow to more than 0.8 inch (20 mm), which is unusual among spiders, as males are almost always smaller than the females.

The water spider builds an underwater retreat held in place by a curved platform of silk that is then filled with air carried down from the surface—the whole structure resembles a sort of diving bell. Once it is filled, oxygen levels are maintained by oxygen from the water and bubbles from green plants diffusing into the bell, while carbon dioxide diffuses out into the surrounding water. Most activities take place within the bell, including mating, egg laying and consumption of prey. Young spiders do not make air bells but instead take over empty snail shells, which they fill with air.

Water spiders prefer living in still or slow-moving water and can be found all over Britain and northern Europe; they are very locally distributed but frequently abundant in those areas. This spider is absent from North America.

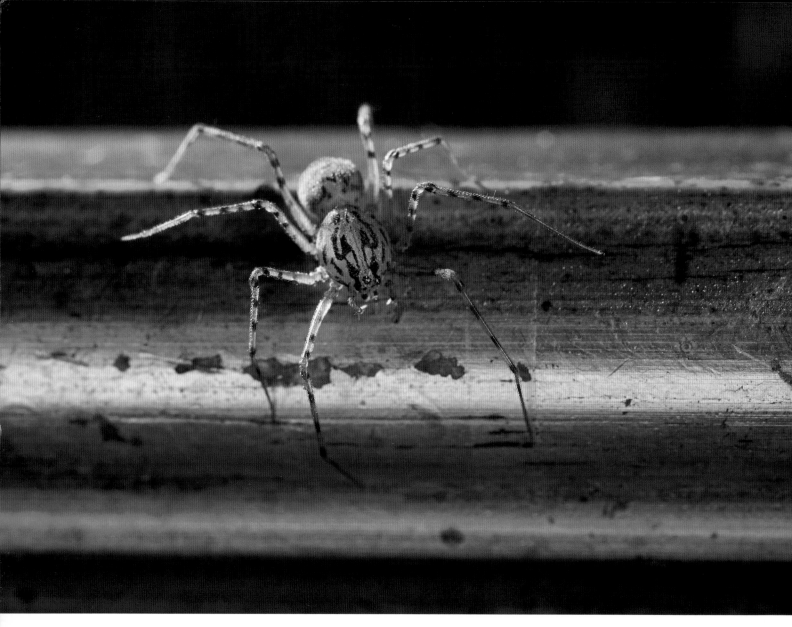

Spitting spider hunting on guilded picture frame.

Spitting spider (*Scytodes thoracica*)

Scytodes from Greek "marbled"; *thoracica* from Greek "chest"

This extraordinary spider was not discovered in Britain until 1816; during the next 120 years only six more specimens were found, all in southern counties. Since then the range of this scytodid has spread well into the Midlands and is probably increasing. It is almost certainly an import from the warmer regions of Europe; in Britain it can survive only inside houses, usually old ones, where it was probably introduced along with antique furniture. *Scytodes* can be found in many parts of the world, including North America, and as long as it is warm enough, at any time of the year.

The really astonishing thing about this spider is the unique way it catches and immobilizes prey. As twilight descends, *Scytodes* emerges from its daytime refuge behind picture frames and furniture to promenade the walls with its characteristic slow, measured gait. When it's about 0.4 inch (10 mm) from its prey, all you see is a quick jerk and then a struggling insect. On closer examination the victim can be seen to be tied down by a zigzag of 10 or 20 viscous threads on each side of its body, rather like Gulliver during his visit to Lilliput. The action is far too rapid to be seen by the unaided human eye, and even under a microscope the bonds are difficult to make out without special lighting.

The key to the mechanism that performs this trick is contained within the domed carapace, which houses two enormous glands, one loaded with poison and the other with a gummy substance. These are connected via ducts to holes at the tip of each fang. With a sudden contraction of muscles, the gum and venom are discharged under pressure through the fangs, which simultaneously oscillate rapidly from side to side, creating a controlled jet.

Scytodes can now deal with its victim at leisure without needing to wrap the body in a blanket of web. After a succession of small bites the struggling insect is subdued, allowing the spider to drag its prey free from the sticky bonds. Once digestive juices have been pumped into the insect, the body contents can be sucked out, leaving nothing but an undamaged empty husk behind.

The squirting technique can also be used for defense against spiders larger than itself, such as *Pholcus*. This unique ability, combined with *Scytodes'* capacity to move stealthily around the threads of larger and more aggressive spiders, ensures its safety in otherwise perilous situations.

When there is little food available in the winter, this spider remains concealed in cracks and crevices. It is long-lived, taking two or three years to become an adult, and with luck can eventually live to the ripe old age of four or five.

A spitting spider immobilizing prey on glazed glass.

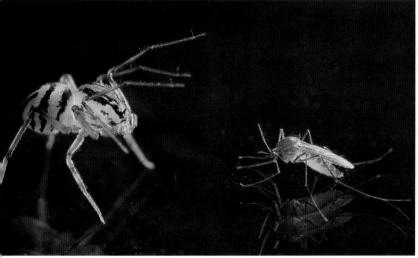

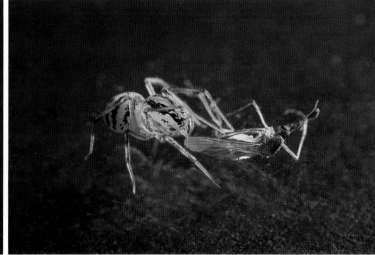

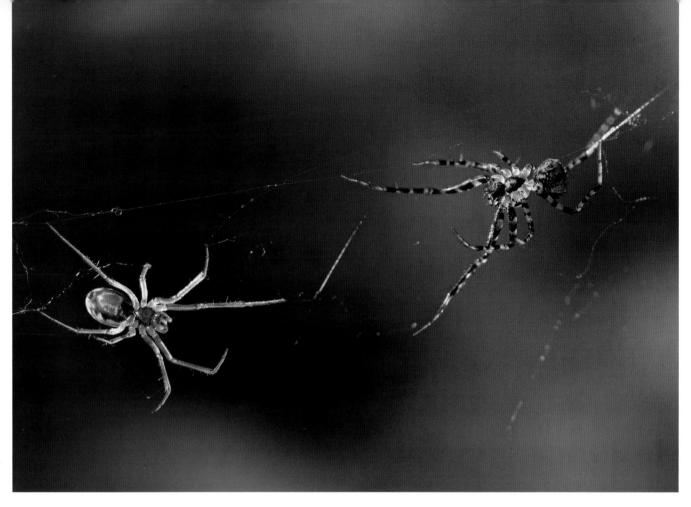

Pirate spider (right) approaching a hammock-web spider.

Pirate spider (*Ero cambridgei*)

Ero from Greek "Eros," God of Love;
cambridgei from O. Prichard Cambridge,
19th-century arachnologist

Rather than stalking, chasing, ambushing or trapping prey like other spiders, pirate spiders lead a nomadic existence. These members of the Mimetidae family creep around stealthily rather like *Scytodes,* seeking out the webs of other spiders, especially those of theridiids, the ubiquitous *Achaearanea* (American house spider) being a favorite.

The little pirate will surreptitiously enter the tangled lines of the theridiid web and attract the attention of the occupant by plucking at the threads. Sensing potential prey or perhaps a mate, the web's owner investigates, and at exactly the right moment *Ero* grasps one of the theridiid's legs and bites the victim's femur. The effect of its extremely virulent venom—a venom specialized to kill spiders rapidly—is almost instantaneous, and the victor proceeds to suck the body juices out of the tiny hole it has made in the relatively large prey. On some occasions, though, the tables are turned and pirate becomes a victim of its own seduction.

Ero is the only genus of Mimetidae in northern Europe, this species being found amid low vegetation, trees and bushes. It spends its time wandering around in search of the webs of similar-sized spiders to invade. *E. cambridgei* is widespread and fairly common. Altogether there are four *Ero* species in northern Europe and more than a dozen in North America.

➤ This little pirate spider (*Ero* sp.) cannot really be appreciated unless magnified.

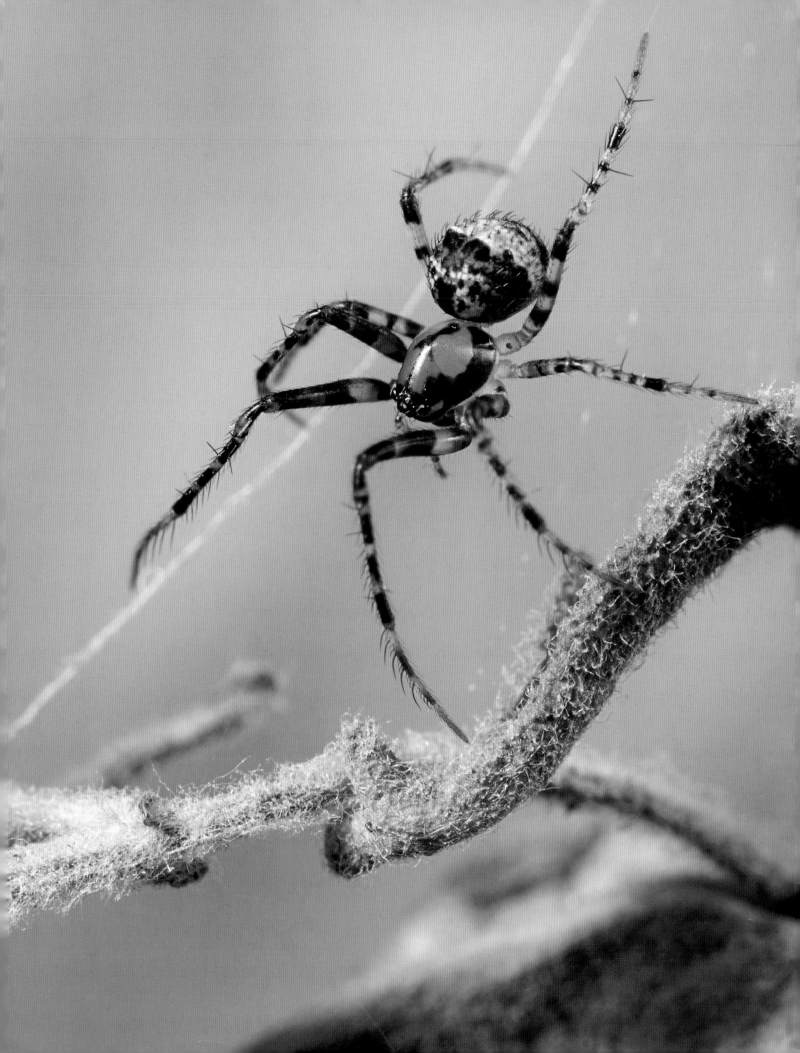

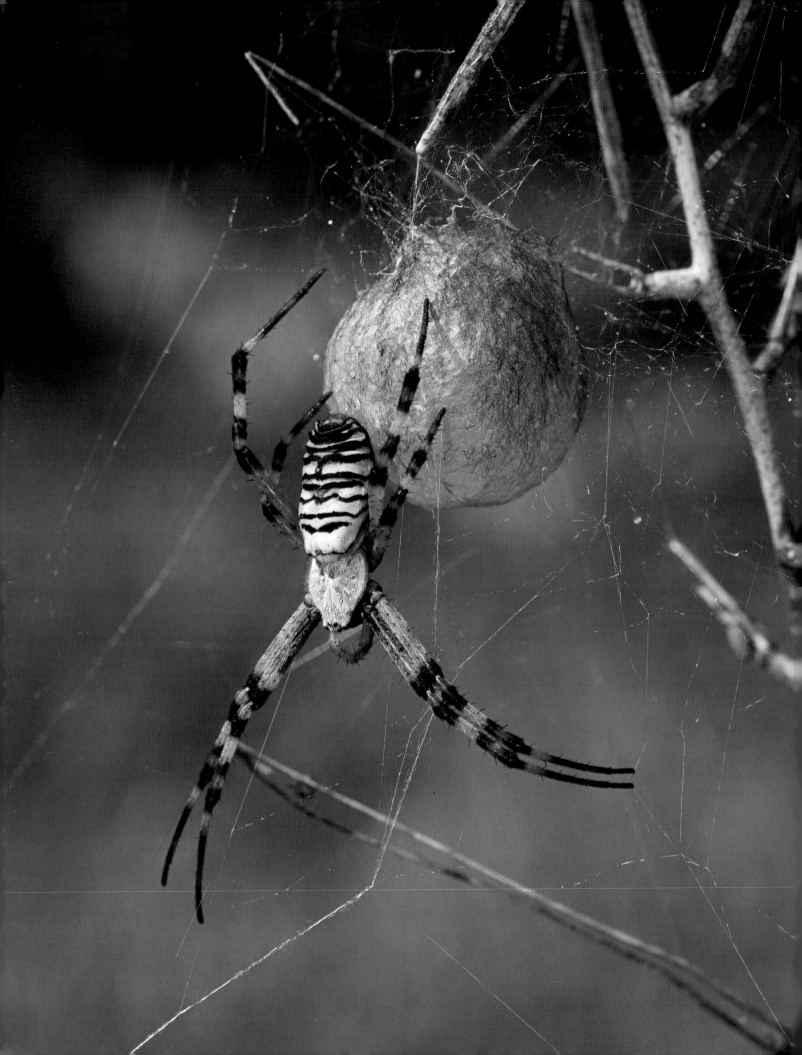

10 Photographing Spiders

This final section offers some basic help for those who may wish to try recording spiders using a camera. It assumes a rudimentary understanding of photography and photographic techniques, and many good books and a variety of field courses can provide both elementary and detailed guidance about all the aspects of photographic theory and wildlife photography.

Taking pictures of spiders is little different from photographing other small, active animals. You'll face the same challenges of exposure, focusing and sharpness. Fortunately, though, many of the technical obstacles that used to plague photographers, particularly those associated with close-up work, have been largely eliminated by modern equipment.

The first question you should ask yourself is what you are trying to achieve. You may wish to record spiders found on your travels, show spider behavior, create artistic masterpieces or perhaps a combination of all three. Knowing your goal will help with your general approach and the selection of suitable equipment for the task.

Film versus digital

Before launching into cameras, a word about digital photography. A few years back I would not have hesitated to say that film is the best medium in terms of image quality for wildlife photography, especially if medium format is used—it won hands down over digital. Now the tables have turned, and digital photography surpasses film not only in cost and convenience but, in my opinion, quality too. A few diehards still prefer film, and I can understand their emotional attachment to this great medium. However, while film may still have a few subtle advantages, they are hardly enough to justify struggling on with it any longer. I haven't exposed film since I tested the first truly high-resolution 35 mm digital camera (the Canon EOS 1DS) in

◄ Female wasp spider with cocoon.

2002—I was bowled over by the quality. More than 95 percent of the photographs in this book were taken using digital cameras.

The advantages of digital photography that are relevant to wildlife photography are summarized as follows.

Detail

A 10 megapixel or larger camera is generally capable of producing as much or more detail than the slowest, finest-grained 35 mm films available. Megapixels are not everything, though, as other aspects such as physical size of the chip, bit depth, lens design, camera circuitry and software also play crucial roles as a far as quality is concerned.

Noise and Grain

If noise can be kept under control, the image tones produced digitally are smoother than film, as are the transitions between tones, the best digital cameras being capable of generating less noise (graininess, in film terms) than film. This depends largely on the number of pixels and the relative size of the chip.

Speed of Results

One massive advantage of digital over film is that the image can be examined immediately after the picture has been taken, or, with cameras that support "live view" on the LCD, before the picture is exposed. Now we don't have to wait for days for the film to be processed to check any of the technical aspects of the image. Was the shot correctly exposed? Did the camera or spider move during the exposure? Have you focused in the correct place? All this and more

is apparent immediately after the shot. The exposure can be checked in the field by examining the image on the camera's LCD monitor, or better still by referring to the histogram (a chart graphically depicting the tone levels from shadows to highlights). Composition and lighting too can be assessed on the LCD screen. If this is not sufficient—fine detail can be difficult to see in camera—the image can be transferred onto a computer where, with suitable software, all these factors can be carefully examined in minute detail.

File Types

The files generated by digital cameras come in two main types, JPEG and RAW, but a spider book is not the best place to explain their pros and cons. Suffice to say that if speed and minimum hassle are important, then JPEG files are the best option. If RAW files are used, they first have to be converted in a RAW conversion program to TIFF or JPEG files before they can be used effectively. The important point about RAW files is that during their conversion it is possible to make all manner of adjustments to image parameters such as exposure, contrast and color balance, with no or minimal loss in quality. This is a considerable advantage if your camera settings were lacking in precision or the finest quality is considered paramount.

Retouching and Spotting

Digital images are easily spotted and retouched using a computer. A word of warning, though— it is pointless to make adjustments to color, tone and contrast unless they are made on a good quality and regularly calibrated monitor. Otherwise you will be chasing your tail.

Expense and Pollution

One of the main advantages of digital origination is the huge savings in film and processing. You can be as trigger-happy as you like in the knowledge that it's not making a large hole in your pocket. As long as you don't buy the most expensive digital camera available, it is quite possible to save its initial cost by not having to worry about buying and developing film. And, of course, nasty processing chemicals are not been being spewed into the environment.

Cameras

The most suitable camera for spider photography will depend on what sort of photographs you are after and the quality expected. At the bottom of the quality scale are the compact cameras, although these days they are capable of astonishingly good results, with sufficient megapixels to produce reasonable 8×10 prints. They do not suffer from parallax problems, and most have lenses capable of close-up focusing suitable for recording large spiders, but if pictures of small spiders such as the Linyphiidae are important, forget compacts.

Compacts also have two other fundamental disadvantages. There is an appreciable delay between the time the camera release button is pressed and the exposure is made—up to half a second or so on some models. While this may not seem like a lot, an enormous amount can happen during this time. With a static spider on a calm day you may get away with it, but as you can imagine, a restless spider or a puff of wind will wreak havoc on your potential masterpiece.

At the opposite end of the quality scale are the medium-format cameras. These have film or chip sizes two or three times the area of the 35 mm format (36 × 24 mm), the number of megapixels ranging from around 20 mp to 50 mp. The larger format means larger image magnification is needed, with a corresponding reduction in depth of field. Their potential quality is staggering, but if spider photography is your aim in life, such quality might be considered overkill, as the improvement will become noticeable only in huge reproductions. In addition, medium-format cameras tend to leave a large hole in your pocket, particularly when equipped with hugely expensive digital backs. Moreover, these monster cameras, together with their heavy lenses, are very cumbersome and impractical for field use, especially for spider action photography.

That leaves us with the much lighter, cheaper and more flexible 35 mm single-lens reflexes (SLRS) or their digital counterparts, DSLRS. These cameras view the subject through the lens rather than a viewfinder and are ideal for most wildlife photography, especially close-up and long-range telephoto work.

A few top-quality DSLRS use the full-frame 36 × 24 mm chip, but the majority make do with a smaller one, about two-thirds the area of the 35 mm format. Both chip sizes are capable of superb results, especially those with higher pixel counts. Potentially full-frame chips can accommodate a larger number of pixels and/or use larger pixels, which produces less noise (graininess). But an advantage of cameras with smaller chips is that the lenses can be made smaller, lighter and a little cheaper than those designed for the full 35 mm frame. When photographing spiders in their natural habitat there is something to be said for the smaller, lighter models, as they are easier to maneuver amid vegetation. Another plus is the greater depth of field available with the smaller

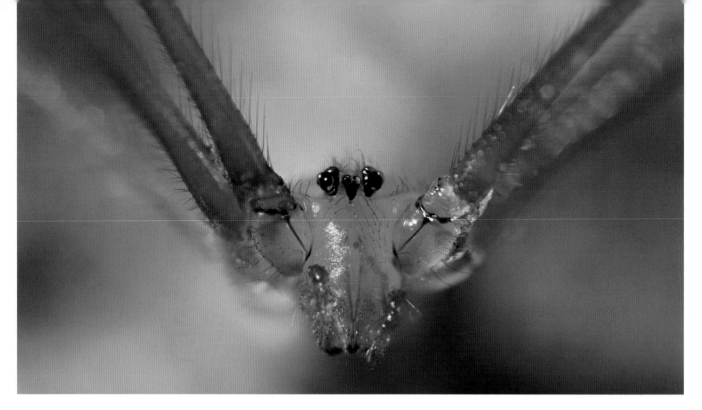

Face of daddy longlegs spider showing 'stalky' eyes.

format. However, there is a small aesthetic penalty to this, in that the larger the format (and thereby the greater the image magnification), the more blurred and less distracting the background becomes, although this is also influenced by other factors such as aperture (f-stop). I use both sizes, preferring the larger format and the extra pixels for ultimate quality.

Autofocus

The use of autofocus (AF) is a huge benefit for certain types of nature photography, especially when long telephoto lenses are employed for mammals and birds. When used for macro work, however, AF is an irritation rather than a blessing, particularly at higher magnifications. Every time there is any fore or aft movement of the lens or subject, the AF mechanism hunts backward and forward in its efforts to find a suitable point on which to lock. This becomes very trying when working with a handheld in the field, especially since the autofocus will usually stop at the first point of focus it reaches.

Manual focus is usually by far the best option, allowing you to decide the point of focus within the composition.

Exposure Settings

Most cameras these days have auto-everything, with multiple program modes for tackling every situation. These are fine for family snapshots but are of little value for serious spider photography. The two most useful modes for macro photography are Aperture Priority (you set the f-stop, the camera sets the shutter speed) and Manual (you set both f-stop and shutter speed). I use nothing else but these two modes, but it is important that the camera also has a quick and easy way to adjust the exposure value in both directions to compensate for subjects that the camera considers abnormal—such as pale spiders on dark backgrounds or vice versa. The manual setting (M) is often the best solution, as it allows total control over both shutter speed and aperture, but it does require a little experimentation and experience to use to its full potential.

Lenses for spider photography

The majority of spider photography requires image magnifications of between one-fifth and twice natural size (reproduction ratios 1:5 to 2:1). The easiest way to focus up to life-size (1:1) is to use a special lens designed for close focusing—a macro lens. This has a built-in adjustable extension tube that allows helical focusing from infinity to 1:1, although most modern lenses achieve this by internal focusing.

An important aspect to consider when choosing a macro lens is its focal length: the longer the focal length, the longer the working distance (distance between lens and subject). As a rough guide, depending on the lens construction, at 1:1 the working distance is double the focal length. Thus a 50 mm lens will provide a working distance of about 100 mm (4 inches), doubling to 200 mm (8 inches) with a 100 mm lens, while a 200 mm macro lens will allow you to work about 400 mm (16 inches) from the subject. Clearly, the longer the focal length, the easier it is to approach the spider without alarming it, and the easier to position the tripod and lights (when needed) so that your body and camera don't obscure the light. Another advantage of the longer lens is that, as focal length increases, differential focus also increases (the amount the background is thrown out of focus), thereby enhancing the pictorial quality by softening background clutter.

There are times when a shorter lens has advantages, for example, when high magnifications of well over 1:1 (life size) are achieved by adding extension tubes or bellows to obtain the required reproduction ratios. One or two manufacturers provide specialist lenses with lots of helical focusing movement, allowing magnifications of up to around five times—ideal for minute spiders and anatomical details. Under these conditions other difficulties surface, such as the cramped working distance and the narrow depth of field, now measured in fractions of a millimeter.

Sharpness and depth of field

Obtaining sufficient depth of field is always a challenge with macro photography, particularly with spiders. Unlike butterflies and moths, where you normally focus on the plane of their wings, spiders possess more depth; unless photographed directly from above, the depth of field necessary to cover from one side to the other is impossibly wide at high magnifications. Bear in mind that at a magnification of 1:1 and an aperture of f/16 the depth is only about 1 mm—this does not give you much to play with! Stopping down much further does not really help either, as overall sharpness will suffer because of diffraction. One solution is to make do with a lower magnification and rely on some enlargement of the image later. This limitation can be seen in many of the larger reproductions in this book showing lateral views: rarely are both front and rear legs in sharp focus.

As well as subject movement, all camera shake and vibration need to be minimized. This becomes worse as magnification and lens focal length increase and as shutter speed lengthens. A tripod or beanbag together with a remote release are invaluable when exposing with daylight, while the better-quality cameras are equipped with a mirror lock to eliminate vibration caused by the mirror slapping about inside, although this is less of a problem than it used to be.

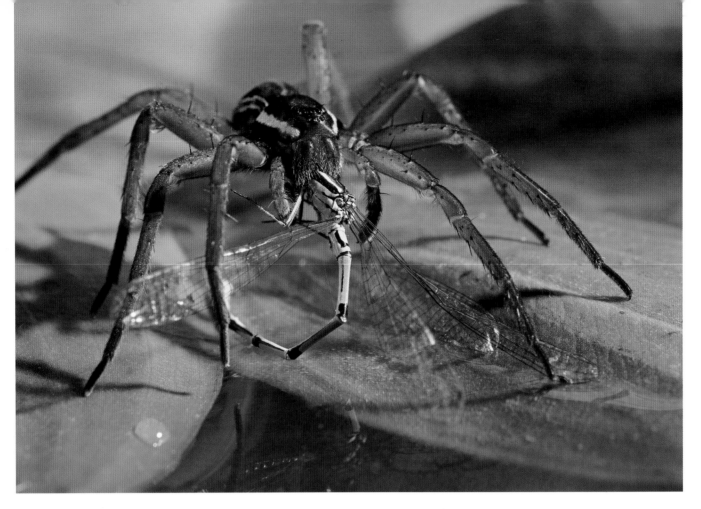

Raft spider feeding on blue damselfly.

Grassroot jungle photography

In a perfect world it would be splendid to be able to take faultless pictures of spiders in their natural habitat by available light, without the use of a tripod. Unfortunately this may not be possible until perhaps an ultrasensitive noiseless chip is developed, allowing ISO speeds of 50,000, thus permitting small apertures and high shutter speeds to be used at all times—some years away, I reckon! Meanwhile we will all have to battle on with the reality of working within the limitations of current equipment, coping with small, active, nervous creatures that rarely hang around long enough for us to select the best viewpoint, erect a tripod and focus. They will either see our movements or be disturbed by the vibrations of our activities. And then there is the wind to contend with—unless conditions are dead calm, pinsharp images are unlikely. Another difficulty that arises with macro photography, particularly in windy conditions, is that the distance between the camera and the subject is constantly changing, maybe only by fractions of a millimeter, but this will result in the image shifting in and out of focus as we attempt to frame the picture—an issue that becomes exasperatingly self-evident when we try.

There are times when conditions are perfect; for instance, windless early mornings and heavy dews are ideal for web photography. At such times the sun is low on the horizon, providing not only a gentle light with long, soft shadows and modeling but also backlight or texture—perfect for moody photography generally. Exposure times are too long to expect consistently sharp images when using daylight and handholding the camera, so a sturdy tripod is mandatory. When operating at ground level you may get away with just a beanbag.

Clearly then, daylight is frequently far from ideal for much spider photography, as the outcome is likely to be disappointing. What is more, whereas dull, murky conditions tend to produce pictures lacking in life, a more common and challenging situation arises when direct sunlight creates far more contrast than the digital sensor or film can cope with, producing pictures with burned-out highlights and/or deep shadows lacking detail. There are three ways of dealing with this. One is to hold a large diffuser between sun and subject to soften the direct sunlight. Another is to fill in the shadows by reflecting light from silver foil, a mirror or other suitable reflecting material. A third solution is to use a flashgun as close as possible to the lens axis. All this presupposes that the spider is perfectly happy to stay put while all this activity is going on around it. Don't forget, many species are very susceptible to movement and vibration. One of the secrets is to approach spiders very slowly in the first instance and set up the photographic paraphernalia in slow motion. Extreme patience is a prerequisite of spider photography, as in most wildlife photography.

Flashing spiders and lighting

More often than not the best answer is to use flash as the sole light source; this arrests all subject and camera movement and you have full control of the lighting. But the trouble with flash is that unless it is sympathetically handled, the results can look ghastly, producing photographs that are unnatural and "flashy," with the subject lacking any shape or texture. The very word *photography* means painting with light. If this concept is borne in mind, then your photography could take on a new lease of life. The natural world is illuminated by the sun and sky—if the picture appears to have been exposed with flash, then something is wrong.

Spiders are three-dimensional, but we are trying to represent their solid form using a two-dimensional medium. So we need as much help as possible to compensate for this restriction, and skillful lighting is the only way to manage this. Many nature pictures exposed with flash, even those that often win competitions, suffer from appalling "flash management"—usually the result of positioning the flashgun on camera, using two flashguns mounted at 45 degrees on each side of the lens or, worse still, employing the dreaded ring flash! There may be rare occasions when "dead" lighting is unavoidable, but we should try to circumvent this whenever possible.

To emulate the sun we need to start with a single modeling light to provide shape and texture. Its position and angle will depend on what we are trying to achieve, the position of the spider relative to the camera, and its tone. The important point is that the lighting should emphasize the cylindrical body and legs so that one side is brighter than the other. Any additional light to fill in the shadows must not kill the modeling or produce ugly and confusing secondary shadows. For most purposes a lighting ratio of around 3:1 will provide enough detail on the shadow side.

How we fill in the shadows will depend on circumstances; frequently a simple foil reflector is sufficient, while on other occasions a second flash-head may be more practical or effective. Frequently soft light is preferable to direct light if, for instance, you are trying to emulate a thin veil of cloud over the sun and gentle shadows. Such lighting can produce lovely images, eliminating some of the harshness produced by direct sunlight or flash, but

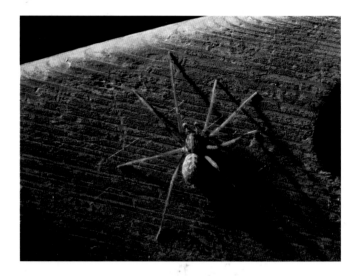

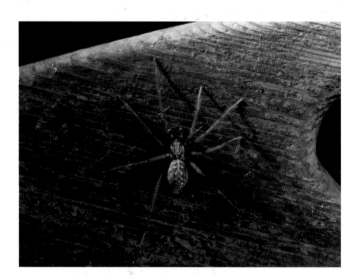

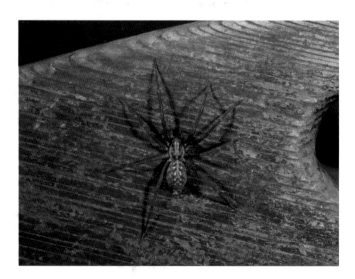

remember that soft, diffused shadows are not the same as flat lighting—shaping the subject is still your aim. The only exception might be for scientific recording, when a quick and easy way of producing standardized lighting may be necessary. In these circumstances, a flash on the camera or a ring flash is the surest way of achieving shadowless, flat and characterless images, but they are very unnatural and never look attractive.

Sometimes more flash-heads can be added to provide specific effects such as backlighting or to illuminate the background, but avoid destroying the overall modeling or creating conflicting shadows. In nature there is only one sun in the sky, producing one set of shadows; in its absence there is very soft shadow produced by a gigantic reflector—the sky. Often the simpler the lighting, the better. The vast majority of the spiders illustrated in this book were exposed using a single flash-head and a foil reflector; only a few benefited from an extra flash-head instead of the reflector and/or a separate light for the background.

House spiders (*Tegenaria domestica*), illustrating basic lighting.

⅄ Single modeling light from side. The effect is dramatic and emphasizes shape and texture. Note the roundness of the body, its hairs and the coarseness of the wood surface. Also the effect is in keeping with the nocturnal way of life and creepiness of this spider. However, there is no detail in the shadows.

▸ Here the modeling light is in exactly the same position as before, but a reflector has been added on the opposite side to fill in the shadows, thereby reducing contrast. Both the modeling and texture have been retained so the spider still looks three-dimensional, but now in a more subtle way.

◂ Two lights were used at 45 degrees on each side. This has resulted in a shapeless cardboard-cutout spider. The lighting also demonstrates what happens with cross-lighting: shadows fall on both sides of the subject. In summary, the photograph lacks information as well as being unnatural and aesthetically dull.

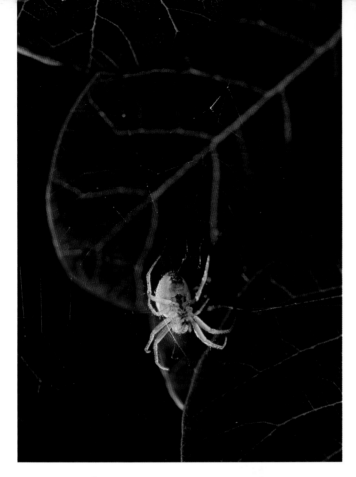

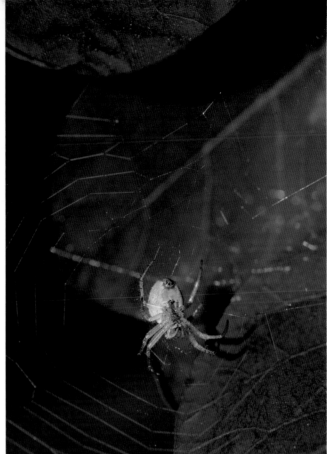

"Painting with light": these two pictures of an orb-web spider (*A. cucurbitina*) and web in a smoke bush demonstrate the huge difference lighting can make to a photograph.

▲ This is an example of a precisely positioned modeling light, backlight and a reflector, resulting in a three-dimensional and moody ambience.

▲ The same subject is lit with a single light close to the camera axis. The result is flat and less interesting, but it does show the colors of the smoke bush leaves as they usually appear to us; frequently pictorial requirements need to be balanced with other considerations.

One way of photographing spiders in their habitat is to purchase a dedicated macro flash unit. This is made up of two flash heads supported by adjustable brackets. The default position for the two lamps is on each side of the lens, which produces flat cross-lighting. However, if one of the lamps is moved well away from the camera using an adjustable extension bracket so that the spider is lit from the best angle, while the power of the fill-in lamp is reduced, then results will improve significantly.

TTL Flash Metering

Before the days of flash metering, flash photography was rather a black art. There was no practical means of measuring the output of a flash-head, so arriving at the correct exposure was a matter of relying on the vagaries of guide numbers and a lot of trial and error. To make matters worse, the whole system—as much as it was a system—completely broke down with close-up photography. The reasons were twofold: first, guide numbers are notoriously inaccurate when a light source is close to the subject. Second, compensation was required to allow for the extra lens extension—or bellows extension, as it was popularly known—a phenomenon that applied particularly to lenses without internal focusing. The ensuing calculations necessary invariably delayed proceedings, by which time the animal had most likely vanished!

Nowadays through-the-lens (TTL) flash metering has come to our rescue, completely eliminating those irksome concerns. Ingenious electronics allow the camera and flashgun to talk to each another: when sufficient light from the flash has entered the camera, the flash is quenched, producing a correctly exposed image. All very clever stuff and done at the speed of light, allowing anybody with a suitable combination of flash and camera to take photographs of insects and spiders without worrying too much about technique. TTL flash metering is not foolproof, however; like ambient light TTL metering, the system still relies on the subject's being mid-toned. It can also be defeated when backgrounds are some distance beyond the subject. You also need to be aware that compensation cannot be made by adjusting the aperture, since the flash will then try to make a compensation to compensate for your compensation! Instead, adjustments have to be made to either the flashgun's output or the camera's flash compensation control. To understand how these functions operate together, the camera and flash unit instruction manuals should be consulted—if you can make sense of them!

Spiders in the studio

Versatile working methods are essential when photographing spiders—you cannot rely on any single approach. There are many reasons why it is not always practical to photograph spiders outside. Wind, rain, the precision needed for high-magnification shots and specialized work such as high-speed photography, or sometimes just convenience are among the reasons for collecting your specimen and shooting in the studio. If handled skillfully it should be virtually impossible to differentiate between studio and outdoor invertebrate photography, but obtaining convincing results requires considerably more expertise than "shooting from the hip" in the wild. I will go further by saying that flash photography performed in natural habitats can look more artificial than accomplished studio work. When the picture is finally completed, nothing about it should give the game away, either to expert arachnologists or skilled nature photographers.

There are two main ingredients for successful studio photography. The first is knowledge of the subject: the spider's typical habitat, its behavior and family traits and its likely reaction in the studio. The set you create should reflect the spider's natural surroundings, ideally incorporating vegetation from around the vicinity where the spider was found. Fortunately most spiders are small creatures and so only a handful of material has to be taken away. The second ingredient is once again our friend lighting and its importance in matching the quality of that imparted by the sun, sky and clouds. Black backgrounds can often be avoided by using suitable backdrops positioned some way behind the subject area and, if necessary, lit with a separate flash-head, a technique that I sometimes employ for outdoor photography as well. The photographs in this book are a combination, about 50/50, of both studio and outdoor shots.

Handling spiders

Perhaps more than insects, spiders seem to have an uncanny ability to vanish entirely, often creeping into a tiny crevice or dodging behind a leaf. Jumping and hunting spiders should be watched at all times—unless settled they can disappear in the blink of an

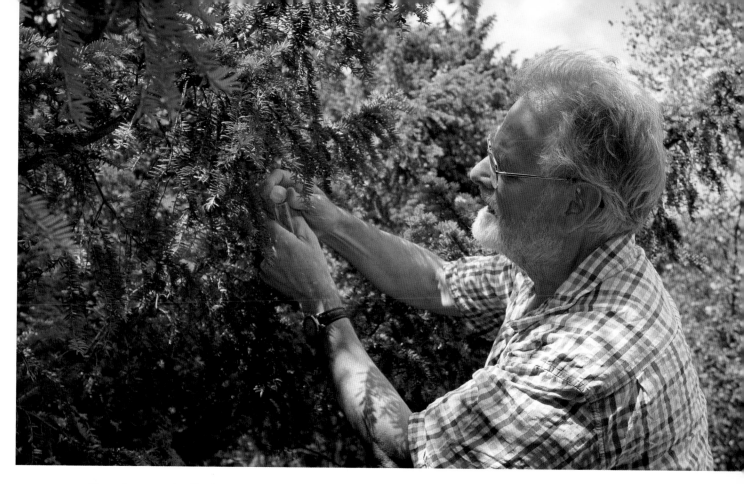

The author returning *Hyptiotes* to its natural habitat.

eye. Handling small spiders is not only taxing for the eyes, but these creatures are also constantly generating silk on which they strive to balloon to freedom. Even an apparently draftless room has sufficient air movement to waft them away and out of sight. To deal with them and the more wayward larger species, I often spread a white sheet under the working area to make them easier to spot once they "vanish." Another essential spider-handling accessory is a camel-hair brush, which can be used to encourage obstinate individuals into the right place without risk of damaging the specimen.

The art of spider photography

Here is not the place to discuss the aesthetics of nature photography, beyond saying that, in my view, space around the main subject generally enhances the picture. If distracting elements are avoided, space improves the overall pictorial qualities of most wildlife photographs. There are those who will give you contrary advice: "Crop in close for impact." Of course, when homing in on specific detail or when the spider is surrounded by irrelevant or confusing background, tight cropping is fine, but animals look more natural and at home when given a little elbow room. Wildlife, spiders included, cannot be looked at in isolation from their surroundings, especially as the combination often provides useful clues to identification and habits.

One final point: If I take a spider from the wild, I try to return it. This makes me feel better, and perhaps the spider too, and it's good to think that my models survived to produce offspring or provide food for some other animal, and thereby help to sustain life.

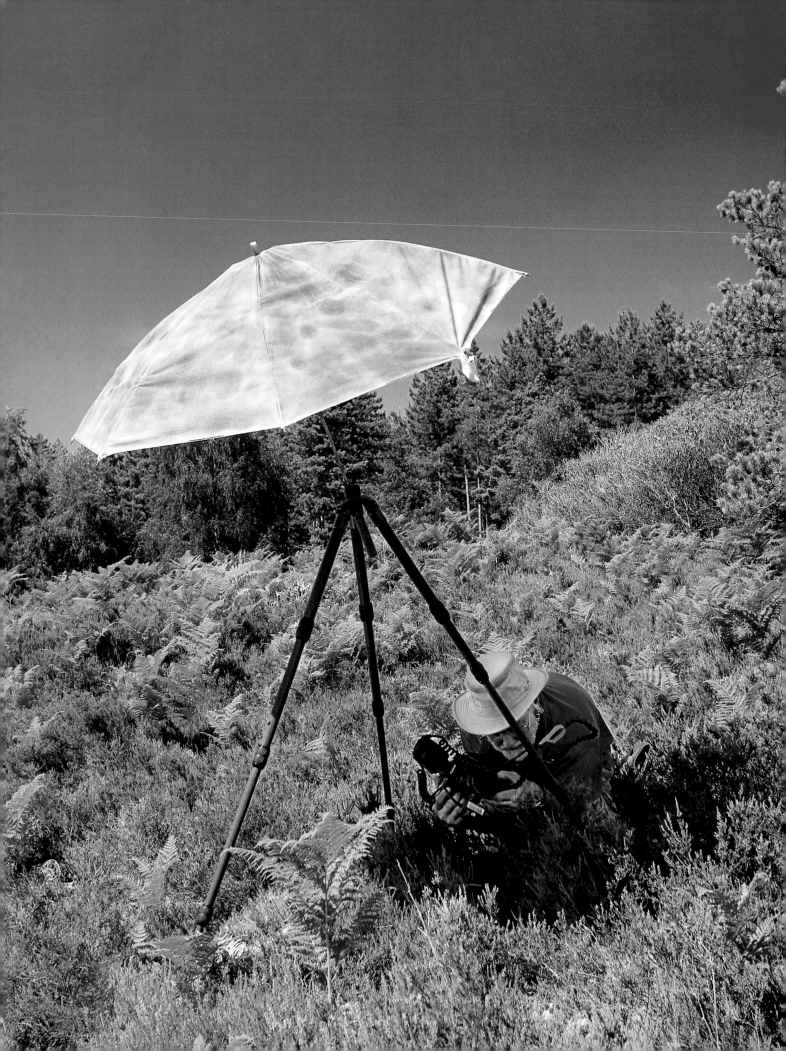

Postscript

I t seems odd that, having suffered from arachnophobia since the tender age of four, when I was bitten by a spider, I should end up writing a book about these creatures. Fortunately, after being immersed in the things for over two years, my primordial instincts were largely overcome by the more cerebral passions of natural history, a long-standing interest in photography, and particularly a deep reverence for all life, however apparently insignificant or menacing. That is not to say that I don't still view large, fast spiders with a little suspicion, but after perhaps the initial shock of first sighting, rationality takes over.

Before I started on this project my knowledge of spiders was scant, so my inability to identify the vast majority of them proved very frustrating—a fact not helped by the scarcity of suitable books on the subject at that time. Unlike bird books, those on spiders are not bestsellers.

Life changed when my wife, in an effort to cure my horror of these creatures, enrolled me in a short summer course on spiders run by the Field Studies Council, an excellent organization that holds courses all over England on a wide variety of natural history and conservation-based subjects.

The course proved a revelation. It was run by Tony Russell Smith, a tweed-jacketed world expert on spiders with an infectious enthusiasm for the subject. I was also surrounded by passionate spider fans, most of whom knew much more about the subject than I. Our time was divided among classroom lectures, searching for specimens in the spider-rich local countryside, and peering down microscopes to examine our catch in an effort to identify them. On one occasion, while I was examining a freshly pickled specimen under the binocular microscope—where the spider appears the size of a dinner plate—the supposedly dead creature suddenly twitched violently. I involuntarily shot back in my chair with a cry. The whole class looked around—and my secret was out!

◄ The author photographing the ladybird spider (*Eresus*) in its habitat.

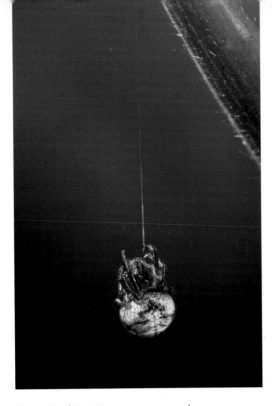

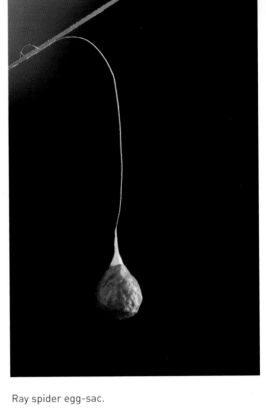

Ray spider (*Theridiosoma gemmosum*).

Ray spider egg-sac.

It was while we were on one of the field trips that a fellow student found *Hyptiotes,* the triangle spider, a small, rare and mysterious spider that I had only read about in W.S. Bristowe's inimitable book *The World of Spiders*. Sadly, this new-found specimen was destined to be pickled in spirits before being subjected to microscopic examination; however, I managed to inveigle my colleague to part with his prize for photography at home. I had never seen pictures of this remarkable little spider in its web, let alone any illustrating the novel technique it has evolved for catching prey. Subsequently it took nearly three weeks to encourage the creature to build a web in a photographically viable position in its favorite habitat, amid the branches of a yew tree, and to record a sequence of prey capture: these appear on page 135–137.

This early success encouraged me to attempt to record other spiders that have adopted equally intriguing hunting techniques. It also began to dawn on me that the subject had potential for an unusual book, though the plan had a major snag. As my knowledge of spiders

was still limited, my ability to find specimens, particularly the more obscure and rare species, would severely restrict any successful outcome. With this in mind I contacted Evan Jones, at that time merely a naturalist acquaintance who I remembered had a formidable field knowledge of spiders. As soon as I explained my goal he jumped at the chance to get involved, thus marking the beginning of a deep friendship and an enjoyable two-year venture culminating in this book.

From spring to summer for the following two years we went on regular spider forays, sometimes to local haunts but often farther afield to other parts of the country in our search for rare and unusual spiders. At such times Evan was in his element—when not sweeping the vegetation or beating the understory with nets and collecting trays, he was on his hands and knees amid the roots of heather in his hunt for some rare or obscure spider, leaving me struggling in his wake. During this time I never ceased to wonder at his uncanny ability to find and identify often the tiniest of spiders, and thanks to his enthusiasm and innate ability to impart knowledge I soon learned much about these alluring animals.

An example of Evan's enthusiastic energy occurred after my discovery of the minute egg-sac of a rare and strange spider I had only read about, *Theridiosoma gemmosum*. That I spotted the thing at all was a miracle, as it is little bigger than the head of a pin. The egg-sac is easier to find than the spider itself, which lives very low down, almost at ground level, in the thickest vegetation imaginable among dark, dank undergrowth. The spider, only slightly larger than its egg-sac, is unusual in that it catches prey in its delicate half-opened, umbrella-like orb web in a similar manner to *Hyptiotes*.

When I returned home and called Evan to brag about my lucky find, he became extremely excited and dropped whatever he was doing to arrive on my doorstep within the hour, after a 40-mile drive! Without delay I escorted him to the spot near my woodland pond and showed him the egg-sac. Five minutes later he found the spider. To me it was an almost invisible silver speck. Photographs of both the spider and its egg-sac can be seen opposite.

There are many blessings to having worked on this project, not least of which are all the memories it holds of hunting for specimens in glorious countryside and sometimes strange places. On several occasions the spiders were rare or curious species that I had only read about in books.

One scorching day in early summer we drove to a secret half-acre patch of strangely ideal habitat on a military range in a remote spot in the south of England, to see and photograph the ladybird spider, *Eresus cinnaberinus*. This is the rarest and most spectacular of European spiders, which until 1979 was thought to be extinct in Britain because of habitat destruction. Having first acquired a special pass, we were met by biologist Ian Hughes, who is charged by the organization Natural England to watch over this exquisite gem of a spider and encourage it to breed and expand its tiny range. In 1994 there were only 56 webs on the site, but thanks to Ian's breeding program the number is steadily increasing. The only thing protecting this apparently unique habitat from the 50-ton tanks that periodically thunder by is a low, dilapidated wire-net fence—it was an incongruous location but I felt privileged to be there. My silver umbrella served as both photographic reflector and shade from the fierce sun on that memorable day. Photographs of the spider and its habitat appear on pages 176–179 and 198, respectively.

Another spider trip a few months later, to the Houses of Parliament in London, attracted somewhat unwelcome attention. On this occasion I was trying to photograph *Segestria florentina*, a large and fearsome spider that lives in holes and crevices of stone buildings around certain ports and docks (page 168–169). The sight of two suspicious-looking characters equipped with tripods, cameras, long lenses and flash equipment drew the attention of the security police, who perhaps suspected that we were planting sticks of dynamite in the walls of the building. We were allowed to continue with our operation only after a long and enthusiastic explanation about the life of this spider. When we enticed one of these menacing creatures out of its lair by tweaking a trip line with a blade of grass, our macho interrogators beat a hasty retreat.

After two years of living, breathing and photographing spiders it was a sad day when the book was completed, but my fascination for these astonishing animals will never come to an end.

Acknowledgments

This book would not have been possible without the practical support and enthusiasm of Evan Jones. He was not only responsible for finding many of the spiders included here but he taught me much about the lives of these fascinating creatures. My thanks also go to Ian Hughes for allowing me to glimpse and photograph the ladybird spider, Britain's rarest spider. Ian has the awesome task of protecting and expanding the range of this spider within its miniscule hush-hush habitat.

I am also most grateful to spider expert Chris Spilling, president of the British Arachnological Society, who was kind enough to check the manuscript prior to submission to the publishers.

My special thanks go to my wife, Liz, who in spite of having to put up with boxes of spiders dotted throughout the house, was still willing to prepare gourmet picnics for the many forays in the field. She also frequently came to my rescue when I was faced with a gigantic house spider in the bath!

Finally my gratitude goes to Lionel Koffler from Firefly Books, who was brave enough to publish a book about spiders, and to all his staff for the hard work devoted to the production of this beautiful book.

Bibliography

Bristowe, W. S. *The World of Spiders*. London: Collins, 1958.
A delightful read with equally delightful drawings. A must for those interested in British spiders. It includes many of Bristowe's observations, particularly on spider courtship and mating behavior.

Forster, Ray and Lyn Forster. *Spiders of New Zealand and Their Worldwide Kin*. Dunedin: University of Otago Press, 1999.
A large-format and lavishly illustrated book with excellent line drawings. Especially rich on general spider biology.

Gertsch, Willis John. *American Spiders*. Kentucky: Van Nostrand Reinhold, 1979.
Similar to Bristowe's *World of Spiders,* informative but perhaps with less magic.

Jocqué, R. and A. S. Dippenaar-Schoeman. *Spider Families of the World*. Tervuren: Royal Museum for Central Africa, 2006.
A concise, descriptive overview of currently known spider families of the world.

Jones, Dick. *The Country Life Guide to Spiders of Britain and Northern Europe*. London: Country Life Books, 1983.
A useful field guide to the spiders of Britain and Northern Europe with 350 photographic records and short descriptions to aid in their identification.

Levi, Herbert and Lorna Levi. *Spiders and Their Kin*. New York: Golden Press, 1986.
A little gem of a booklet with pages of lifelike drawings of spiders of the world.

Roberts, Michael J. *Spiders of Britain and Northern Europe.* London: Collins, 1995.
Excellent for the identification of British and European spiders. Over 450 species described and painted by the author.

Ubick, Darrell, Pierre Paquin, Paula Cushing and Vince Roth. *Spiders of North America: An Identification Manual.* New York: American Arachnological Society, 2005.
A large-format guide to North American spider identification to genus level, copiously illustrated with genitalia. Much information on taxonomic history, but perhaps too academic for some.

Useful Websites

American Arachnological Society www.americanarachnology.org

British Arachnological Society www.britishspiders.org.uk

European Spiders identification www.eurospiders.com

Spider Bites in the UK www.nhm.ac.uk/nature-online/life/insects-spiders/spiderbites/

The Arachnology Homepage www.arachnology.be/Arachnology.html

Index